Here lived
V. SACKVILLE-WEST
who made this garden
Born at Knole 9 March 1892
Died at Sissinghurst 2 June 1962

Gardening
at
Sissinghurst

Gardening at
Sissinghurst

Tony Lord

PUBLISHED IN ASSOCIATION WITH
THE NATIONAL TRUST

FRANCES LINCOLN

To Graham Stuart Thomas,
whose work has enriched the lives of generations of gardeners and
enhanced the beauty of so many gardens, including Sissinghurst.

Frances Lincoln Limited
4 Torriano Mews, Torriano Avenue
London NW5 2RZ
in association with the National Trust (Enterprises) Ltd
36 Queen Anne's Gate
London SW1H 9AS

Gardening at Sissinghurst
Copyright © Frances Lincoln Limited 1995
Text copyright © Tony Lord 1995
Photographs copyright © Tony Lord 1995
Watercolours copyright © Frances Lincoln Limited 1995

First Frances Lincoln edition: 1995

British Library Cataloguing in Publication Data
A catalogue record for this book is available from the British Library

ISBN 0 7112 0991 X

Printed and bound in Italy by New Interlitho S.p.A.

9 8 7 6 5 4 3 2

Half-title page: The wooden seat beneath the tower arch with Harold's
memorial to Vita.
Frontispiece: The tower seen from the Cottage Garden with mulleins,
coreopsis and Papaver commutatum.

The view across the Rose Garden's yew Rondel to the bacchante statue in the
Lime Walk illustrates Sissinghurst's 'perfect proportion between the classic
and the romantic'.

Contents

The statue of Dionysus, replaced by the National Trust in July 1995 after the original crumbled.

An Overview

Framed in English oaks and basking in an autumnal sunrise, the gazebo overlooks the Kentish Weald.

1886 Harold Nicolson born, 21st November, Teheran, third son of Sir Arthur Nicolson (later Lord Carnock) and his wife, Catherine.

1892 Vita Sackville-West born, 9th March, Knole, Kent, only child of Lionel, 3rd Lord Sackville, and his wife, Victoria.

c.1900 Probable planting date of original Orchard trees and filberts in Nuttery.

1910 Vita and Harold meet.

1913 Vita's engagement to Harold announced 5th August; Harold and Vita marry on 1st October; they make their first garden at Cospoli near Constantinople.

1914 Harold and Vita return to England 21st June, bringing with them three bishops plaque (now in Bishops' Gate) and marble bowl (now in Herb Garden); their first son, Benedict (Ben), born 6th August, Knole.

1915 Harold and Vita buy Long Barn, Kent; a second son stillborn.

1917 Their youngest son, Nigel, born 19th January, Ebury Street, London.

1918–21 Love affair between Vita and Violet Trefusis.

1930 Vita buys Sissinghurst; cottages cleared from Top Courtyard; Lion Pond (now Sunken Garden) made in Lower Courtyard; Moat Wall unearthed and Nuttery cleared.

1931 Lake completed to south-east of garden; entrance arch from forecourt reopened; Top Courtyard lawn sown and Lower Courtyard lawn turfed; paths laid in Cottage Garden and Priest's House garden (now White Garden) where beds planted, with mostly shrub roses in south half, predominantly Hybrid Teas in box-edged beds to north; clearing of rubbish completed throughout almost all the garden.

1932 Harold and Vita let Long Barn and move in to Sissinghurst; path laid from entrance arch to tower and four Irish yews planted; Lady Sackville gives six Bagatelle vases; avenue of poplars planted along approach to forecourt; A.R. Powys employed as architect; Yew Walk planted; axis along Nuttery and future Lime Walk devised and hornbeam hedges planted; Harold plants foxgloves from wood through Nuttery; Moat Walk turfed and at its western end Sissinghurst Crescent built to Harold's design; kitchen garden (now Rose Garden) fenced; yew hedges planted around Rondel and between kitchen garden and Cottage Garden.

1933 Central path of kitchen garden laid out and box hedges planted. Erechtheum built.

1934 Yew hedges of Herb Garden planted; four Irish yews planted in Cottage Garden; Rondel lawn sown; magnolia bed planted in Lower Courtyard.

1935 Improvements to living accommodation completed; Powys Wall built in kitchen garden and Long Border path paved; Top Courtyard north wall built and paving installed in front of entrance range; little virgin statue placed to the north of Priest's House garden.

1936 Lime Walk paved and limes planted.

1937 The Rondel planted with shrub roses from Priest's House garden; Chinese jar placed at centre of Priest's House garden; Greek column from Shanganagh Castle placed in Delos; Orchard planted as wild garden with perimeter walk; forecourt paved and flanking pleached limes planted.

1938 Vita plants first herbs in Herb Garden; carpet of polyanthus completed through Nuttery.

1939 Outbreak of World War II; Jack Vass becomes Head Gardener; Lion Pond in Sunken Garden drained to make bed.

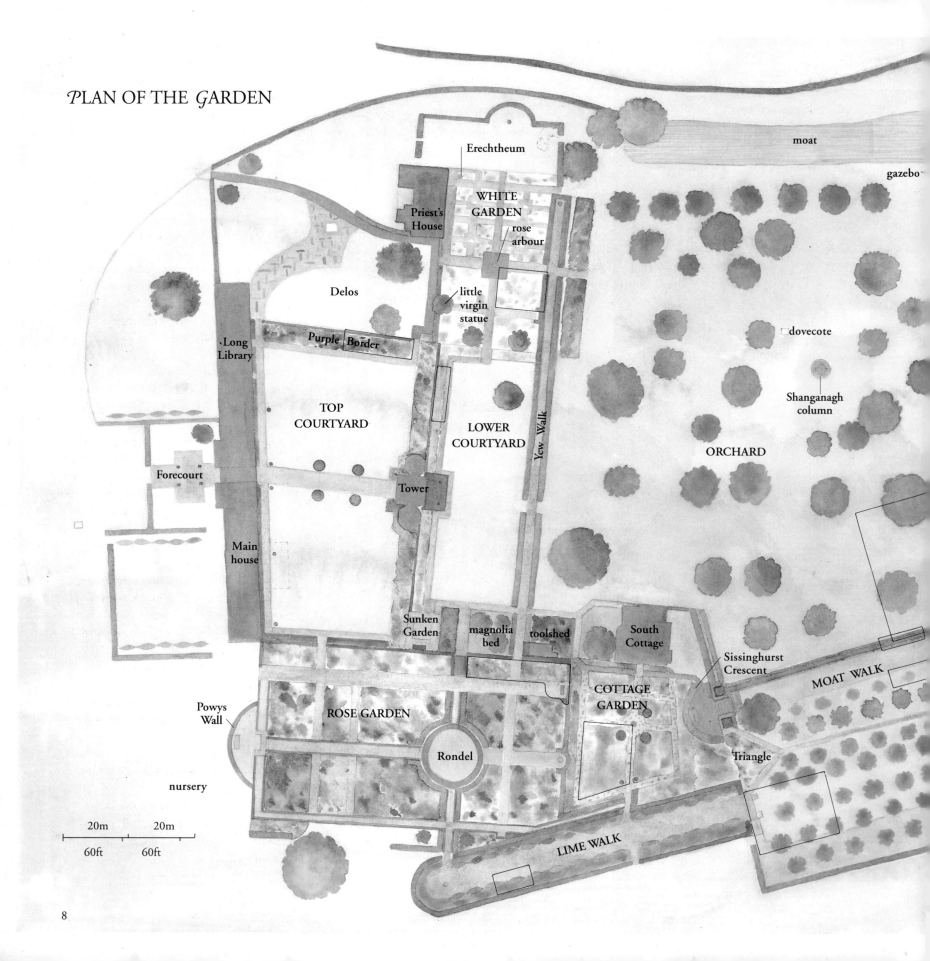

PLAN OF THE GARDEN

moat

gazebo

Erechtheum

WHITE
GARDEN

rose
arbour

Priest's
House

Delos

little
virgin
statue

dovecote

Purple Border

Long
Library

TOP
COURTYARD

LOWER
COURTYARD

Shanganagh
column

Yew Walk

ORCHARD

Forecourt

Tower

Main
house

Sunken
Garden

magnolia
bed

toolshed

South
Cottage

Sissinghurst
Crescent

MOAT WALK

Powys
Wall

ROSE GARDEN

COTTAGE
GARDEN

Rondel

Triangle

nursery

20m   20m

LIME WALK

60ft   60ft

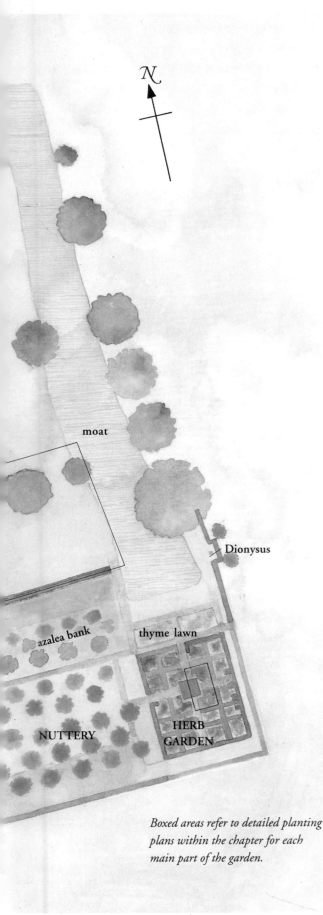

N

moat

Dionysus

azalea bank   thyme lawn

NUTTERY   HERB
GARDEN

Boxed areas refer to detailed planting
plans within the chapter for each
main part of the garden.

1941 Jack Vass leaves to join Royal Air Force.

1944 Iron gate placed between Top Courtyard and Rose Garden; Harold becomes member of National Trust's Council.

1945 War ends; Harold loses seat in Parliament.

1946 Harold starts notebook of Lime Walk planting; statue of Dionysus installed; Jack Vass returns to Sissinghurst and begins restoration of parts of garden neglected during the war.

1948 Vita plants her thyme lawn and azaleas along Moat Walk; she becomes founder member of National Trust's Gardens Committee.

1950 Priest's House garden replanted to become the White Garden and little virgin statue moved beneath weeping silver pear.

1952 Harold receives a knighthood.

1954 Dovecote installed.

1957 Jack Vass leaves; Ronald Platt becomes Head Gardener.

1959 Ronald Platt leaves; Pam Schwerdt and Sibylle Kreutzberger employed as joint Head Gardeners. Visitor numbers *c.* 6000.

1962 Vita dies at Sissinghurst on 2nd June; Nigel inherits.

1963 Cold winter kills many of the garden's tender plants; Sissinghurst Crescent box hedge cut back on Cottage Garden side to regrow.

1966 Visitor numbers reach 28,000.

1967 Pots from Siena placed along entrance range paths and down the Lime Walk; 17th April, Sissinghurst transferred to National Trust, with Graham Stuart Thomas as Gardens Adviser; Moat Walk side of Sissinghurst Crescent hedge cut back; Cambridge glasshouse provided; visitor numbers reach 47,000; box hedges in east half of Rose Garden replanted.

1968 Harold dies at Sissinghurst on 1st May; box hedges in west half of Rose Garden replanted; steps renewed and paving extended between Moat Walk and Orchard; visitor numbers 57,000.

1968-9 Paving laid in the west half of the Rose Garden.

1969 Inside and top of Yew Walk hedges cut back; gazebo completed in memory of Harold; paving around Thyme Lawn; Herb Garden repaved; concrete path through Nuttery repaved with York stone.

1970 White Garden levels corrected, a quarter of box edgings replanted and all paving relaid; rose arbour designed by Nigel; major repairs to buildings and walls begun; concrete paving in Herb Garden replaced with York stone and grass paths paved with brick; rejuvenation of azaleas along Moat Walk begins; revetment of moat replaced; polyanthus in Nuttery show increasing signs of replant disease; drainage scheme throughout most of the garden (incorporating, from 1972, taps for watering) starts with moat outlet and Orchard.

1971 Wall between Top Courtyard and Rose Garden rebuilt; paths and edgings in Top Courtyard relaid.

1975 Outside of Yew Walk hedges cut back; Nuttery underplanted with woodland plants following death of polyanthus.

1976-8 Outside of Rondel hedge cut back; Lime Walk repaved with York stone; Lime Walk trees replaced (spring 1977) with semi-mature trees; most trees die from summer drought following excessive winter wet and are replaced with young trees.

1978-9 New car park made and screening and shelter belts planted.

1981 Inside of Rondel hedge cut back and paving laid round Rondel lawn (final stage of path improvement and restoration).

1984 Catalogue of plants in the garden compiled by the National Trust.

1985 Jim Marshall takes over from Graham Stuart Thomas as Gardens Adviser.

1987 Great Storm causes loss of Orchard trees, large trees in park field and weeping silver pear in White Garden; many trees, including pear, replaced.

1991 Sarah Cook takes over as Head Gardener; visitor numbers 197,000.

1992 Timed ticket system introduced; visitor numbers fall to 153,000.

1994 Sarah Cook appointed to new role of Property Manager.

1995 Statue of Dionysus replaced.

Sissinghurst
Past, Present and Future

Harold and Vita photographed by Cecil Beaton.

The story of Harold Nicolson and Vita Sackville-West, their unconventional marriage and their garden at Sissinghurst has been told before, by such excellent authors as Nigel Nicolson, Victoria Glendinning, Anne Scott-James and Jane Brown. The aim of this volume is to concentrate on the garden, how it was made and how it has survived. The planting is discussed in depth, as are the techniques used to maintain the whole to such a high standard.

Some influential gardeners do not consider Sissinghurst to be a garden of the first rank. In my opinion they are quite wrong: they are mistaking understatement and restraint in design for weakness. Moreover, great gardens do not depend on design alone. Planting and romance are equally important; and all can be eroded if resources, particularly of skilled and sensitive staff, are lacking. The garden at Sissinghurst is strong in all four areas. True, its romance might be trumped by Italy's Ninfa, or the cleverness of its design, unhampered by restraints of existing enclosures and awkward axes, by Hidcote in Gloucestershire, the great gardens of France or other Italian gardens. But few are so pleasing overall. The continued popularity of Sissinghurst is evidence of the survival of its spirit and beauty.

✑

Since childhood, Vita had been susceptible to the charms of the garden at Knole in Kent, home of her parents Lord and Lady Sackville. She married Harold Nicolson on 1st October 1913, and together they made their first garden at Cospoli near Constantinople, where Harold was serving as a diplomat. They returned to England in June 1914 and bought Long Barn, their home at Weald, only two miles from Vita's beloved Knole, in the spring of 1915. Here Vita learnt about plants while Harold developed his skills as a garden designer. As they were to do later at Sissinghurst, they divided their garden into separate 'rooms', some of them planned for a restricted range of colours. Their friend Sir Edwin Lutyens helped Harold to devise a plan for a small parterre garden of L-shaped beds.

Vita's passion for plants was shaped by her love of old Dutch flower paintings and by the choice species she saw on her travels, sometimes with Harold, to places such as Persia and the Alps. The romantic associations of flowers with the past, painters and faraway countries were to influence her choice of planting at Sissinghurst in the years to come.

By 1930, the Nicolsons had become worried about proposed developments to the farm adjoining Long Barn and had been considering a move. On 4th April, Vita and her younger son Nigel went to see Sissinghurst, then little more than a series of ruinous buildings surrounded by derelict farmland. In the sixteenth century, Sissinghurst had belonged to Sir John Baker, whose daughter Cecily married Sir Thomas Sackville, later owner of Knole. Thus for centuries Sissinghurst had been owned by Vita's ancestors. Overwhelmed by its romance and ignoring all the difficulties, she told Harold she had found the ideal home. He visited with their other son Ben the next day and was charmed but daunted by the problems and probable expense. For weeks he vacillated, writing to Vita on 24th April:

'My view is:

(a) That it is most unwise of us to get Sissinghurst. It costs us £12,000 to buy and will cost another good £15,000 to put in order. This will mean nearly £30,000 before we have done with it. For £30,000 we could buy a beautiful place replete with park, garage, h. and c., central heating, historical associations, and two lodges r. and l.

(b) That it is most wise of us to buy Sissinghurst. Through its veins pulses the blood of the Sackville dynasty. True it is that it comes through the female line – but then we are both feminist, and after all Knole came in the same way. It is, for you, an ancestral mansion: that makes up for company's water and h. and c.

(c) It is in Kent. It is in a part of Kent we like. It is self-contained. I could make a lake. The boys could ride.

(d) We like it.'

Harold acquiesced. On 7th May Vita bought Sissinghurst. But though work on both the buildings and the garden started almost immediately, it was not until 1932 that Harold and Vita were able to let Long Barn and move in. At that point they employed as their architect Albert Reginald Powys, the Secretary of the Society for the Preservation of Ancient Buildings, who had probably come to their notice through the recent campaign against the plundering of ancient buildings for reassembly elsewhere. Powys was responsible not only for making Sissinghurst's buildings habitable but for building some of the garden's walls, most notably the curved one in the Rose Garden that bears his name.

The making of the garden proceeded rapidly; by the outbreak of war in 1939, the basic character of each area, except the White Garden and the Thyme Lawn, had been established. In 1953, Vita set out their roles and objectives in an article in the journal of the Royal Horticultural Society:

'I could never have done it myself. Fortunately I had, through marriage, the ideal collaborator. Harold Nicolson should have been a garden-architect in another life. He has a natural taste for symmetry, and an ingenuity for forcing focal points or long-distance views where everything seemed against him, a capacity I totally lacked. We did, however, agree entirely on what was to be the main principle of the garden: a combination of long axial walks . . . and the more intimate surprise of small geometrical gardens opening off them, rather as the rooms of an enormous house would open off the arterial corridors. There should be the strictest formality of design, with the maximum informality in planting.'

Seldom does a single person excel at both garden design and planting – Beatrix Farrand being a rare exception – and few great gardens have been made by one person alone. Most are the result of collaboration: the partnership of Gertrude Jekyll and Edwin Lutyens is perhaps the most famous example; at Hidcote, Lawrence Johnston laid down the bones of the garden with substantial help from Norah Lindsay in the planting. And Sissinghurst has always been seen as the product of a creative tension between the Apollonian order and control of Harold's formal design and the Dionysian exuberance of Vita's planting. This is indeed, in broad terms, how it was. However, it would be simplistic to regard Harold solely as the garden designer and Vita as the provider of the planting. Nigel Nicolson recalls them consulting, Harold asking Vita how she would plant whatever design he had in mind. And although Nigel feels that Harold was much more of a plantsman than Vita was a designer, it should be acknowledged that it is perhaps through Vita's influence that the garden is so restrained; Harold's more imaginative suggestions for solutions to design problems were sometimes dismissed by Vita in favour of something simpler. All the hedges were flat-topped and, except for the yew buttresses in the Herb Garden, without any piers or finials. Only in the box parterre of the White Garden, the yew buttresses of the Herb Garden and perhaps the design of Sissinghurst Crescent is there any adornment, anything other than the most basic treatment. Another exception dates from the 1960s when, at Nigel Nicolson's suggestion, the hedges on either side of the opening through the Yew Walk were stepped up, to strengthen this part of the vista from the tower to Dionysus. In each of these cases, few would dispute that a more elaborate design has been justified. Throughout the garden, the addition of well-chosen statues, urns and vases as focal points, bringing with them the romance of the past, is made the more telling by the simplicity of the surrounding framework.

Jane Brown has identified the restraint of Sissinghurst as one of its most noteworthy features:

'Along with the plethora of imitations of the English classical revival style comes a whole host of familiar furnishings, which it is well to note that Sissinghurst does *not* have: it has no long grass walk flanked by double borders, no pergola, no pools or fountains, no trellis walks or arbours, and no topiary twists or triangles. There are no white-painted seats, no Versailles tubs, there is no iris nor laburnum tunnel, no balustraded terrace or columned temple, and there are very definitely no Japanese touches or *trompe l'oeil* effects. There are plenty of such things in other gardens.'

This apparent simplicity is deceptive, leading some to suggest that there is little to the design, that the Nicolsons merely threw up a few walls and hedges to complete existing enclosures, and scattered a few statues. This is plainly not so. Consider as an example the axis from the White Garden to the head of the Lime Walk: this entire sequence is built up from one original feature that predated their arrival: the doorway at the south end of the Lower Courtyard. This determined the position of the Bishops' Gate and the wall that contains it, the *clairvoyée* at the farthest end of the White Garden, the Rondel and the statue at the head of the Lime Walk. Harold's treatment of the irregularly shaped White Garden to make it look rectangular, his clever handling of the Lime Walk axis and his use of the statue of Dionysus to terminate both the Moat Walk and tower vistas, were masterly. It is a tribute to his skill that visitors today find it so logical that it is hard to believe its enclosures and axes were not always there. There are few aspects of the design that fail to satisfy completely.

Much has been made of Sissinghurst as a series of 'garden rooms', a term that Vita herself used but which has since become a cliché. However, Vita and Harold certainly saw the garden thus and Harold greatly valued what he called Sissinghurst's 'succession of privacies'. Most of the enclosures already existed when Sissinghurst was bought, or at least had three of their four 'walls'. If Sissinghurst had not had the capacity to be made into such rooms, it would not have offered the Nicolsons the potential for the sort of garden they liked and they might never have bought it.

Gardens of this kind were not new; there are many of this period or a little earlier that are similarly subdivided: Snowshill, Rodmarton and Hidcote spring to mind. But what makes the garden compartments at Sissinghurst genuine rooms is the way they were used. Harold and Vita lived in their garden as though it were a house; it linked the fragmented buildings of Sissinghurst together, the bedrooms and sitting room in the South Cottage to the dining room in the Priest's House, the library to Vita's study in the tower. They spent as much time out of doors as they did inside, so that garden areas truly served as rooms: the Top Courtyard was an entrance hall, the White Garden a dining room, the Cottage Garden another sitting room for Harold, and the Lime Walk his long gallery.

The photographs of the garden in Vita's day are the most reliable guide to her style of planting. Her gardening notebook contains other clues, lists of plants she liked and those she ordered from nurseries. Her *Observer* articles are a rather less trustworthy guide, for she occasionally wrote about other styles of planting which she admired but seems never to have adopted at Sissinghurst.

The Rose Garden, as it appears in old photographs and remains today, shows the hallmarks of her style: she preferred soft and unstructured masses; little use of bold foliage or contrasting form; no 'punctuation plants'; only sparing use of variegated plants; few colour contrasts (an exception being soft orange and blue, a combination also used at Long Barn). Vita's love of the floral arrangements of the Dutch masters, their abundance and romance, the unstructured tumble of flowers, is evidence of her taste. In the Rose Garden we still see Vita's overflowing and exuberant planting, relying little on form or foliage. However, the lack of varied flower colour in the White Garden forced her to use foliage effects and in the Cottage Garden the tender plants which supplied the hot colours often had bold leaves.

The catalogue of plants in the garden compiled by the National Trust in 1984 gives more information about Vita's plants. It has been annotated by Pam Schwerdt and Sibylle Kreutzberger, Head Gardeners from 1959 to 1991, with those plants that were in the same position in 1959 and also with those grown in the garden at that time though not in the same place. The catalogue shows that, although many shrubs and wall plants remain where they were in Vita's time, less than one-third of the plants now at Sissinghurst were there in 1959. In spite of such wholesale changes to the planting, neither the Trust nor the gardeners have wanted to change the character of the garden. Pam and Sibylle always aimed to stay within the original spirit of each area to retain the style of Vita's planting.

The substantial change in the plants used is the result of a policy of flexibility within unchanging guidelines: since Vita's time, the gardeners have constantly revised the planting, replacing unsuccessful plants with better varieties and trying to achieve an attractive display in each of the garden's areas for as much of the visiting season as possible. This policy has proved a creative stimulus, allowing the garden to be refreshed constantly and renewed from year to year. As Pam Schwerdt says, 'Had Lady Nicolson been alive, she would always have been adding plants. We were always so thankful that somewhere along the line somebody decided that Sissinghurst was going to be a place where we would go on adding rather than that someone would absolutely stop the clock.'

Dawn over Sissinghurst. Seen from the south-west, the timeless view of fields, hedgerows, woods and ancestral oaks remains unchanged by modern agriculture. Some young oaks can be seen in planting guards.

The planting plans throughout this book should therefore be considered as a qualitative guide to the planting rather than as a prescription. They show the planting as of 1994, yet even by the following season a substantial proportion of the plants had been moved to different positions. This is one of the characteristics that makes repeated visits to Sissinghurst so rewarding: though the atmosphere of each garden room will remain the same, many of the plant associations will be different. There is probably no other garden in the world in which, over the last thirty years, so many successful plant associations have been assembled.

~

It is often said that Harold and Vita were snobs. It is certainly true that they preferred to associate with intellectuals. But though Harold disliked gaudy and overused flowers, neither of them was a horticultural snob. Vita was in fact fascinated by novelties: Pam and Sibylle remember with amused affection her excitement at the new asbestos roof for the cow shed and her pale green plastic bathroom curtains decorated with sailing boats. Gardening novelties aroused her interest too, whether they were gadgets or new colour 'breaks' such as bright orange or bicoloured roses; these all made good copy for her weekly *Observer* articles, though her interest in new things did not always extend beyond a trial period.

Vita's notebook contains many jottings of the best new Hybrid Teas and Floribundas, some of them clearly intended for Sissinghurst rather than just as material for her articles. Some survive in the garden to this day. Nor did she dislike double flowers: she was particularly fond of double primroses and wrote of the double varieties of the florists' flowers of old arousing her worst feelings of envy. However, she did hate any flower that was coarse or clumsy.

There are snobs who set up Vita as a garden goddess of unimpeachable taste and insist that her horticultural preferences must therefore match their own. Such people often believe, as did Miss Jekyll, that good gardening is solely the province of the armigerous classes, that no professional gardener is capable of exercising artistry in the garden and gardens run solely by professionals are doomed rapidly to reach the nadir of soulless bad taste. Such opinions are as ridiculous as they are odious. It is absurd to suggest that horticulturists who devote themselves single-mindedly to the creation of beautiful gardens cannot achieve artistic standards to match those of owners who dabble in their borders for a few hours a week and

Harold's lake, created in 1931 with help from Ben and Nigel, seen beyond the Cottage Garden and Lime Walk from the tower. The magnificent oaks that surround the garden enhance many views from within and strengthen the sense of Sissinghurst's continuity with an ancient past.

lack the horticultural knowledge and technique to maximize their gardens' beauty. It may be rare for horticulturists to subjugate their own preferences to the styles of planting already possessed by a garden, but that is exactly what Sissinghurst's gardeners have done since the Nicolsons' time. Many assume that all the garden's most beautiful plant associations were created by Vita, and any less successful ones by the gardeners. This is a fallacy: although the style and spirit of Vita's garden remain, the planting has been so frequently and so comprehensively rearranged that few of its individual groupings have endured; the associations we see, though in Vita's style, are predominantly the creation of the gardeners.

As gardeners departed to fight in the war, it became hard to maintain the whole garden. Jack Vass, who became Head Gardener in October 1939, left to join the Royal Air Force in 1941, telling Vita that whatever else was allowed to decline, the hedges must be kept in good order; everything else could be reclaimed in time. Vass's return to Sissinghurst in 1946 heralded the rebirth of the garden; the restoration of the planting and the extra maturity of shrubs and trees ensured that Sissinghurst was more beautiful than ever. But by the time Vass left in 1957, Harold and Vita's health and energy were declining. Standards in the garden slipped: hedges became too tall and too broad, destroying proportions and narrowing vistas; perennial weeds colonized large areas; rose pruning was inadequate; routine replanting was neglected so that the balance between key plants was lost. So little organic matter had been added to the ground that soil structure suffered and the plants struggled.

To most garden visitors in the late fifties, Sissinghurst seemed more free and more romantic than ever. But professional horticulturists who remember it from this time recall that the garden seemed to have reached the point at which excessive freedom and informality were about to give way to chaotic ugliness and, before long, oblivion. Their enjoyment of the garden was spoilt by their knowledge that, however lovely its appearance, it could not continue to exist without monumental and sustained effort and the utmost skill. Such a state of near wildness, in which gardeners have to fight a perpetual rearguard action against advancing weeds, to struggle with excessively wide and high hedges, wastes much time that could better be spent on the delicate balances of fine planting. This is the most transient of states, nearly impossible to maintain and almost always leading to the final disappearance of all that is good and fair; such an ephemeral condition may only be enjoyed for a very few years and deprives future generations of a more lasting and sustainable beauty. Sissinghurst as it was in the late 1950s looked unlikely to survive.

The arrival of Pam Schwerdt and Sibylle Kreutzberger was a happy chance that proved to be Sissinghurst's salvation. Both had trained from 1949 at Waterperry Horticultural School in Oxfordshire, which was run by the formidable Miss Beatrix Havergal who was renowned for teaching the growing of plants and garden craftsmanship to the highest standards. After two years' training, both worked on the staff (though Sibylle worked away for a time before returning to Waterperry). Nearly ten years after their arrival, Pam and Sibylle felt that life there was 'rather like being at boarding school forever'.

They decided that they would like to start a nursery, perhaps in the neglected walled garden of some country estate. An advertisement asking for a suitable nursery site was to be placed in *The Times*, but was delayed until it could be printed at the top of the column on the front page. A five-week strike intervened. Rather than do nothing, Pam and Sibylle wrote to various people, including gardening correspondents, one of whom was Vita, then correspondent for the *Observer*. Vita replied that she knew of no suitable place for a nursery but wished them luck.

A week later, Vita wrote again to say that she was looking for a Head Gardener, but only one. Pam and Sibylle replied that they were two; however, they agreed to visit Sissinghurst on 17th July 1959, though they had little intention of working there. Vita offered to employ them both but they asked to defer their decision until their advertisement had appeared. In the event, over fifty replies yielded not a single place appropriate for nursery and home; they went to Sissinghurst.

In days when work was relatively easy to find, particularly for such highly experienced professionals, Pam and Sibylle worried little about whether they would like the job in the long term: if they had not found it satisfying, they would have resigned and moved elsewhere. Vita was intrigued with her new gardeners and used to suggest to guests that they go to see 'the girls' rather than the garden. Sissinghurst's visitors were also fascinated: Sibylle recalls them pointing and saying 'Look, they've got *lady* gardeners', as though they were at the zoo. The novelty was less popular with the existing gardeners, who had been there for years: they were not used to being told what to do by women. However, Pam and Sibylle felt in no position to give orders to long-established staff, who were left to get on with the jobs they had always done; meanwhile there were many skilled tasks for the new Head Gardeners to tackle. Undaunted by the scale of the undertaking, they worked steadily to improve standards and planting.

Pam and Sibylle received few instructions from Vita and almost none from Harold, who spent the weekdays in London, only returning to Sissinghurst at weekends. Occasionally Vita would buy or be given a new plant; Pam and Sibylle would go around the garden with her to find a suitable site. Comments that 'something must be done' with Irish yews or figs were taken as requests for action, but Vita did not specify the means; the gardeners were trusted to take the appropriate measures. There were no discussions about Vita's theories for planting each of the garden areas;

they took their cue from the style of planting already there. Occasionally they were invited to dinner with the Nicolsons and their guests, an indication that in some ways Harold and Vita were not in the least snobbish, for it was unusual then to dine with one's gardeners.

Pam and Sibylle did not attempt to make major changes to the garden during Vita's lifetime. Perhaps their most significant innovation then was the making of a nursery on the far side of the Rose Garden. Vita was curious and would sit on the edge of the frames, pulling out the labels to read them and often putting them back in the wrong pot. They recall particularly from those years the strange procession that used to cross from the Priest's House to the South Cottage across the Orchard and back: the butler, wearing a white coat and galoshes and accompanied by his wife, would walk to and fro carrying a silver tea tray, a vacuum cleaner or mops and brushes in a curious mix of stateliness and rustic domesticity.

ҩ

Vita had been a founder member of the National Trust's Gardens Committee in 1948 and had supported the Trust enthusiastically, as had Harold who joined its Council in 1944 and was later Vice-Chairman of its Executive Committee. In 1954, Nigel asked her about the future of Sissinghurst: should it be made over to the Trust? The response in her diary was vehement.

'I said, Never, never, never. *Au grand jamais, jamais.* Never, never, never! Not that hard little metal plate at my door! Nigel can do what he likes when I am dead, but so long as I live, no Nat Trust or any other foreign body shall have my darling. No, no. Over my corpse or my ashes, not otherwise. No, no. I felt myself flush with rage. It is bad enough to have lost my Knole, but they shan't take S/hurst from me. That, at least, is my own. I *won't*, they can't make me, I never would.'

But for all the force of this outburst, occasioned by Vita's possessiveness about the places she loved, neither she nor Harold had any hostility towards the Trust, which they had both supported loyally.

Vita died at Sissinghurst on 2nd June 1962. Harold placed a memorial to her under the tower arch: it read 'Here lived V. Sackville-West who made this garden.' On being told the proposed wording, Nigel asked his father if he wasn't being rather hard on himself, for the creation of the garden had been a joint effort in which Harold and Vita had played roles of comparable importance. 'No,' replied Harold, 'it was her garden.' To Harold, his own contribution did not matter; what made Sissinghurst

This view of the Orchard from the tower shows the vista to Dionysus converging with that along the Moat Walk. The poplar avenue to the lake can be seen at the top right.

precious to him were the elements added by Vita. It was the personification in planting of his beloved wife.

Vita left Sissinghurst to Nigel, the more rural of her two sons, who took over the running of the garden. He considered that his 'main desire and duty was to save what she and my father had created, to preserve in perpetuity the garden which, together with her books, is the legacy of her imagination'. Faced with heavy death duties that could not be met out of capital, all of which had been invested in the repair of the buildings and the making of the garden, Nigel had two options: one was to sell the farm, leaving the castle and garden isolated in the middle of someone else's property; the other was to offer the castle and garden to the Treasury in part payment of duty, on the understanding that the property would be transferred to the National Trust. Vita had left Nigel a letter saying that she realized what the financial problems would be and would understand if he wanted to choose this option. Just over a month after Vita's death, Sissinghurst (with Harold's knowledge and consent) was offered to the National Trust.

❧

The transfer to the Trust was not a foregone conclusion, for some members of its Gardens Committee felt that Sissinghurst should not be accepted. Dr George Taylor, the Chairman, thought it 'not one of the great gardens of England'; another member, Vita's friend Alvilde Lees-Milne, protested: 'I and thousands of others put Sissinghurst way above such places as Sheffield Park. It is not only romantic and intimate, as well as full of interest, it also happens to have been created by a great English poet and writer. To my way of thinking it is everything a garden should be.'

Alvilde Lees-Milne's support won the day: Sissinghurst was transferred to the National Trust on 17th April 1967. It is our good fortune that Nigel Nicolson was so determined it should survive, that it had gardeners capable of achieving and maintaining such high standards and that it enjoyed the continued support of the Trust. Without any one of these, Sissinghurst's garden might have been little more than a recollection of a golden past; and without its pre-eminence in the public's affection, the memory of its creators and their literary achievements could not so effectively have been kept alive.

Harold lived for six years after Vita, dying at Sissinghurst on 1st May 1968. As a memorial to him, Nigel and Ben planned a gazebo for the north-east corner of the Orchard. Designed by Nigel with assistance from the architect Francis Pym, it was completed in 1969. With windows along its north-east side facing towards Canterbury, it proved to be an ideal place for Nigel to work. It was also an effective focal point, drawing visitors to this farthest corner of the Orchard.

Since the deaths of Vita and Harold, Nigel Nicolson has continued to play an active part at Sissinghurst, a 'front of house' role in which distinguished visitors are received and much helpful publicity generated. Nigel has written successive editions of the guide book and created the splendid exhibition in the Oast House celebrating his parents, Sissinghurst's past and the creation of its garden. His writing and lectures have played a major part in making Sissinghurst one of the most successful of the National Trust's properties.

One of the most significant changes resulting from the transfer of ownership was the great increase in the numbers of visitors. From 28,000 in 1966, the total rose to 47,000 the following year, the first time Sissinghurst was advertised to National Trust members. In 1968 there was another rise, to 57,000. In that year, the National Trust and the gardeners embarked upon a major programme of work that was to preserve Sissinghurst's built features for generations to come and equip it for the ever-increasing numbers of visitors. The crumbling vinery, tomato house and orchid house were replaced with a new glasshouse. Then there was no potting shed. The gardeners pleaded that 'you cannot expect to have a banquet without a kitchen'; and a potting shed was erected on the footings of the old orchid house. Other facilities, including a toolshed, a double garage for machinery, a lock-up chemical store and a washroom were provided for the gardeners. Walls were repointed and roofs mended; uneven paving, most of it laid on bare soil, was reset on a solid base throughout the garden, removing toe-tripping changes of level; grass paths, where they were regularly worn away by the thousands of visitors, were replaced with brick or stone. The scale of such projects would have been beyond all but the most affluent and determined of private owners. Otherwise, the gardeners were pleased to find that they were allowed to get on with maintaining the garden as they had done for the previous nine years, with the minimum of interference. They continued to refine the planting, removing poor varieties and adding good new ones, as Vita would have wished.

Harold and Vita's aim was never to make at Sissinghurst a great garden for posterity; they intended it solely as a place for their own pleasure and enjoyment. Its transition from family garden to one of world importance inevitably demanded alterations to its fabric and planting. In a public garden with so many visitors, it was not acceptable to have loose paving stones and uneven levels; seedlings no longer flowered in cracks in the paving, nor could plants sprawl gracefully on to the paths without being trampled. There are those who consider that such changes erode the romance of the garden, replacing its slightly ramshackle charm with a hard professionalism. Some feel that this amounts to unjustifiable interference with the garden's character; others will think that the garden's change of use and the public's expectations of perfection have made such alterations essential.

Pam and Sibylle consider the arrival of the garden centre in the 1960s to have brought about the greatest change in gardening during their time at Sissinghurst. In 1959, it was difficult to track down the choicest varieties from nurseries which advertised little and sent their catalogues only to a select few clients. Almost all plants were sold bare-rooted (though Sissinghurst's surplus plants were sold to the public in pots long before this became the norm). Now that it is relatively simple to track down any plant through British, European or American Plant Finders, it is easy to forget just how much effort was needed to search out the choice varieties used to enhance Sissinghurst's planting throughout the 1960s and 1970s. The gardeners always resisted adding large numbers of popular genera such as hosta or hemerocallis which would have had a noticeable impact on the character of the planting; only a few of the finest have been used.

Pam and Sibylle repeated groups of the same plants, sometimes with odd plants away from the group or occasionally straddling a path. Such effects are used in moderation. They have, however, made one general and most important change to the nature of the planting. Originally each area had its moment of beauty; when this passed, Harold and Vita could move on elsewhere. In spring there were the Lime Walk, Nuttery and Orchard. In early summer, the Rose Garden and Herb Garden reached their peak, followed by the White Garden and courtyards. Late summer and early autumn saw a second flush of bloom in the Rose Garden. Only the Cottage Garden, its colour scheme depending on oranges and reds rare among hardy plants and more frequent among long-flowering tender varieties, made a significant display throughout summer and into autumn.

Unlike Harold and Vita, visitors expect every area to be full of flower throughout the year. Pam and Sibylle's success in meeting this expectation has had implications far beyond Sissinghurst. By preferring long-flowering varieties and by championing tender perennials, they have made most of the garden rooms colourful from spring to autumn without diminishing the impact of the display at their original intended season. They were among the first to incorporate a wide range of tender perennials such as salvias, verbenas and argyranthemums in mixed planting, and they recognized, as Miss Jekyll had done some decades before, the value of dahlias. Most gardeners in the British Isles now follow their example. There is no doubt that it has become so widely accepted that planting can, and should, perform from spring to autumn that few gardeners today would even contemplate the single-season garden. For those of us with but one garden room, this has been an undoubted advance.

Pam and Sibylle kept detailed records of planting and major tasks while they were at Sissinghurst in a series of notebooks. A diary for 1959–61 records their work while Vita was alive. Volumes for 1965–79 are entitled, with tongue firmly in cheek, 'Great Thoughts'; they include not just a

Pam Schwerdt (left) and Sibylle Kreutzberger in their Cotswold garden.

note of what plants were obtained, their sources and where they were planted, but reminders for the gardeners of what needed to be done around the garden. The staggering number of plants marked 'scrap', 'reduce' or 'redo' is evidence of their endless perfectionism. These volumes, though more extensive and ruthlessly critical, are much in the spirit of Vita's own garden notebook and those recording Harold's changes to the Lime Walk.

By the late 1980s, Pam and Sibylle felt that they would like to retire while they were young enough to make their own garden and a new life away from Sissinghurst. A suitable Head Gardener had to be found, knowledgeable in all the techniques used in the garden and sympathetic to its traditions of planting. Sarah Cook had trained in the Decorative section of the Alpine and Herbaceous Department at Kew under Assistant Curator Brian Halliwell before joining Sissinghurst's staff for four years from 1984. There followed a period as Head Gardener at Upton House in Warwickshire, notable for its dramatic terraced garden which achieved much of its tremendous potential during her years there. Sarah returned to Sissinghurst in autumn 1990 to work in tandem with Pam and Sibylle before taking over as Head Gardener in the New Year of 1991.

Throughout the 1980s, visitor numbers had crept ever higher until in 1991 they reached 197,000. Particularly at weekends, the garden became unbearably crowded; much of the turf was regularly worn away. Sissinghurst was a victim of its own success. A timed ticket system was introduced in 1992 to discourage the periodic overcrowding of the garden and limit the number of visitors to about 400 at any one time. Though this helped to spread the load, numbers remain high and seem likely to average at an annual figure of around 180,000.

Though Sarah Cook plans no major change in the management of the garden, there have been some developments since 1991. Just as most great gardens have been made by a creative partnership between two people, so few good gardens maintain high standards through direction by a single gardener; almost all depend on the interplay of ideas from two sympathetic but not identically minded protagonists. Thus Harold and Vita created Sissinghurst; Pam and Sibylle enriched it and ensured its survival for another generation. Sarah recognizes the need for an assistant of high calibre with whom she can evaluate standards and planting and assess what needs to be done over the coming weeks, months and years. Assistant Head Gardener Alexis Datta, who was appointed in 1991, now fills this role; she and Sarah have regular 'fault-finding' tours of the garden, analysing successes and failures and noting what action is necessary, in a way that is analogous to Pam and Sibylle's record of the garden's requirements in their 'Great Thoughts' notebooks.

A seventh gardener has also been added to the team, allowing outer areas such as the car park, formerly maintained by contractors, to be tackled by the gardeners. This makes possible longer grass and a more natural finish than the close cut which was all the contractors' machines could provide. The extra staffing also means that one of the gardeners has had time to specialize in machinery maintenance.

Though the staffing has changed from two Head Gardeners plus four staff in Pam and Sibylle's time to one Head Gardener plus six today, the hours spent in the garden have not changed greatly: the working week has been reduced from forty-four to thirty-nine hours and the gardeners now have longer holidays. More efficient machinery has helped, such as the new mower used in the Orchard, which can cut and pick up long grass, saving the effort of raking it off by hand. Volunteers provide welcome help with deadheading, and might in future be used for some other tasks, though of course there is no substitute for trained, skilled, experienced gardeners, who must always do the bulk of the work.

In 1994, Sarah Cook was appointed to the new role of Property Manager, which she now combines with that of Head Gardener. She co-ordinates the various activities at Sissinghurst, such as the shop, restaurant, visitor services, functions and building projects, with the running of the garden. This inevitably takes about two days a week of her time (though this has been offset to some extent by the employment of a part-time gardener), and she is not complacent about the difficulties it involves: she believes strongly that a garden cannot be run from an office and that head gardeners must work with their staff to learn what the garden needs and to pass on experience, information and enthusiasm; and she continues to spend as much time as possible in the garden. But she feels that combining the two roles helps ensure that the garden remains central to Sissinghurst's existence rather than one of several potentially competing enterprises.

Sarah Cook is the first to admit that her own methods of gardening and planting differ a little from those of Pam and Sibylle and that she is still learning about the garden. There are bound to be slight differences of approach, though she is committed to keeping the traditions of Sissinghurst and its spirit intact. The planting must continually be revitalized, not just by rearranging the existing plants but by constantly searching for good new varieties, as her predecessors had done.

☙

Much has been written in recent times of the stagnation of garden design. Complaining that the time has come to move away from Gertrude Jekyll's precepts for informal planting within a formal framework, critics frequently champion whimsical, badly planted and often profoundly ugly alternatives whose chief and sometimes only virtue is that they are different. Yet the continued popularity of Sissinghurst gives the clearest indication that this now-traditional style has not been surpassed: though it is labour-intensive, it is simply the most beautiful style we have: that is why the vast majority of gardeners and garden visitors find it so pleasing. By all means let us have innovatory styles; but I for one do not want to follow a new fashion until there is one that can match Sissinghurst in beauty.

National Trust gardens, including Sissinghurst, are sometimes the subject of spiteful comments about 'gardening by committee'. Yet Sissinghurst's planting has never been planned by more than two gardeners, and has always been vital and patently individual. It is sometimes suggested that regular visits from the Trust's Gardens Advisers bring uniformity; this too is unjust. Sissinghurst's Gardens Adviser, Jim Marshall, has little need to suggest what Sarah Cook or her staff should plant, though he gives information and encouragement in many other ways and brings to the garden a fresh eye. Nor does Jim or any other Gardens Adviser impose his or her own taste on any Trust garden: it is essential to select planting based solely on the traditions and character of the garden itself.

It is doubtful whether any organization other than the National Trust would have had the sensitivity and resources to keep the garden so alive,

Nigel Nicolson on the tower steps. The owner of Sissinghurst from Vita's death until its transfer to the National Trust, Nigel ran the estate and garden for some five years. He still lives there, and continues to support Sissinghurst *actively in many ways. The pots on the steps beside him hold* agapanthus, Lobelia richardsonii *and* Felicia amelloides *'Variegata', while the Bagatelle vases behind are planted with* Artemisia schmidtiana *'Nana'.*

to be enjoyed by so many. The expertise and commitment applied to tasks such as the repair of the walls, the re-laying of paths and the recasting of the bronze Bagatelle vases after their theft from the garden have been exemplary. The Trust's commissioning and reinstatement in July 1995 of a replica of the statue of Dionysus after the plaster of Paris original had crumbled are proof that the commitment continues.

Thus three happy circumstances have ensured the survival and enrichment of the garden since its creators' time. One is the foresight and continued generosity of Nigel Nicolson. The second is the single-minded

perseverance, industry and professionalism of Pam Schwerdt and Sibylle Kreutzberger. Not only have they kept alive the planting and the spirit of the garden but they have changed the way we all plant. Thirdly, the National Trust has given support for the gardeners, expertise for maintenance of the fabric, access and facilities for visitors, and a guarantee that the garden will continue to be enjoyed by countless thousands.

Sissinghurst's greatest inheritance is the vision of Harold and Vita, without whom the garden would not have existed. It survives today as a poignant reminder of their lives, and their horticultural and literary achievements.

The Top Courtyard

Sissinghurst's tower glows in the setting sun. Irish yews, trained with military precision, stand sentinel along Vita's precious sweep of paving; in the distance, Dionysus marks the end of the view. To the right, the South Cottage lurks behind magnolias.

The Top Courtyard is Sissinghurst's entrance hall. Setting the tone for the tour of the garden, the visitor is shown generously planted walls and borders around fine green lawn, and offered a choice of routes: there is the imposing vista beneath the tower through the Orchard towards Dionysus, the glimpse of the Rose Garden to the right, or the more mysterious entrance to the left, beyond which lies Delos and the White Garden. The temptations to rush on are great but should be resisted: the courtyard has its own attractions, not least the Purple Border, which are worth savouring for a while before venturing further.

It is an extraordinary coincidence that even as a child Vita had dreamed of having her own tower, a solitary place in which she could write and reflect. Here was just such a tower, no mere tacked-on turret but a vertiginous, romantic, rose-red Elizabethan rocket poised for take-off, soaring skyward, seemingly unattached and unrelated to the rest of Sissinghurst's more earth-bound fragments. Of course, the gardener pays a price for such architectural extravagance in ferocious wind turbulence.

The courtyard was cleared of the tumbledown Victorian cottages in its southern half in 1930, allowing the lawn to be sown in 1931. The central path was flagged with York stone in 1932 and four Irish yews were planted to stand sentinel along it in the same year. In a letter to their architect, A.R. Powys, Harold reported, 'We have put in our gigantic yews. From now on we shall watch them die gradually.' Even in the earliest photographs they appear to be large and picturesquely craggy in outline. In the same year, Harold and Vita consulted Powys about a wall to enclose the north end of the courtyard: Harold favoured something elaborately architectural but Vita wanted simplicity; Powys's suggestion of a loggia was rejected and the present wall was built in 1935.

In that same year they turned their attention to paving along the front of the courtyard range; Harold had preferred a terrace but this was difficult to reconcile with the plain and unadorned path from entrance to tower which Vita called 'my precious sweep'. Yet again, simplicity won the day and a path level with the lawn was chosen instead, necessitating once more the ploughing, levelling and reseeding of the turf. There was some debate about the best width for the path: Powys advised 2.7m/9ft; Harold and Vita wavered between preferring this and opting for a narrower path 1.8m/6ft wide. The York stone slabs were placed on the ground to the full width to show the effect; Harold and Vita opted for the narrower path. In spite of twice having been moved out from the wall to give more room for the wall shrubs, the path now seems rather pinched; with hindsight, the wider option might have been better, giving just the right amount of room for plants, benches, pedestrians and pots.

The lawn was neglected during the war but in 1946, with the return of Jack Vass, it was dug up and resown for a third time using sweepings from the hayracks in the barn. The resulting coarse turf took many years of exemplary culture to encourage the finer grass species and improve its appearance and resistance to wear. All the routes into the garden pass through the courtyard, demanding particular attention to the turf if it is to withstand such heavy wear.

Some of the earliest planting predates the present colour scheme and still survives, such as the bushes of *Rosa* 'Geranium' in the Purple Border, its flowers not of scarlet lake as its name suggests but of a rose red that harmonizes with the buildings' Tudor brick.

❧

The Purple Border is the courtyard's greatest gardening glory, conceived in a colour that was anathema to Miss Jekyll, which is perhaps why Vita chose it. She proved that in spite of that great lady's misgivings, such hues could be blended to give a rich and satisfying tapestry of colour. However, it is true that purple is difficult; it can seem sullen and lifeless. Though it can look sumptuous in dull weather, it is not flattered by sunlight, particularly when the sun is high in the sky, as it is during the garden's opening hours. In 1959 the border held a much more limited range of plants than we find today: there were onions such as *Allium stipitatum* and *A. sphaerocephalon*, purple smoke bush, *Thalictrum delavayi*, *Dahlia* 'Edinburgh' and miscellaneous seedlings of Michaelmas daisy and *Campanula lactiflora* of variable, and often inferior, quality. Of the few flowers that were not mauve or purple, the pure rich blue of *Anchusa* 'Loddon Royalist' did not blend happily and was removed; there was no attempt to provide a spring display, and few flowers for late summer and autumn; the walls held only about three clematis. In their early years at Sissinghurst, Pam and Sibylle encouraged Vita to enhance the range of plants, adding *Eryngium* × *tripartitum*, *Campanula glomerata* 'Superba' and *Persicaria bistorta* 'Superba'. Vita herself returned triumphant from

Great Dixter bearing four clematis that were to prove invaluable for carrying the border's colour scheme up to the top of the wall.

The gardeners worked continually to eliminate second-rate seedlings from the border and to extend the colour range: magenta was supplied by *Geranium psilostemon* and liatris; bistorts, *Dierama pulcherrimum* and *Dianthus amurensis* added lilac-pink; lavender-blues ranged from pale *Clematis* 'Perle d'Azur', eryngium and the best of the *Campanula lactiflora* seedlings to deep *Lavandula angustifolia* 'Hidcote'; tall cardoons and the lavender added a touch of silver foliage to leaven the scheme. Purple foliage, provided by *Vitis vinifera* 'Purpurea' and *Cotinus coggygria* 'Foliis Purpureis', is used sparingly; an excess could make the whole scheme intolerably leaden. The resulting recipe achieves a delicate balance, maintaining the richness Vita foresaw but adding sufficient light and bright tones to save this feast from stodgy indigestibility, aided late in the season by the piquant contrast of scarlet rose hips.

There is no reason why such planting should not provide a generous spring display, using tulips and biennial wallflowers to occupy gaps which the perennials fill later. Wallflower 'Ruby Gem' (syn. 'Purple Queen') is grown in the nursery and planted out in the autumn to accompany tulips such as 'Blue Parrot', 'Pandion', 'Dairy Maid' and 'Greuze'; the tulips remain in situ from year to year, though it is occasionally necessary to top them up by adding more bulbs. Such early flowers can be worked throughout the entire depth of the border; as the foliage of the tulips dies, it is engulfed by larger-growing perennials. Some of the permanent plants chime in with the early display, including Dwarf Bearded irises and perennial wallflowers such as *Erysimum* 'Constant Cheer' and *E.* 'Mrs L.K. Elmhirst'. However, it must be owned that incorporating such early planting with summer flowers has to be done with conviction and panache: scattered dots of flowers as bright as tulips and wallflowers can look infuriatingly spotty, failing to achieve any interplay with each other or flow of colours along the border. Planting for spring is costly, both in the labour needed to grow and plant wallflowers and in the price of bulbs. The gardeners strive to ensure that there is enough display to make it effective.

Since Vita and Harold's day, the border has been made to perform as well in late summer and autumn as it does at its intended apogee in early summer. The choicest asters, some tender salvias and a wider range of dahlias have proved invaluable in achieving this. Late-flowering plants such as dahlias must be started early under glass if they are to attain the necessary bulk to fill their stations and are almost in flower by the time they replace the wallflowers. Though there is no intention or desire to make the border evenly banked, it is difficult to keep its length filled for the whole of the prolonged season. There must be no lacunae to interrupt the counterpoint of colours and textures.

PLAN *Planting in the east end of the Purple Border in 1994. Differing flower sizes, from tiny silver-blue C. × jouiniana 'Praecox' to quite large lilac 'Victoria', along with the varied colours, help create an attractive tapestry to carry the border's colour scheme to the top of the wall.*

BELOW LEFT *The small flowers of* Viticella clematis *'Leonidas' mingle with larger 'Madame Julia Correvon'.*

BELOW RIGHT *The cherry-red flowers of* Rosa *'Geranium', a plant which predates the purple colour scheme.*

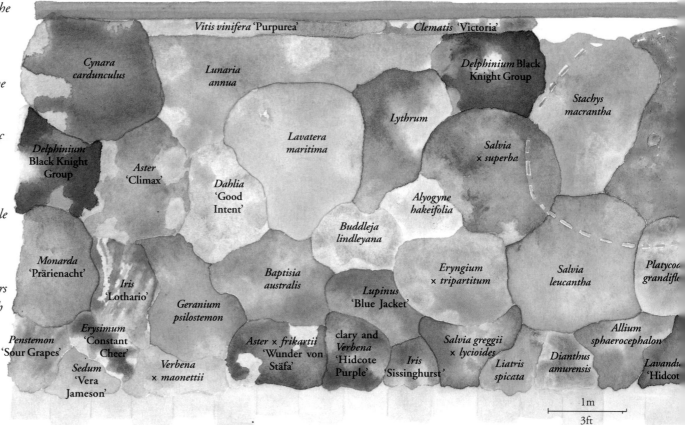

Vitis vinifera 'Purpurea'
Clematis 'Victoria'
Cynara cardunculus
Lunaria annua
Delphinium Black Knight Group
Stachys macrantha
Lythrum
Delphinium Black Knight Group
Aster 'Climax'
Lavatera maritima
Salvia × *superba*
Dahlia 'Good Intent'
Alyogyne hakeifolia
Buddleja lindleyana
Monarda 'Prärienacht'
Baptisia australis
Eryngium × *tripartitum*
Salvia leucantha
Platycoc grandiflo
Iris 'Lothario'
Geranium psilostemon
Lupinus 'Blue Jacket'
Penstemon 'Sour Grapes'
Erysimum 'Constant Cheer'
Aster × *frikartii* 'Wunder von Stäfa'
clary and *Verbena* 'Hidcote Purple'
Salvia greggii × *lycioides*
Allium sphaerocephalon
Sedum 'Vera Jameson'
Verbena × *maonettii*
Iris 'Sissinghurst'
Liatris spicata
Dianthus amurensis
Lavandu 'Hidcot

1m
3ft

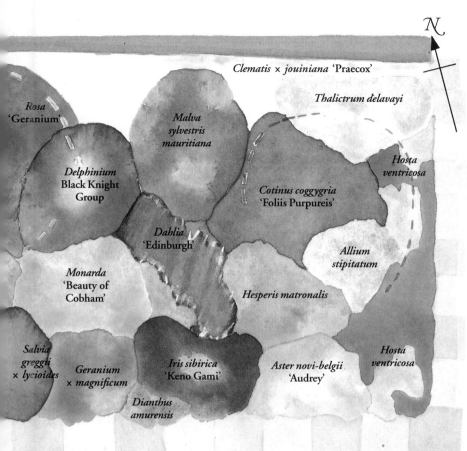

Clematis × jouiniana 'Praecox'

Thalictrum delavayi

Rosa 'Geranium'

Malva sylvestris mauritiana

Hosta ventricosa

Delphinium Black Knight Group

Cotinus coggygria 'Foliis Purpureis'

Dahlia 'Edinburgh'

Allium stipitatum

Monarda 'Beauty of Cobham'

Hesperis matronalis

Salvia greggii × lycioides

Geranium × magnificum

Iris sibirica 'Keno Gami'

Aster novi-belgii 'Audrey'

Hosta ventricosa

Dianthus amurensis

RIGHT ABOVE *Vinous-purple* Allium sphaerocephalon, *magenta liatris and lythrum occupy the red end of the Purple Border's spectrum, while* Salvia × superba *is near the centre of its colour range.* Clematis 'Perle d'Azur' *and sweet pea* 'Noel Sutton' *are at the blue end, and silver* Eryngium × tripartitum *will turn steely blue as the inflorescences age.*

RIGHT *A view into the border showing fragrant lupin 'Blue Jacket' and sweet rocket with the bold foliage of cardoons behind. The lupin is outstanding for its long primary and plentiful secondary spikes, ensuring several weeks of continuous flowering.*

The border in high summer at the peak of its display before the hips of Rosa 'Geranium' reveal their contrasting colour. Tall roses and Cotinus coggygria 'Foliis Purpureis' give a varied profile quite different from the evenly banked herbaceous borders that Vita disliked. Some plants, such as lavender 'Hidcote' (right) and Knautia macedonica (left), sprawl forward to soften the line of the stone edging. Though most plants are supported by hazel brushwood, the stakes are scarcely visible except in Aster × frikartii 'Wunder von Stäfa', which has yet to grow to hide them. In the corner of the courtyard, the solid shape of the flowering ash, seen dark against the morning sun, provides the border with a visual full stop.

27

LEFT *Looking southwards from the tower arch.* Rosa *'Geranium' is seen with* Rosmarinus officinalis *'Sissinghurst Blue' in the foreground.* Verbena bonariensis *threads itself through silver* Helichrysum petiolare *and* Artemisia 'Powis Castle' *at the front of the border.* Aster × frikartii *'Mönch' to the right, also used in the moat wall border and Rose Garden, again proves its usefulness.*

RIGHT *From the tower arch looking north towards the Priest's House. The same rose 'Geranium' appears to the right. The upright stems of rosemary 'Sissinghurst Blue' provide attractive texture. At the corner a flowering ash adds welcome height while,* below, Aster turbinellus *stands by the entrance to Delos.*

As elsewhere around the garden, the planting is constantly revised and reworked, as shown by a comparison of the planting plan for 1994 with that for 1993 shown in my previous book *Best Borders*. As many as a third of the groups can be moved from year to year. Even moving a single variety can throw out a whole series of plant associations, making an entire chain of recombinations necessary if all plants are to be effectively juxtaposed. Sarah Cook continues the tradition of constantly seeking out new and worthy plants; recent additions have included *Alyogyne hakeifolia*, *Malva sylvestris* var. *mauritiana* and a deep purple hybrid salvia (*S. greggii × lycioides*) which though not showy has fascinating richness and intensity.

Throughout the summer, plants are deadheaded as they approach the end of their floraison; if they have been correctly staked, the brushwood that supports them will stay hidden beneath the remaining foliage. Often, as for *Salvia × superba*, deadheading will encourage a second flush of flower. In some cases, as for *Geranium × magnificum* or *G. psilostemon*, the stakes must extend above the basal foliage and it is necessary to cut the group to the ground when it has finished flowering; new foliage is soon produced to keep the clump well furnished for the rest of the season. Such plants are placed in front of later-flowering plants; when cut down, the later blossom can appear behind the freshly grown foliage of the regrown clumps.

Thus it is possible to have some taller early flowering plants farther forward than might otherwise be possible.

A modicum of pest and disease control is essential, often tackled with the same sprays used for the roses. Mallows suffer from rust and are treated with a systemic fungicide; capsids on caryopteris, blackfly on cardoons and tarsonemid mites on Michaelmas daisies would destroy any flowers if left unchecked. The mites prevent blooms from developing on *Aster novi-belgii* cultivars and might also be responsible for distorted blooms of other aster species; they must be controlled by a monthly spray from late spring.

❧

The presence of the tower sets up powerful downdraughts that make careful staking essential in all the borders, using the same range of techniques described for the White Garden (see pages 141-5). Climbers on the walls must also be carefully tied in to their supports. The clematis are tied into 15cm/6in mesh pig wire every couple of weeks during the growing season with paper-covered wire twist ties. The vertical strands of the pig wire prevent the clematis from slipping too far sideways, avoiding kinking of the stems that can cause wounds through which clematis wilt disease can penetrate. The netting is wrapped over the top of the wall, allowing the

clematis to hold on to the top of the wall rather than being blown forward by the wind to form a bulky and unsightly quiff as it approaches the coping.

The two lengths of border to either side of the tower provide a similar range of flower colours to the Purple Border though their west-facing aspect receives less sun, requiring subtle differences in the range of plants. Fewer spring flowers are used here and several large shrubs such as escallonia, *Rubus odoratus* and purple-berried callicarpa interrupt the interplay of colours with wide expanses of green for all but their short season of display. Shrubs are used more here than in the Purple Border because the planting must be able to withstand the fierce buffeting of the downdraughts caused by the tower.

Though these borders are full of interesting plants and maintained to an equally high standard, it is the rather showier Purple Border that grabs visitors' attention the moment they enter the courtyard, drawing them magnetically towards its counterpoints, chords and carillons of colour. This imbalance is slightly unnerving: the tower borders are neither quite the same as the Purple Border nor entirely different. However, if they were made to equal the Purple Border in colour content and scale, the visitor might worry that the shady aquilegia border flanking the entrance to the Rose Garden did not match the others in hue and intensity.

Just south of the tower are yet more plants of *Rosa* 'Geranium', replacements for those planted here by Vita. In this southern section of border, Vita had planted Michaelmas daisies which were allowed to self-seed and run wild. She came to loathe these and resented time spent by the gardeners reducing or removing them, so they invaded further, blighting yet more border with their mildew-ridden weediness. It was not until after Vita's death that the gardeners eliminated the seedlings entirely, allowing only the choicest asters throughout the garden; graceful *A. turbinellus* is one of the most satisfactory, used near the entrance to Delos, with airy flowers of deep mauve borne over foliage that is perfectly free of mildew.

The east-facing wall of the entrance range is clad with a variety of climbers. Some of them, such as *Magnolia grandiflora* and, by the library door, vermilion *Chaenomeles × superba* 'Knap Hill Scarlet', are traditional, others, such as *Lonicera splendida* and the showier male form of *Ribes laurifolium*, more unusual. Slightly tender subjects such as *Solanum crispum* 'Glasnevin', ceanothus and hoherias have occasionally been cut to the ground or lost in cold winters as the morning sun rapidly thaws their frozen branches, splitting cells and bark asunder. Even the relatively hardy rose 'Mermaid' was killed here in 1985. After this severest of recent winters, the gardeners used seed-raised maurandyas and cobaeas to clothe the bare walls quickly.

Rose 'Allen Chandler' is perhaps something of a surprise here, its bright scarlet, loosely formed blooms seeming scarcely the sort of thing Vita would have liked; but it is a 'good doer' and shows spectacularly against the brick as many duskier and more subtle varieties would not. Another excellent rose, 'Blossomtime', sent by Hilda Murrell, grows in the south-west corner of the courtyard. Pam and Sibylle consider it to be underrated: its quartered blooms mix well with old varieties; it produces a second flush of bloom and is resistant to mildew.

The courtyard's shady north-facing border is predominantly a site for showing off the choicest wall plants. Morello cherries had grown here but were not pruned for several years; by 1959 they had grown high above the wall. Their flowers that Vita had enjoyed were yearly stripped by birds and they had become too large to be restored by pruning. Several plants of *Viburnum plicatum* were planted in between the cherries; as they filled the wall, the cherries were removed. The whole wall became unstable and had to be rebuilt by the National Trust in 1971. The viburnums and other wall plants were detached and the wall was dismantled and made again, adding two buttresses on the Rose Garden side and facing the exterior of the wall with original bricks. Few visitors were able to see any change to the wall, though some of the more observant thought that it might have been repointed. The viburnums succumbed to old age in 1994; the section of border where they grew has since been sterilized with dazomet and the viburnums replanted.

In front of the wall shrubs is a border of long-spurred aquilegias in a wide variety of colours intended to furnish the base of the wall shrubs; scarcely changed since Vita's day, this is one of very few areas at Sissinghurst where there is little attempt to add other plants for early or late display. The aquilegias remain in leaf from spring until the autumn so there are few opportunities for interplanting, save for an early spring display of chionodoxa; their flowering is delayed by the border's shady aspect so that they are still in bloom when the garden opens to the public. The aquilegias are a mixture including some McKana Hybrids and other seedlings from around the garden, the colours balanced to avoid an excess of blue. The gardeners widened the paving leading to the iron gate here, eliminating worn patches in the turf at the approach to the gate.

❧

The edging to the Purple Border was originally a single row of slabs, not wide enough to serve as a path, causing wear to the adjacent lawn. The gardeners added an extra row of slabs but visitor numbers increased and the grass was worn away once more. Paving and lawn were then not perfectly level with each other and were separated by an ugly 15cm/6in gulley that needed constant edging and weeding; the gulley governed the position of footfall from paving to lawn, concentrating the wear in one threadbare strip. When the paths and edgings were relaid in 1971, three-quarters of both the north and south sides of the lawn were raised, making the turf fractionally higher than the stones so that the mower could run over the edge. The gulley was filled in and the York stone edging broadened to its present width and aligned with the library door. This made the border's western end considerably deeper, allowing more generous group sizes and a more gradual banking of groups towards the back of the border.

The visual improvement and the saving in labour caused by such simple measures was immense and the wear was reduced to a manageable level. The lawns are checked weekly for wear and any bare patches that start to appear are cordoned off with canes and string and repaired by inserting plugs of hard-wearing grass (Mommersteeg MM50 plus MM14 mixes). These 'hair transplants' are grown in the nursery in trays of cells and blend quickly and imperceptibly with the existing grass. *Clematis* 'Alice Fisk' trained up poles in the south tower border regularly draws crowds of gasping onlookers, creating a balding area (the gardeners call it an 'admiration patch') that is cured in the same way.

A Ransomes Matador 60cm/24in cylinder mower is currently used to cut both these and the Lower Courtyard lawns. However, as all these lawns take a great deal of traffic and are more than usually prone to compaction, this might be replaced by a lighter model. During mild spells in early spring when the lawns are relatively wet, the grass is sometimes topped with a rotary mower, which prevents it getting too long and avoids causing compaction. Because the lawn is not perfectly rectangular, it is cut diagonally to mask its irregularity, cutting it at 2cm/1in once a week. The height of cut might be considered excessive in a private garden but is essential if the lawn is to withstand such heavy wear. Each stripe consists of a double mower width so that the stripes are not too small in proportion to the total area.

Troy Smith, who is responsible for lawns in both the courtyards, would prefer to be able to cut twice a week, particularly in late spring when fertilizer has speeded the grass's growth. However, the busy schedule does not allow time for this counsel of perfection: lawns are cut on a Wednesday, allowing the rest of the week for edging and other tidying jobs so that the whole garden is neat for the weekend. A Little Wonder edger is used, taking only five minutes to edge the courtyard. Troy is scathing about such contraptions and thinks that all are noisy and difficult to use; however, he admits that this one is as good as any and that they still offer a considerable saving in time and effort over edging by hand. The lawn is scarified in autumn to remove accumulated thatch and is also spiked with a Sisis Auto Turfman, then and periodically throughout the year, to improve surface aeration and drainage.

The south-east corner with (left) Clematis montana *var.* sericea *and (right) the layered branches of two* Viburnum plicatum *'Lanarth'. Four months later both viburnums had died; in such cases honey fungus is usually suspected, though old age is equally likely. The border of long-spurred aquilegias is a charming and unsophisticated feature.*

Spring fertilizers have varied over the years. Recently the gardeners have experimented with slow-release sorts, though a bad experience on the Moat Walk has made them cautious: heavy traffic caused the prills (resin-coated granules of fertilizer) to break open, scorching the already bruised grass. Soil analysis has shown that nitrogen is not deficient: high-N feeds that favour coarse grasses over finer sorts are avoided, likewise in autumn when a dressing of sulphate of potash alone is used.

Vita had been fascinated by selective weedkillers and used them with relish. In June 1954 she wrote:

'The weeds in the lawn are all curly. Dandelions, plantains and the daisy leaves have all turned upwards as though they were raising small hands to heaven in one last despairing prayer. In a few weeks' time I hope, heartlessly, that they will have disappeared and their place be taken by a nice clean sward of irreproachable turf, so mistakenly supposed by overseas visitors to demand four centuries in the making. . . . Instead of crawling about on all fours in solitary bad temper and incipient lumbago with a trowel or a broken kitchen knife, you may now promenade in a leisurely way, saunter up and down, sprinkling selective death from a watering-can as you converse with the friends who have come to tea.'

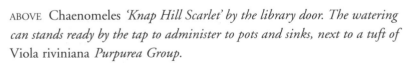

ABOVE Chaenomeles *'Knap Hill Scarlet' by the library door. The watering can stands ready by the tap to administer to pots and sinks, next to a tuft of* Viola riviniana *Purpurea Group.*

LEFT *Bright scarlet rose 'Allen Chandler' is to either side of the entrance range. To the right is* Ceanothus *'Percy Picton', echoed on the left by* C. *'Southmead' next to rose 'Meg'. The pots contain a choice clone of the tender Canary Island-endemic* Pericallis lanata, *a parent of the florists' cineraria. Left of the arch is the old Climbing Tea rose 'Gloire de Dijon' ; in the far corner is the excellent modern repeat-flowering 'Blossomtime'.*

TOP RIGHT Osteospermum ecklonis *'Prostratum' in the sink and, on the ground beneath, aquilegias and a young* Abutilon × suntense, *with* Erysimum *'Constant Cheer' and the bold glossy leaves of* Magnolia grandiflora *to the right.*

ABOVE RIGHT *A blue auricula of exceptional quality, selected from seedlings by Pam and Sibylle. Grown for several years, its vigour has declined, the usual consequence of the gradual accumulation of virus diseases. Its use was abandoned in 1995; Sarah will either raise seedlings from it and select the best progeny or have the virus removed by tissue culture.*

A fiery sunset lights the entrance arch and the tower beyond. The Lower Courtyard, Yew Walk and Orchard can be glimpsed through the tower arch. The awkward shift of axis, a typical example of what Harold considered 'the magnificent but constantly obtuse' nature of Sissinghurst, is the result of the entrance range being set at an angle to the tower. Above the arch are the arms of the Sackville-West family to the left and the Baker family to the right, placed there by Harold in the 1930s.

In these environmentally conscious days, we have come to mistrust the selectivity of such death. Fortunately with low ambient weed populations, full-scale invasions are rare; small incursions by clover are dealt with by spot applications of a translocated selective weedkiller. Vita's enthusiasm for selective weedkillers seems to have been short-lived for by 1959 they were no longer employed; only sodium chlorate was used, applied around the well in Delos, along the outside drive and around the barn.

Vita and Harold had found a number of stone sinks in Sissinghurst's outbuildings when they arrived, perhaps dating back to the Victorian workhouse laundry here, the source also of the coppers, one of which remains the centrepiece of the Cottage Garden. They realized that the sinks could be used to grow jewel-like alpines and bulbs, plants that would otherwise not fit easily into the larger scale of the garden. In November 1932 Harold discussed with A.R. Powys a plan to create a formal yew-hedged garden straddling the axis from tower to moat, jutting into the Orchard from the Yew Walk; the purpose of the garden would have been to display a series of 'alpine tables', planted in much the same way as the sinks were in the following years. Powys was gently sceptical, suggesting that tall hedges would not let in enough light for the alpines. Furthermore, this enclosure would not look satisfactory seen from the outside, from the South Cottage or the Orchard. The plan was abandoned and the alpines grown instead in sinks where we see them today.

It is probable that Vita was guided in the planting and culture of alpines in sinks by Will Ingwersen who, with his father Walter, ran a nursery famed for its exhibits of alpines in troughs and sinks at Birch Farm, on William Robinson's Gravetye estate. Aware that not all her readers had or were able to maintain large gardens, Vita extolled the virtues of this gardening in miniature, writing comprehensive articles about the subject in 1949 and 1954 as well as making frequent references to suitable plants; crocuses, irises and saxifrages seem to have been particular favourites.

However, by 1959 the sinks contained only a few crocuses, dwarf and bulbous irises. With the refurbishment of the entrance range in the early 1960s, the sinks were reset on their supporting piers and the plants renewed; the planting was in the same simple but effective style we see now, with seldom more than one or two different plants in each. Today perennials such as *Osteospermum ecklonis*, *Aquilegia glandulosa* and *Euphorbia myrsinites* flourish in the shallow soil, seeming perfectly in scale with their home. Slow-release fertilizer is incorporated in the compost and the sinks are regularly watered; usually once a week is enough. A particularly choice blue auricula raised in the garden was used until recently to fill one of the sinks but has declined in vigour. Its place is now taken by *Tulipa linifolia* (Batalinii Group) 'Bronze Charm' in spring, with lavender-blue *Nemesia caerulea* 'Percy Picton' for summer. The gardeners prefer this white-eyed nemesia to other rich lavender varieties: all the others have yellow eyes that are too small and of the wrong tone for an effective colour contrast; they just make the flowers seem grubby. *Gazania* 'Freddie' also enjoys the sinks' restricted root-run and a summer baking.

Outside the entrance to the Top Courtyard, the magnificent bronze Bagatelle vases which had belonged to Vita's mother, Lady Sackville, were planted in Vita's day with *Portulaca grandiflora*, brought to Sissinghurst after the war by Jack Vass. Though successful in hot dry summers, the portulaca never opened in dull weather. *Plecostachys serpyllifolia* (syn. *Helichrysum microphyllum*) now drapes itself gracefully over the vases in summer, with blue pansies for spring.

The pots Vita and Harold used along the entrance range path were not protected from frost in winter and by the mid 1960s had started to disintegrate. In 1967, Nigel Nicolson chanced upon some splendid pots lying by the roadside outside a large pottery near Siena. He ordered sixteen and arranged for them to be shipped home to Sissinghurst where they replaced the originals both along the entrance range path and down the Lime Walk. Decorated with generous swags and the Medici arms, their colour blends perfectly with Sissinghurst's brick. Pam and Sibylle used to plant them in summer with heliotrope which seldom throve, resenting the afternoon shade. Over the years several alternatives have been tried: deep blue petunias, the most richly scented colour, were sometimes combined with *Helichrysum petiolare* 'Limelight'; occasionally *Tradescantia pallida* 'Purpurea' was used; in recent years, vivid *Pericallis lanata* (syn. *Senecio heritieri*), its magenta flowers set off by a central white zone and grey foliage, has been planted, with *Verbena* 'Kemerton' to trail over the edge. Pansy 'Senator Blue with Blotch' is used for an early display, planted in mid spring once the pots' protective tarpaulins are removed.

The pots are filled with a peat-based compost containing heavy grit to which a slow-release fertilizer is added. It proved good for both pots and outside vases as it is water-retentive and, like the sinks, they seldom need to be watered more than once a week. For 1995, Sarah used fewer pericallis and introduced small-flowered trailing *Petunia integrifolia*, its numerous blooms more gracious than most modern hybrids.

の

The Top Courtyard provides a tantalizing foretaste of the delights the garden has in store. Though it contains one of the garden's most famed and successful set pieces, the Purple Border, its planting is relatively subdued: there is no attempt to upstage the brilliance of the White Garden or the Cottage Garden, or the soft abundance of Sissinghurst's roses. There is much for us all to learn from the gardeners' solutions to problems of culture in this difficult site.

The view from the Top Courtyard across the Lower Courtyard through the tower arch was given extra strength and significance by the addition, in 1946, of the statue of Dionysus on the far side of the moat. This vista now rivals the axis from the White Garden across the Rondel to the head of the Lime Walk in importance, and the simplicity of the treatment of the narrow opening in the Yew Walk seems almost too restrained. A pot of hedychium and Plecostachys serpyllifolia *in a Bagatelle vase can be glimpsed to left and right.*

The Lower Courtyard

The tower lit by the setting sun, with Macleaya microcarpa *in the foreground.*

Situated at the crossing of the two main axes, this spacious room is the formal heart of the garden. Beautiful plants furnish the three walls; clematis and roses in rich abundance illustrate the range of pruning and training techniques that are needed to produce the best results. There is no attempt in the Lower Courtyard to achieve maximum colour or impact: this is a 'decompression chamber' in which to relax between the excitements of Sissinghurst's set pieces.

Turf must be cultivated to the highest standards and the yew be crisp, well furnished and flourishing if the contrast of this formal space with its thoroughly informal planting is to be telling. The Yew Walk has suffered from most of the problems of such hedges, needing drastic pruning to maintain vistas, to keep the walk navigable and to prevent its hedges from becoming threadbare at the base.

The first feature to be created here, in the courtyard's south-west corner, was the Lion Pond, made in 1930 and, save for the moat, the garden's only water feature. The lawn was turfed the following year. In 1932 Harold and Vita enclosed the Lower Courtyard from the Orchard beyond by planting the Yew Walk. The west side of the Yew Walk was planted that spring and the east side the following autumn. The positioning of the walk might be considered odd, for it gives the Lower Courtyard a strangely elongated shape, at right angles to the axis from tower to moat, bisecting the original courtyard of the Tudor house. It has been suggested that Harold and Vita's courtyard should have coincided exactly with the original one to make a more satisfying, more or less square enclosure; however, this would have added substantially to the area of high-maintenance gardening and taken a large bite out of their beloved Orchard.

Also in 1932 a catalpa was planted in the larger northern part of the lawn, furnishing it and helping to make north and south seem comparable in size. The following year saw the arrival of two lead urns from Vita's mother, Lady Sackville, first placed on the tower steps; these have subsequently been replaced by two Bagatelle vases, also a gift from Lady Sackville. The urns are now on the Rose Garden's semicircular terrace. In 1934 magnolias from Hilliers nursery were planted in the south-eastern bed, known to this day as the magnolia bed. The Lion Pond, which failed to hold water, was drained in 1939; it is now the Sunken Garden. Vita's ideas for a colour scheme here of white with a touch of pink were not implemented, perhaps because of the war. After the war, the most significant change to the courtyard was the strengthening of the axis from tower to moat, achieved by adding the statue of Dionysus in 1946; sited just beyond the moat, this formed the perfect termination both to the garden's main vista through the tower and to the view along the Moat Walk.

The statue of the bacchante was formerly the focal point of the Yew Walk at its north end. But when the statue at the west end of the Lime Walk fell and broke, the bacchante, a good match for Bacchus among the nuts, was moved there in its stead. Harold then bought a white marble statue for the Yew Walk but this was replaced by Nigel some years later with the vase that is there today.

⁓

At the time the Yew Walk was being planted, Harold had planned to make more enclosures east of the walk, referred to in his letters to A.R. Powys as the Yew Gardens, which were to have covered a total area 12m/40ft square. He had considered that there were two possible widths for the breach in the walk through which the vista from tower to Dionysus is directed, either that of the whole tower, or 2.5m/8ft, the width of the tower arch. Powys thought the wider opening to be more generous, though he suggested 'posts' of yew within the gap, to give continuity to the yew hedges and enclosure to the Yew Gardens. Perhaps Powys was thinking of a similar arrangement to that on the Cedar Lawn at Montacute in Somerset; the house here had been rescued from demolition in 1931 by the Society for the Preservation of Ancient Buildings of which he was Secretary. Harold and Vita opted for the simplest treatment and the narrower width. The idea for the Yew Gardens was apparently abandoned soon after, but had Harold made these small garden rooms, this more constricted gap would have been as good a solution as any; however, in the context of the courtyard and the Orchard beyond, it seems rather pinched, particularly as the yews grow out, reducing the opening. The gap in the hedge between the proposed Yew Gardens and the Orchard was to have been a mere 60cm/2ft, utterly inadequate for a major vista. At that time there was no statue of Dionysus beyond to mark the termination of the vista. This suggests that Harold and Vita then considered the vista from the White Garden to the Rose Garden to be the garden's main axis and the route from tower to moat to be of minor importance, which is perhaps why the courtyard's

long shape then seemed to be preferable.

The severe simplicity of the Yew Walk and its linear form make it a complete contrast with all the garden's other component areas, never more effective than when emerging from its gloom into the bright and bounteous beauty of the White Garden. One is reminded of dark tunnels in eighteenth-century English landscape gardens, the terror of their dank, dripping blackness followed by the relief of emerging blinking into daylight. However, it must be owned that the walk is dark and claustrophobic, too narrow for two people to walk comfortably side by side. As Powys commented to Harold, it was scarcely broad enough for the original grass path to grow in its dark depths; nor had Harold allowed for the inevitable widening of the hedges with age. Harold was oblivious to such criticism, replying that he had been told that grass would grow, though he would not mind if it died: he and Vita wanted eventually to pave the path, for 'stone against yew is a lovely thing'.

The walk is undeniably narrow, but to have made it wider would have created other problems: moving the west side out would have made the courtyard even more worryingly elongated; moving the east side would have required the removal of the toolshed, unless this were to be left jutting obtrusively into the walk. One wonders nevertheless if the toolshed should not have been sacrificed and the entrance to the Rose Garden widened by a foot or so to make the walk rather more generously proportioned and to let in more light for the struggling yews.

⁓

A stone path soon replaced grass along the Yew Walk, at first barely half the width of the present paving. By the early 1960s, the yews had grown out across the vista to Dionysus, nearly blocking it; the gardeners cut them back on either side, restoring the vista to its original proportions.

By 1969, the hedges all along the Yew Walk had become so wide that the path was obstructed; inside the walk, the yews were dying at the base and the courtyard lawn was robbed of 1.2m/4ft of its width, making it noticeably narrower than was desirable. The gardeners decided to take drastic action: in March 1969 the hedges were cut back within the walk, a brave policy at a time when this technique was not established. The height of the hedges was also reduced by 60cm/2ft, letting more light into the walk to encourage the yews to regrow. Some had misgivings, fearing the hedges would never be the same again, but they responded at once.

None of this would have been possible had the yews not been generously fed in the previous year and drainage along the walk improved: regrowth can be patchy unless yew is in vigorous good health. Initially, pruning left short lengths of branch attached to the main stem; these did not grow and had to be cut back to the trunk, proving to the gardeners that the response

ABOVE Ceanothus × veitchianus *helps frame the view along the Yew Walk from the Rose Garden. Shafts of light across openings from the Orchard to the Lower Courtyard and White Garden encourage the visitor to explore.*

ABOVE RIGHT Macleaya microcarpa *and* Alstroemeria ligtu *hybrids in the Sunken Garden, planted by Vita, harmonize with the Tudor brick walls.*

came from the main stem rather than the laterals. To the relief of all, the hedges quickly sprouted.

The gardeners felt that the view of the hedges from the tower steps was so crucial that it should be impaired by hedge restoration for the shortest possible time. It was six years before the hedges were dense enough from top to toe for their outer sides to be cut back. This is a longer period than usual, a result of the shade and drought created by the large catalpa at the north end of the walk and the Orchard trees to the east, combined with poor drainage. The catalpa, beneath which Harold often used to sit and read, died before the restoration of the hedges was complete, allowing their outer sides to furnish much more quickly than their inner sides had done.

The extra breadth won within the walk allowed the stone path to be widened. This repaving also gave an opportunity to flatten some irritating bumps and dips and allowed the removal of a 30cm/1ft step, an inconvenience to gardeners with barrows, a vexation to visitors and a blemish to the walk's pure simplicity. Thus the walk assumed the same continuous and gradual slope as the Cottage Garden, Lower Courtyard and White Garden, instead of being separated from these by an annoying step. Now that the paving is even for the entire length and width of the walk, the gardeners are able to clip the hedges with geometrical precision using a wooden template resting on the path. This incorporates a few degrees of batter, though all openings through the hedges are given absolutely vertical sides.

The disadvantage of hedges that are fatter and taller than they should be lies not just in the effect this has on garden proportions and design: an extra 60cm/2ft of height and 1.2m/4ft of width can double the work of clipping, for the tops of hedges are always the most difficult part to cut. Furthermore, a wide hedge is much more likely to be broken apart or distorted by a heavy fall of snow. Though the gardeners try to clip off as much as possible of each annual increment of growth, the hedges inevitably become slightly wider each year.

Pam and Sibylle feel that in a garden on the confined scale of Sissinghurst, it would probably be necessary to cut the yews to the bone every thirty or so years to maintain the garden's proportions. Throughout the world, yews will generally respond well to severe pruning wherever they are hardy. However, temperate north-west Europe is an exception: summers here do not always sufficiently ripen the wood for regrowth to occur and a proportion of trees fails to respond. Even in Yorkshire, as little as 300km/200 miles north of Sissinghurst, it is likely that up to fifty per cent of yews will die if they are treated thus. It is sometimes assumed that because yew trees will tolerate poor conditions in dry shade, yew hedges can be grown in the same situations. This is a recipe for abject failure: if they are subjected to starvation, drought, poor drainage or excessive shade, they will inevitably look moth-eaten and lack the intensity of rich green that is their chief glory, the reason they are such an effective foil for flowers. Good drainage and annual feeding are vital.

In the early 1970s, land drains were laid in the Lower Courtyard leading through the Orchard to the moat, helping to disperse the occasional torrents that descended from the Top Courtyard down the tower steps and improving the health of the yews. The replacement catalpa blew over, and the whitebeam planted subsequently died.

Behind the magnolia bed, though slates have been hidden within the wall to stop questing roots from invading the brickwork, there is sufficient root-run above the slates to grow carmine wallflowers in spring, followed

Schizostylis coccinea *'Sunrise', which flowers in early autumn before the garden closes to the public, with* Fuchsia magellanica *'Variegata' and phygelius; all three tone with the brickwork and terracotta pots. Silver-leaved* Plecostachys serpyllifolia *grows in the Bagatelle vases on the steps.*

Though the Lower Courtyard has no overall colour scheme, in some areas hues have been chosen to harmonize with key plants. The box hedge around the magnolia bed was so bulky before it was cut back that it occupied most of the bed and cast the rest into dense shade. Once the hedge had been reduced and restored to its proper proportions, planting was chosen to complement Magnolia liliiflora 'Nigra', its flowers of rich pink with a vinous red reverse opening from upright buds borne like candles on a Christmas tree. Drifts of the Barnhaven strain of Primula sieboldii in pink and carmine intermingle with the dusky pink pendent flowers of dicentra.

Above the entrance to the Rose Garden the wall is lightly clad with swags of Clematis × vedrariensis; this is no mean feat for a climber that, like its parent C. montana, is prone to form itself into dense and inelegant masses in which the individual beauty of the flowers is lost in the sheer profusion of blooms.

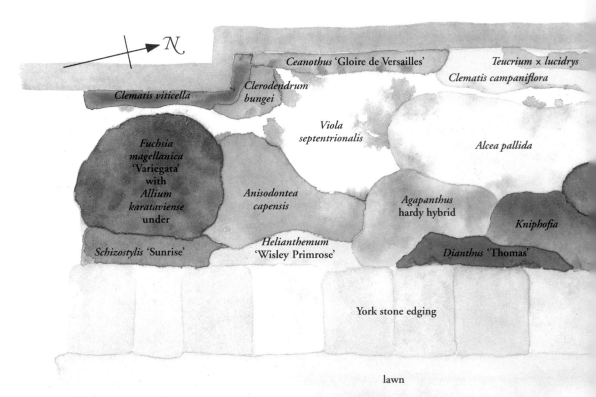

Ceanothus 'Gloire de Versailles'

Teucrium × lucidrys

Clematis campaniflora

Clerodendrum bungei

Clematis viticella

Viola septentrionalis

Alcea pallida

Fuchsia magellanica 'Variegata' with Allium karataviense under

Anisodontea capensis

Agapanthus hardy hybrid

Kniphofia

Schizostylis 'Sunrise'

Helianthemum 'Wisley Primrose'

Dianthus 'Thomas'

York stone edging

lawn

in summer by trails of *Lophospermum scandens* liberally hung with wine-red trumpets. The gardeners had grown this in pots in the glasshouse, trying to persuade it to clamber up stakes; it refused to climb. Left to hang over the side of the bench, it willingly made a cascade of shoots. With customary precision, the gardeners found it perhaps the only site in the garden where its flower colour and habit are ideally suited.

The gardeners implemented a spring colour scheme toning with the pinks of primulas and magnolias, changing in summer to hotter tones. At one time *Primula pulverulenta* and *Meconopsis grandis* were grown here but did not enjoy the conditions. The subsequent scheme included gentian-blue *Salvia patens*, creamy *Kniphofia* 'Little Maid' and scarlet *Lobelia* × *speciosa* with vermilion *Crocosmia* 'Lucifer' supplying bold foliage contrast. The lead trough was planted with *Dicentra spectabilis* for spring followed by fuchsias ('Margaret' originally, the dark-leaved Triphylla variety 'Thalia' in more recent years). Now in spring the yellow-greens of euphorbia and dagger-leaved *Iris pseudacorus* 'Variegata' dominate, with *Coronilla valentina* subsp. *glauca* in the trough.

Pam and Sibylle derived their technique for pruning *C. montana* and its allies from Burford House, John Treasure's Worcestershire garden, in which *C.m.* var. *rubens* was used to clothe a balustrade, spurred back every year immediately after flowering to prevent it overwhelming the architecture of its support. Used on a tripod at Sissinghurst for a time, *C.m.* 'Picton's Variety' was similarly pruned without becoming uncontrollably large. Such clematis flower on the previous season's growth and so must be pruned immediately after flowering if they are to make replacement shoots. In a confined space, annual pruning is essential; however, on larger areas of wall, the gardeners find pruning once every two or three years is sufficient to prevent their growth from becoming too dense. It is important to retain some flowering spurs towards the base of the plant to furnish it as completely as possible.

Most of the other clematis in the courtyard are Viticella, Texensis or Jackmanii hybrids, cut back hard in late autumn each year and regularly spread across the wall and tied in as they grow during spring and early summer. The gardeners use 'twizzlers', paper-covered wire ties, and find them easier to use than twine, which would have to be cut while teetering on top of steps or ladders: there is less risk of breaking the brittle young shoots than if struggling with string; the inconspicuous dull green colour of the ties is another advantage. The tiny flowers of *Clematis* × *triternata* 'Rubromarginata' add variety and a rich vanilla scent, while a few other sorts, such as *C. campaniflora*, tumble over the wall from the Top Courtyard.

The walls hold a considerable assortment of roses, needing varied methods of pruning and training. As elsewhere at Sissinghurst, the routine of other work around the garden makes it impossible to prune Ramblers in late summer after flowering; they must wait until the garden closes in mid autumn. Climbing roses are pruned at the same time and not left until spring as tradition decrees: border work cannot begin until jobs needing a

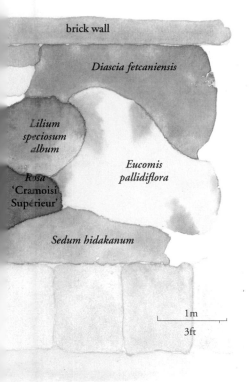

brick wall

Diascia fetcaniensis

Lilium
speciosum
album

Rosa
'Cramoisi
Supérieur'

Eucomis
pallidiflora

Sedum hidakanum

1m
3ft

OPPOSITE *Turkish hollyhock* Alcea pallida *lights up the section of border shown on the plan, surrounded by* Clematis viticella, Ceanothus *'Gloire de Versailles' and hardy agapanthus.*

PLAN *The east-facing border contains plants to flower from spring to autumn. Lower species such as diascias and violas are used at the back, their spaces being filled by wall plants as the season advances. The teucrium grows in the loose lime mortar of the wall.*

RIGHT *Pots of tender plants in flower brought out from the greenhouse are used here on the tower steps and by the Bishops' Gate.* Hedychium gardneranium, *a relative of ginger, is not quite hardy enough to survive the winter in the Cottage Garden but performs admirably in pots, furnished beneath with* Felicia amelloides 'Variegata'.

ladder have been completed and errant rose shoots tied in so they are not damaged by wind. There is also the advantage of finishing fiddly training and tying before the onset of finger-freezing winter.

On the walls it is only China roses such as *R. × odorata* 'Mutabilis' that are pruned in spring. The Ramblers are treated in various ways. Most of the previous year's wood is removed from those roses, such as 'Emily Gray' and *Rosa wichuraiana*, that produce an abundance of new stems; remaining shoots are trained out across the wall. Some Ramblers make fewer shoots and approach climbing Hybrid Teas in their habit of growth, major stems being able to flower in their second season; thus the likes of 'New Dawn', 'Easlea's Golden Rambler' and 'Doctor W. Van Fleet' can be pruned less severely, shortening but not entirely removing the most vigorous of the stems that have flowered.

The sparser stems of climbing Hybrid Teas can be a problem, particularly in varieties such as 'Cupid' that produce a few stout shoots growing directly away from the wall. These must be trained in to the wall in their first season while they are still pliant. When new climbing Hybrid Teas are planted they are not pruned hard in their first year, the gardeners preferring to wait until there are at least two good new shoots before removing the old wood. Stems are pulled over in an arc, the more horizontal position encouraging production of flowering laterals. In successive years, the stems are pulled lower so that at any one time, the upper and central part of their panel of wall will be occupied by the youngest stems with the oldest

stems down below. As in the Rose Garden, a proportion of the old wood is removed to encourage strong growth shoots from the base to build a good and renewable framework.

Other wall plants need different treatment. *Ceanothus × delileanus* 'Gloire de Versailles' has long growths that are shortened in autumn; all flowering shoots are spurred back each spring and the framework is tied in to the wall; earlier pruning can cause dieback. *Vitex negundo* is also spurred back in spring. *Celastrus orbiculatus* is grown for its butter-yellow autumn colour and its capsules which split open to reveal glistening scarlet seeds; it is pruned in early winter, leaving some older wood to bear fruit and flowers. Usually this species produces male and female flowers on separate plants; fortunately the Sissinghurst plant is hermaphrodite, so fruiting is possible with only one plant.

The long east-facing border to either side of the tower suffers from wind turbulence almost as much as its counterpart in the Top Courtyard on the other side of the wall. However, except on rare occasions when a spring north-east wind shrivels unfurling shoots, this is the most sheltered of the garden's borders and the place chosen for plants of doubtful hardiness. In front of the mainly tender shrubs are some of the garden's most extraordinary plants, rare species or choice forms that demand to be inspected at close quarters and benefit from the rain shadow cast by the wall. Most are in the same colour range of red or pink through to blue that is found in the Rose Garden.

Few plants here survive from Vita's time; many were lost in the cold winter following her death in 1962. A large *Hoheria lyallii* at the south end of the border is one survivor, with several unusual roscoeas and the astonishing *Allium schubertii* sheltering under its petticoats; though the bulb itself is hardy, the foliage of the allium and its starburst of dusky pink flowers can be shrivelled by late frosts. Also south of the tower is the spiny *Cynara baetica* subsp. *maroccana* (syn. *C. hystrix*), a smaller cousin of the cardoon and globe artichoke, its large thistle head surrounded by long, sharp, violet bracts. This is not an easy plant in the English climate and resents winter wet; the gardeners occasionally renew the plants from seed, produced only in hot dry summers. The wall behind supports a mound of white *Convolvulus cneorum*; planted in the border, this grew too vigorously, its leaves a dull grey instead of their customary silver satin, and was always killed by winter cold and wet; in the starved conditions of the wall, its growth is tough and hardy and it survives even the harshest weather. Noteworthy among the border's bulbs are the South African *Eucomis* species: pale yellow-green *E. pallidiflora* was first grown as *E. pole-evansii*, a much rarer, taller and more tender species usually misidentified in British gardens. The purple-flushed forms of *E. comosa* were the gardeners' selections from seed-raised plants.

The entrance to the White Garden is known as the Bishops' Gate, a reference to the marble plaque of three bishops, brought by Harold and Vita from Constantinople in 1914. The section of border between this and the east-facing wall, christened the Living Desert by the gardeners after the Disney film, is the garden's most sun-baked spot. In Vita's day, much of it was overshadowed by a large *Malus* 'Eleyi' leaning over from the Top Courtyard and filled by a sizeable myrtle, which died in the cold winter of 1962–3. Mesembryanthemums used to be grown along the front but were only successful in sunny summers. The gardeners decided to sterilize the soil, add grit to improve the drainage and devote the space to rather tender plants, especially bulbs, that would appreciate a hot, dry position. Here are extravagantly spotted tigridias, *Cypella herbertii*, *Nerine bowdenii*, silky-leaved *Oxalis obtusa* and the dwarf alpine thistle *Carlina acaulis* subsp. *simplex* (syn. *C. a. caulescens*). One of the showiest plants here, the coral tree (*Erythrina crista-galli*), is protected by a covering of bracken in winter

TOP LEFT TO RIGHT Eucomis pallidiflora *with* Lilium speciosum; Roscoea cautleyoides *'Kew Beauty'*; Lophospermum scandens.

CENTRE Allium schubertii *growing beneath* Hoheria lyallii; Puya alpestris.

BOTTOM Cynara baetica *subsp.* maroccana; Erythrina crista-galli; Clematis *'Etoile Rose'* with rose *'Albertine'*.

and pruned after the bracken has been removed in spring. Over the gate grows the single-flowered Hybrid Tea rose 'Irish Elegance', a survivor from Vita's time. The gardeners attribute its longevity to the severe pruning needed to prevent it from hiding the bishops plaque. The section of border east of the gate used to be shaded by the catalpa and was occupied principally by wintersweet, *Chimonanthus praecox*, which Vita used to pick every day it was in bloom. Unattractive for the rest of the year, it served no purpose after her death and was replaced. Dusky deep coral rose 'Comtesse du Cayla' was moved from the toolshed bed where Vita had combined it with 'Masquerade' and *Rosa × odorata* 'Mutabilis'. A particularly fine form of evergreen *Carpenteria californica* from local plantsman Jack Elliott covers the wall behind. Though it is reasonably hardy in Kent, and has survived the severest weather here, cold winters can scorch its foliage, making it seem to be in terminal decline. At the foot of the tower, grey-leaved *Convolvulus althaeoides* subsp. *tenuissimus* thrusts through the paving each year, covering itself with flowers of rich, deep old rose. The bronze Bagatelle vases on the tower steps were filled for a time with *Artemisia schmidtiana* 'Nana' for both spring and summer but its silky silver foliage proved irresistible to visitors who patted it to death. Glaucous *Acaena affinis* has been planted here and also *Campanula isophylla* 'Mayi', which is pretty but proved brittle. *Plecostachys serpyllifolia* (syn. *Helichrysum microphyllum*) has also been used recently.

Pots of choice and tender plants are brought out from the glasshouses when in flower and used on the tower steps or by the Bishops' Gate. Perhaps the most remarkable of these is the Chilean relative of the pineapple, *Puya alpestris*, grown from seed collected in the wild by Clarence Elliott in the late 1920s. Its extraordinary peacock-green flowers drip with nectar, an effective lure in the wild to pollinating hummingbirds. Plants flower only once every two or three years and can then die so at least two are kept, saving the seed and re-raising after flowering.

❧

The Lower Courtyard forms an effective crossing point of the garden's axes, a restful interlude along the tour of the garden surrounded by interesting and beautiful plants. However, its design seems to ignore the increased strength of the axis eastward from the tower since the addition of the statue of Dionysus; the courtyard's elongated shape at right angles to the new axis is no longer entirely harmonious. We might expect that this would worry Harold and that he would have wanted to resolve such problems by some Lutyens-inspired trick of design. But Vita would not have wanted the simplicity of the whole garden to be compromised by any architectonic legerdemain. Whatever loss we perceive must be balanced against the gain, the power of the garden's pure and simple beauty.

The Rose Garden

From left to right: the fine Pemberton Hybrid Musk 'Felicia'; the relatively rare Bourbon 'Madame Lauriol de Barny', trained as a tall bush to show off its flat blooms (Vita suspected its namesake 'belonged to the haute cocotterie of Paris'); the unusual Hybrid Perpetual 'Baron Girod de l'Ain'; Rosa nutkana 'Plena', a large, informal Shrub rose.

Of all Sissinghurst's flowers, it was the roses that most captured Vita's imagination, their colours gorgeous or delicate, their textures of velvet or satin, with evocative fragrance and generously abundant blooms borne in early summer, Vita's favourite time of year. The science and art of pruning and training old roses and Hybrid Musks have developed to exemplary standards at Sissinghurst over the years. So too has the companion planting, chosen both to complement the roses and to extend the season of display. There have been continual refinements to the structure of the Rose Garden, its paths and hedges, both to enhance its proportions and to enable it to withstand the high numbers of visitors.

It was some time after Harold and Vita had moved to Sissinghurst that the Rose Garden was planted, having been used as the kitchen garden from 1932–7. In 1932, Harold and Vita fenced its boundaries and planted the yew Rondel, assisted by Nigel who held the cane and string that was to define its circumference. This important transept of the garden's main cross axis from the White Garden to the head of the Lime Walk was perhaps intended to screen the main route around the garden from anything as prosaic as peas and potatoes. Now the Rondel hides most of the Rose Garden from view along this route, effectively dividing the Rose Garden in two but rendering the two halves more human in scale and giving each more of the seclusion that Vita and Harold so valued.

Harold's diary for 29th September 1933 records further developments: 'Measure central path in the kitchen garden and Gwen [Harold's sister] helps me. Finally Vita refuses to abide by our decision or to remove the miserable little trees which stand in the way of my design. The romantic temperament as usual obstructing the classic.' The central path, then of

grass, was edged with box and cross paths were made. The path to the east was now terminated with a Roman altar. Also sited with Nigel's assistance, it was intended to be aligned with the Yew Walk; however, Nigel's handkerchief-topped bamboo cane and string were significantly out of line. This error seems not to have offended Harold's preference for perfect geometry, though it might not have been apparent until the hedges had grown. Perhaps he realized that there were benefits: had the line been straight, it would have slanted disconcertingly across the Rose Garden's axis, cutting this half of the garden into four curiously shaped and unevenly sized beds.

In 1934, plans for a wall at the west end were commissioned from their architect, A.R. Powys. Built the following year, this wall – always known as the Powys Wall, after its designer – also had its idiosyncrasies: it does not cross the garden's axis quite at right angles (though the deviation is scarcely noticeable) and it was topped with planting troughs, presumably for climbers to tumble down. Nobody seems to have considered the practical difficulties of watering and weeding on top of a wall, nor the effect of winter frost on the soil in the troughs, which froze, cracking apart the brickwork. Though Powys took great trouble in choosing bricks that would harmonize with existing old walls, the pointing is heavy and unattractive, albeit mercifully now largely covered by climbers.

By 1937, Vita's collection of roses old and new had outgrown its home in the Priest's House garden. The vegetables were ousted from the kitchen garden and roses took their place. Here at last was sufficient room for them to develop to full and floriferous maturity in rich and well-cultivated soil. Much has been written about Vita's roses, not least by Vita

herself. Here it will suffice to say that they are central to Sissinghurst's style of planting and typical of its soft abundance, subtlety and romance.

The planting of the Rose Garden is quite different from that of any other part of the garden and probably most typical of Vita's style. It is episodic, not at all like the Cottage Garden, White Garden or Purple Border where colours, form and texture have been worked into a symphonic whole. Textures are soft with little use of contrasting foliage, save for the dagger leaves of iris. There are almost no 'punctuation plants' like pampas grass (which Vita hated), phormiums or yuccas; one yucca surviving from Vita's time is buried deep in a corner of the Long Border where it scarcely serves as a contrast; a more recent introduction, *Yucca filamentosa* 'Variegata', though an admirable plant, seems uncharacteristically bright and insistent used as a full stop at a corner of one of the beds.

From time to time, Vita wrote about the value of contrasting foliage in the garden. This was not necessarily her own preference for she seems not to have practised such planting in the Rose Garden. However, she recognized the need for more form in the White Garden, in the absence of varied flower colour. Doubtless she was expressing the opinions of those of her peers she most admired, gardeners such as Margery Fish, and suggesting styles of planting she thought might appeal to her readers. This does not mean she felt any need to adopt such styles herself. She seems not to have used what she called 'the most commendable of the spurges', *Euphorbia characias* subsp. *wulfenii* 'Lambrook Gold'. It was not introduced to the Long Border until after Vita's time, but it has become an inseparable part of Sissinghurst tradition, thriving improbably but memorably in the wall beneath one of the windows.

Vita seems to have felt that Harold's strong and simple design provided all the structure that was needed. She never expressed any dissatisfaction with the nebulous and billowing masses of roses that dominated here. That the planting was so unstructured was not a fault: it was her choice. Even today, this characteristic of the Rose Garden is apparent; if it is to retain its individuality, it should remain so. True, not everyone appreciates the style: 'too fluffy' or 'too soft' are occasional comments. Nor do all gardeners like the colours here, subtle, sumptuous or soft, preferring something with more pizzazz. But to strive for universally acceptable taste would be a recipe for anonymous mediocrity; it is to the gardeners' great credit that they have kept Vita's style intact for over thirty years.

During the middle years of the century, Vita's was one of the most influential voices encouraging gardeners to grow the old roses. She was guided in her early gardening days by E.A. Bunyard, himself perhaps the most significant champion of old roses during an age when they were all but forgotten. Other rosarians should not be overlooked, for those who published least were still busy behind the scenes, sharing knowledge and plants, and fostering a love of roses and their history. Lawrence Johnston, the Hon. Robert James, Maud Messel, Arthur Tysilio Johnson, Sir Frederick Stern, Nancy Lindsay, Sacheverell Sitwell, Constance Spry, Hilda Murrell, James Mitchell and Graham Stuart Thomas, all were influential. Mrs Spry was a frequent visitor to Sissinghurst; her taste in flowers and planting was remarkably similar to Vita's. Hilda Murrell sent gifts of roses from her Shrewsbury nursery. To Graham Thomas fell the task of bringing together all the roses that had survived in British gardens and publishing the most authoritative and comprehensive volumes on them since Victorian times.

Vita's love of old roses was never more evocatively expressed than in her foreword to Graham Thomas's *The Old Shrub Roses* in 1955:

'Mr Thomas swept me quite unexpectedly back to those dusky mysterious hours in an Oriental storehouse where the rugs and carpets of Isfahan and Bokhara and Samarcand were unrolled in their dim but sumptuous colouring and richness of texture for our slow delight. Rich they were, rich as a fig broken open, soft as a ripened peach, freckled as an apricot, coral as a pomegranate, bloomy as a bunch of grapes. It is of these that the old roses remind me . . . how right is Mr Thomas when he implies that they have "all the attraction that sentiment, history, botany, or association can lend them" . . . The next need is to discard the idea that roses must be limited to certain accepted and accustomed colours, and to welcome the less familiar purples and lilacs, and the striped, flaked, mottled variations which recall the old Dutch flower-paintings; to approach them, in fact, with open and unprejudiced eyes, and also with a nose that esteems the true scent of a rose warmed by the sun. They have one major fault, and Mr Thomas does not evade it: their flowering period is limited to one glorious month of midsummer. Personally I think they are more than worth it.'

The garden became so crammed with roses that from 1959 onwards there was no attempt to replace any less satisfactory sorts that failed through poor health or old age. Now the roses are less crowded so that their individual beauty can more easily be appreciated. However, most of Vita's roses remain and few varieties have been added so that her collection remains the least changed element of Sissinghurst's planting and a testament to her taste. Vita would doubtless have valued many of the roses raised since her time, perhaps especially David Austin's English Roses, whose flower shapes include all those of the historic roses, though their disease resistance, vigour and wide range of colours surpass these classics. They could probably provide equal beauty at Sissinghurst over a longer period. However, such a change would inevitably erode the character of Vita's planting in a way that substitution of the odd herbaceous plant, tulip or ground cover does not.

With only a few exceptions, the Rose Garden's varieties are of three basic types. First and foremost are the old roses, Gallicas, Damasks, Centifolias, Mosses, Albas, Hybrid Perpetuals and Bourbons, plush crimson-purples, satin-pinks and extravagant stripes, often nostalgically and evocatively named, recalling more gracious times. Vita loved the rich purples with a velvet sheen, 'Cardinal de Richelieu', 'Hippolyte', 'Nuits de Young' and more modern 'Zigeunerknabe' ('Gipsy Boy'), using them together to draw attention to their resplendent tones. Of the Gallica 'Tuscany' she wrote: 'The Velvet Rose. What a combination of words! One almost suffocates in their soft depths, as though one sank into a bed of rose-petals, all thorns ideally stripped away.' It is these colours and rose-pinks along with the amethyst tints of alliums that dominate the Rose Garden to this day.

The Hybrid Musks, most of them raised by the Revd Joseph Pemberton between 1913 and his death in 1926, approach the old roses in importance. These are crosses between Polyantha roses (derived from *Rosa multiflora*) or their Noisette offspring and Hybrid Perpetuals, Hybrid Teas and other

FAR LEFT AND LEFT *More lax Climbing roses, Ramblers and some Bourbons produce abundant flowering laterals if trained spirally around vertical supports. The lowest branches of stiffer shrub roses can be trained to benders, to produce a domed shape.*

PAGES 48–9 *Looking towards the gate to the Top Courtyard. The sumptuous Moss 'Nuits de Young', typical of the old roses Vita loved, makes a suckering group on its own roots; occasional reduction keeps it in scale. Careful pruning and training ensure a spectacular display from Hybrid Musk 'Vanity'. Amethyst Allium cernuum 'Hidcote' and rich pink Phuopsis stylosa straddle the path; Rosa Mundi beyond is backed by handsome fig foliage.*

China derivatives. In spite of their name, the scent for which Pemberton seems to have selected them is inherited mainly from *R. multiflora* and not from the musk rose; their colours include the soft yellows and apricots of the Noisettes as well as gentle pinks and the vibrant carmine 'Vanity'. Many gardeners did not notice how significant and useful these varieties were when they were new; Graham Thomas has noted that 'The few excellent swans were overwhelmed by the geese, and also by popular opinion, which was still rabidly doting on Hybrid Teas and dwarf Polyantha; the achievement was also somewhat overshadowed later by the Poulsen group.' Vita did not overlook their value and championed Hybrid Musks in her *Observer* articles, before they had gained general acceptance; there must be many thousands of gardeners who, like me, were first tempted to try them through her writing. It is curious that Vita did not write more of their useful recurrent blooming, for most also perform well in the autumn if they are correctly pruned.

There is also a small but select handful of Hybrid Tea and Floribunda roses, chosen for exquisite form and colouring. Single apricot 'Mrs Oakley Fisher' is one such, a particular favourite of Vita's. The gardeners have used it in combination with indigo-blue flowers such as fragrant lupin 'Blue Jacket', a mixture of colours that was also a feature in Harold and Vita's previous garden at Long Barn. The best of a batch of seedlings, the lupin is now propagated every few years from cuttings. Pruning back the yew and box hedges gave the gardeners room to develop the colour scheme further, adding *Geranium wallichianum* 'Buxton's Variety', *Kniphofia thomsonii* var. *snowdenii* and *Thalictrum rochebruneanum*. The Hybrid Tea 'Ellen Willmott', similar in colour to 'Mrs Oakley Fisher', was used in the same scheme but is now planted in the Rose Garden's south border. Other bush roses include 'August Seebauer' and, transferred from the White Garden, the single 'White Wings'. Although Vita was not averse to using novel and even gaudy new varieties, she seems to have realized that most had either a flower shape or bright colours that were utterly modern; mixing them with the classic roses of the past would have compromised the Rose Garden's subtlety and romance, its ability to conjure up the delights of gardens of the previous century.

Even so, it is worth remembering that Vita used a substantial planting of 'Masquerade' in the toolshed bed adjacent to the Cottage Garden. This Floribunda is now generally despised for its brash colouring, poor flower shape and ungainly habit. Opening yellow and ageing through orange and red to a blotchy deep salmon, it was unique when introduced in 1949 for the potency of its chameleon colours, which Vita recognized as being useful within the ambit of the Cottage Garden's sunset scheme nearby. Unlike the Rose Garden, this area makes little reference to planting of the past, so modern varieties were perfectly appropriate. Graham Thomas also

feels 'Masquerade' has its uses, and values its second flush of bloom, its colours harmonizing with autumnal schemes.

It must be owned that not everyone loves the old roses. All too often, for each perfect bloom there are three or four in a state of ugliness, their blooms withered or balled with grey mould. Their foliage is undistinguished, their habit ungainly or at best amorphous; unless their pruning is exemplary, their blooms can be few and fleeting. Rosarians and romantics, like Vita, are oblivious to these faults and see only the flawless blooms. But with perfect cultural conditions, pruning and training, the defects of the old roses can substantially be overcome.

෪

All roses can be encouraged to produce flowering sideshoots if their stems are trained as nearly horizontal as possible. At Sissinghurst this is achieved by two main methods, either training the stems spirally up three or four vertical poles or around domes of branches, anchored by sturdy arching hazel boughs called benders. Using either of these two basic shapes helps give structure and unity to the planting.

Jack Vass introduced the use of benders to the garden from Cliveden where he had worked previously. The technique has subsequently been greatly refined by successive gardeners. When Pam and Sibylle arrived in 1959, only one variety, the Hybrid Perpetual 'Ulrich Brunner Fils', was trained in this way, while most roses were supported by vertical stakes.

When, in an *Observer* article, Vita wrote about the use of benders, in effect she described the traditional pegging of Hybrid Perpetuals to produce a flat bed. She was not altogether impressed by the low tyre-shaped bush that resulted, which, she said, reminded her of a lobster pot; she commented that when Jack Vass had finished cutting and tying the Rose Garden looked like a fishing harbour. Pam and Sibylle adapted the technique to produce more densely clad bushes of varied heights. The roses at the front of the beds were trained into domes, so those at the back became more visible and a better balance of shapes was achieved.

The gardeners found it difficult to get suitable hazel stems for the benders until a hazel coppice was planted specifically to produce stakes. Even so, only the shadier parts of the coppice produce the long, straight, unbranched boughs 1.8–3m/6–10ft long that are ideal for this technique. The ends of the stake are pointed using a bill hook and the thicker end made more supple by flexing it, until the whole rod will describe a perfect arc when bent. The two ends of the bow, held vertical, are firmly pushed straight into the ground.

Roses are tied to the outside of the stakes or benders with a three-ply green fillis twine, wound once around the stem and, to stop the tie slipping, twice around the stake. The ties can be fairly tight because they do not last more than a couple of seasons, during which time the rose stems expand little. Originally each main rose stem was tied to its own bender but now far fewer benders are used, the domes being built up by the stems of the roses themselves. Because new rose stems grow within the dome, the top of the dome should be relatively sparsely covered to let in light for the growing shoots. The gardeners vary the height of the domes, preferring to train higher those with nodding flowers such as 'Madame Lauriol de Barny' so that the blooms can more easily be seen.

Where vertical stakes are used, three or four sweet-chestnut poles are laid out as a triangle or diamond with the point directed towards the nearest path rather than parallel to it. The height of the stakes and the distance between them varies according to the variety and the shape required. Some quite short cultivars such as *Rosa gallica* 'Versicolor' are staked, as well as much more vigorous varieties like 'Ispahan' and 'Königin von Dänemark'. The bush roses and a few of the shrub varieties ('Leda', 'Nuits de Young' and *R. gallica* var. *officinalis*) are too short to need support.

Though the benders are renewed every year, it is not always necessary to replace the vertical stakes: if they will withstand a hefty kick without snapping, they are left for another season. Sometimes it is sufficient to replace a single stake and only once every two or three years must the roses be untied and all supports replaced. Roses are not tied straight up the stakes, leaving a tuft on top, because this would not encourage flowering laterals to be produced all the way up the bush. Instead the stems are trained spirally around the supports, occasionally taking one or two stems over the top to clothe it adequately. Roses that make abundant late growth such as 'Magenta' and the Hybrid Musk 'Pax' may need to be tied in before their second flush of bloom in the autumn.

Staking, pruning and retraining must be completed by early winter; then compaction, caused by trampling during pruning, can be relieved by cultivation, and planting can be started without the hindrance of wayward rose stems. This is contrary to convention, which insists that early pruning can lead to sappy young shoots that can be damaged by frost; the gardeners have never found this to be a problem. All dead and weak old wood plus spindly young growths are pruned away and all remaining stems are shortened. Unlike the shrub roses, Hybrid Teas and Chinas are usually pruned in spring, the Chinas in particular being less hardy. The gardeners aim always to encourage a balance between production of flowering wood and renewal growth, achieved by cutting out a proportion of the old wood from the base. As a result, many of the roses planted by Vita almost sixty years ago are still vigorous and capable of producing abundant bloom. Some varieties, such as 'Zéphirine Drouhin', produce such a wealth of new canes that almost all the previous season's growth can be cut out.

In spite of the success of renewal pruning, there are occasional losses and an old bush has to be replaced. The gardeners try not to plant in exactly the same place, adjusting two or three neighbouring groups so that positions are changed but plant associations remain the same. Nevertheless, to avoid poor growth from rose replant disease it is sometimes necessary to sterilize the ground to be planted with roses using dazomet. Unless a contractor is employed, this soil sterilant is not available to the amateur, who must alternatively replace the soil to a depth of at least two spits (45cm/18in) with soil that has not grown roses.

❧

When Pam and Sibylle arrived at Sissinghurst, the roses were not mulched. Vita bought some bags of spent hops and was horrified that the gardeners used them all beneath the roses trained on benders; perhaps she felt that because she could not see the mulch, it was not providing any benefit. But it was here, where the ground was most starved and the weeds least accessible, that it was most useful. The gardeners saw obvious benefits in the improved root systems of the roses: whereas they were once sparse and woody, the humus-rich upper layer of soil became full of a mass of fibrous new roots. Over the years more mulch came to be used. The spent hops were not ideal, being too pale in colour, too easily scattered by birds and latterly becoming scarce and expensive. For some years a fine grade of crushed bark, already matured by being stacked for a time before delivery, was used. Sarah Cook still uses bark in woodland areas, but she feels that it can look out of place among traditional mixed or herbaceous planting in a historic setting. In these areas the gardeners now use compost made in the garden. A dressing of two parts of Kieserite (hydrous magnesium sulphate) to one of potash is used to feed the roses without giving them excess nitrogen. This and the mulch immeasurably improve their vigour, disease resistance and flowering.

In a garden that depends so much on roses, it is not acceptable to have them marred by mildew or defoliated by rust or black spot. The only effective means of control of such diseases, which are efficiently incubated in Sissinghurst's sheltered garden rooms, is sparing use of synthetic pesticides. Spraying against fungal diseases is usually tackled once a fortnight,

Looking towards the entrance to the Top Courtyard. Rose 'Adam Messerich' produces a splendid display in early summer, with some later bloom. Usually classed as a Bourbon, its complex parentage leads some to class it as a Shrub rose. Its lax stems lend themselves to training on vertical poles. Vibrant Geranium psilostemon *harmonizes with its rich pink, while sulphur-yellow* Achillea *'Anthea' provides contrast. The strobilanthes (beneath the geranium) produces violet-blue flowers through late summer and autumn. Behind, giant oat grass* (Stipa gigantea) *shimmers in the setting sun.*

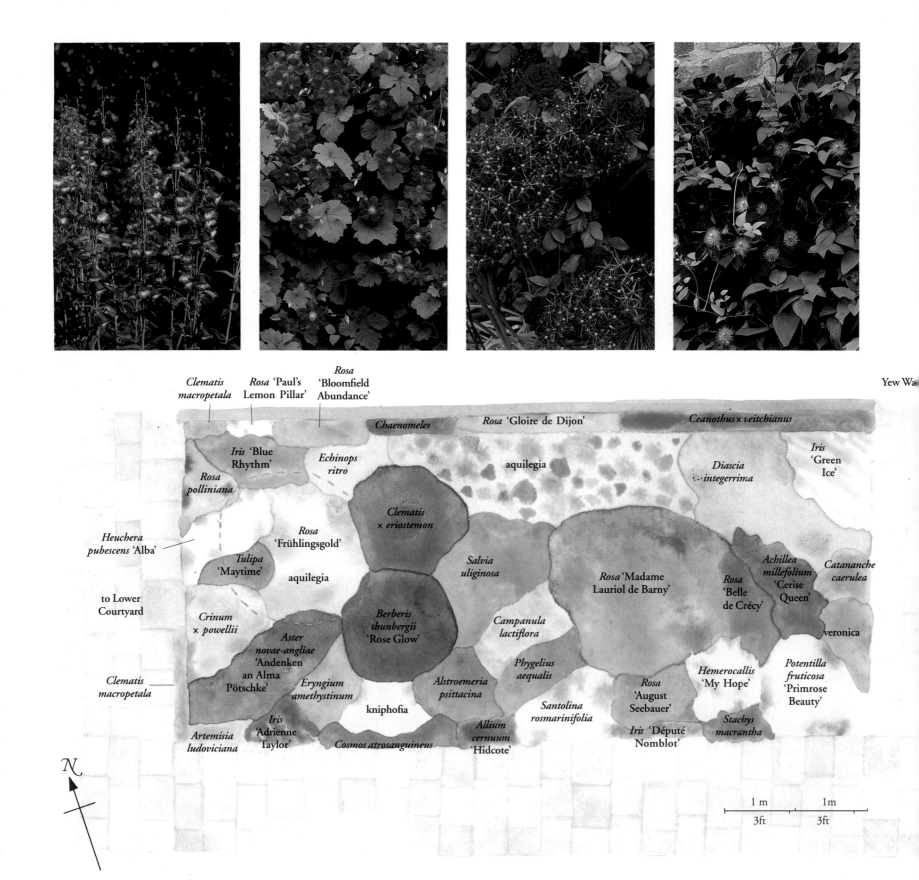

Clematis
macropetala

Rosa 'Paul's
Lemon Pillar'

Rosa
'Bloomfield
Abundance'

Yew Wa

Chaenomeles   Rosa 'Gloire de Dijon'   *Ceanothus × veitchianus*

Iris 'Blue
Rhythm'

*Echinops
ritro*

aquilegia

Iris
'Green
Ice'

*Rosa
polliniana*

*Diascia
integerrima*

*Clematis
× eriostemon*

*Heuchera
pubescens* 'Alba'

*Rosa
'Frühlingsgold'*

*Salvia
uliginosa*

Rosa 'Madame
Lauriol de Barny'

*Achillea
millefolium
'Cerise
Queen'

Rosa
'Belle
de Crécy'

*Catananche
caerulea*

*Tulipa
'Maytime'*

aquilegia

*Crinum
× powellii*

*Berberis
thunbergii
'Rose Glow'*

*Campanula
lactiflora*

veronica

*Aster
novae-angliae
'Andenken
an Alma
Pötschke'*

*Phygelius
aequalis*

*Rosa
'August
Seebauer'*

*Hemerocallis
'My Hope'*

*Potentilla
fruticosa
'Primrose
Beauty'*

to Lower
Courtyard

*Clematis
macropetala*

*Eryngium
amethystinum*

*Alstroemeria
psittacina*

kniphofia

*Santolina
rosmarinifolia*

*Rosa
'Député
Nomblot'*

*Stachys
macrantha*

*Artemisia
ludoviciana*

Iris
'Adrienne
Taylor'

Cosmos atrosanguineus

*Allium
cernuum
'Hidcote'*

N

1 m   1m

3ft   3ft

'Alice Hindley' is one of several penstemons in the Rose Garden used to extend the display throughout summer and into autumn. Flowers of Clematis *'Perle d'Azur' and leaves of* Vitis vinifera *'Purpurea' place themselves with customary poise and elegance against the Powys Wall. In the Long Border,* Allium cristophii *jostles with blooms of Bourbon rose 'Prince Charles'. On the west-facing wall next to the seat, Jackmanii clematis 'Madame Grangé' is supported by horizontal wires. By autumn the silky tassels of* Pennisetum villosum *take on parchment tints, complemented by rich lavender* Caryopteris × clandonensis.

PLAN *This planting shows a wide variation of group sizes; shorter plants such as diascias, phlox and aquilegias are used at the back of the border to fill in beneath roses and wall plants. Like many of the old roses in the garden, 'Madame Lauriol de Barny' and 'La Ville de Bruxelles' are made more generous and substantial by being planted in groups of three, though all three are sometimes trained as a single bush.*

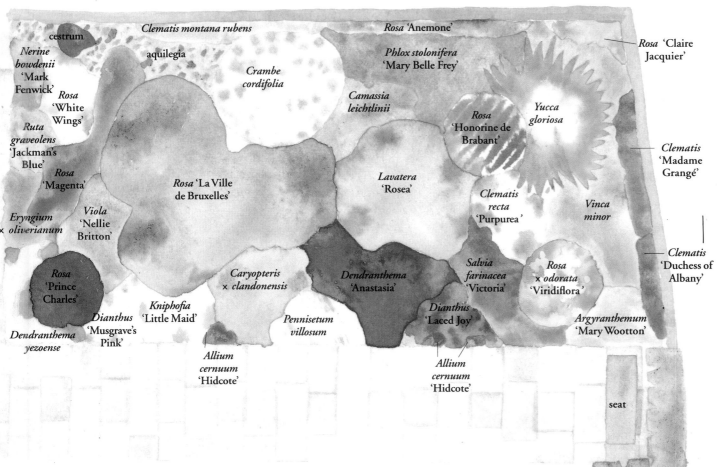

Clematis montana rubens

cestrum

Rosa 'Anemone'

Nerine bowdenii 'Mark Fenwick'

aquilegia

Phlox stolonifera 'Mary Belle Frey'

Rosa 'Claire Jacquier'

Crambe cordifolia

Rosa 'White Wings'

Camassia leichtlinii

Rosa 'Honorine de Brabant'

Yucca gloriosa

Ruta graveolens 'Jackman's Blue'

Clematis 'Madame Grangé'

Rosa 'Magenta'

Rosa 'La Ville de Bruxelles'

Lavatera 'Rosea'

Clematis recta 'Purpurea'

Vinca minor

Eryngium × *oliverianum*

Viola 'Nellie Britton'

Clematis 'Duchess of Albany'

Caryopteris × *clandonensis*

Salvia farinacea 'Victoria'

Rosa × *odorata* 'Viridiflora'

Rosa 'Prince Charles'

Dendranthema 'Anastasia'

Kniphofia 'Little Maid'

Dianthus 'Musgrave's Pink'

Dianthus 'Laced Joy'

Argyranthemum 'Mary Wootton'

Dendranthema yezoense

Pennisetum villosum

Allium cernuum 'Hidcote'

Allium cernuum 'Hidcote'

seat

yew hedge

the chemicals being changed periodically to prevent the pathogens from developing resistance. The season of 1994 was a difficult one, with rain nearly every day in late spring making spraying almost impossible; as a result, black spot was a severe problem.

⅋

The choice of herbaceous plants to furnish the spaces between roses reflects Vita's particular planting style. A few key genera predominate, among them lilies. In 1948 Harold chose to set them against the dark hedges of the Rondel, *Lilium regale* being used in great quantity along with *LL. auratum*, *martagon* and *lancifolium* (syn. *l. tigrinum*). The lilies continued the garden's display for a few precious weeks of high summer, after the best of the roses and before its leanest month: as Vita bemoaned, 'August is always a bad month here – it gets nicer again in September and October.'

When Jack Vass departed in 1957, he was replaced by Ronald Platt, a notable grower, exhibitor and raiser of lilies. One of his varieties, 'Red Max', had been given an Award of Merit by the Royal Horticultural Society and he exhibited *LL. nepalense* and *lankongense* from Sissinghurst at the Society's Lily Show in July 1959. Platt, like Vita, enjoyed growing lilies in pots and these featured prominently during his time at Sissinghurst, though by the time of his departure the lilies had dwindled and disappeared from all the Rose Garden beds. The gardeners have added many lilies over the years; though a few, such as apricot 'Attila', have lasted, most varieties waned after two or three years.

Also set against the dark yew of the Rondel, plumes of pale eremurus have been a dramatic feature of the Rose Garden since at least the 1950s. Sarah Cook finds that they no longer thrive, probably because of soil sickness. Her policy is to buy five large roots each year to ensure that there are always enough to create a spectacle.

Both Harold and Vita loved peonies, though they were not originally included in the Rose Garden planting. A bed of *Paeonia lactiflora* cultivars in the Orchard had resolutely refused to prosper, probably because they disliked the high water table and acid soil. Vita asked Pam and Sibylle to move them to the bed south-west of the Rondel where some of them thrive today. Vita also grew a collection of tree peonies on Delos, a clashing mixture of salmon and carmine, puce and rose pink. The gardeners moved a splendid bright pink variety to the Rose Garden, where it enjoys a brief moment of glory each year next to the statue at the east end of the garden's axis. Like the old roses, this must be pruned to encourage vigorous new growths from the base, to prevent it becoming lanky and keep it healthy and floriferous. It is necessary to stake it to support the weight of the flowers and to prevent snow damage in winter.

Irises were important companions for the roses from the start. In June 1949, Vita wrote of them:

'I am no blind believer in the "improved" modern flower . . . but for the Russell lupins and the bearded irises one must make an exception. Everyone knows, and grows, the lupins; not everyone, I think, has yet realized the extreme beauty of the irises. So as June is just the moment to see them in flower I thought I would remind you of their beauty and their many advantages. Their beauty is beyond dispute. No velvet can rival the richness of their falls; or, let us say, it is to velvet only that we may compare them. That is surely enough to claim for any flower? They suggest velvet, pansies, wine – anything you like, that possesses texture as well as colour.'

From 1959, the gardeners increased the range of iris varieties, introducing some creamy yellow to make the planting seem more alive. Alan Bloom's pale sulphur *Achillea* 'Anthea' has also been added for the same purpose. Irises such as 'Benton Nigel' from Sir Cedric Morris were included and some of the excellent Intermediate varieties raised by John Taylor. Some older cultivars are valued for their floriferousness and scent: among these are 'Shannopin' in murrey and pale amber, introduced by Harold, and fragrant mauve 'London Pride'. Groups seldom need to be completely replanted and are kept vigorous by regular removal of the worn-out older sections of rhizome. Because most irises are planted at the front of the beds where flower stems can easily be snapped off, it is necessary to stake each stem with a split bamboo cane. A few species, such as blue *I. setosa*, are also included.

Other survivors from Harold and Vita's time include Japanese anemones in pink and white, useful for their late flowers, pinks and *Alchemilla mollis*, whose chartreuse provides a piquant contrast for pink and dusky purple roses. The amethyst tones of onions have come to play a greater role than they did in Harold and Vita's time, when only *Allium cernuum* and *A. cristophii* were grown, their colours harmonizing perfectly with the roses. The gardeners were encouraged to use the latter more when a stray seedhead fell among anemones. The allium seedlings throve, proving this to be an ideal combination, the anemones' young foliage hiding the dying leaves of the alliums. When replanting anemones, the trick has been repeated deliberately, though the alliums can sow themselves too thickly and occasionally have to be reduced. *Allium hollandicum*, added for late spring display, has proved excellent, though its tall leaves are not so easy to hide once they become shabby; unless larger-leaved plants such as hostas can be used to screen it, foliage must be removed as flowering begins.

Perhaps the most magical plant association in the Rose Garden is recent. Foxgloves have been used to lure visitors to the far side of the garden since the 1960s, but the combination of white and apricot ones with the blush flowers and deep bronze leaves of *Sambucus nigra* 'Guincho Purple'

The view westwards along the Long Border at the peak of the Rose Garden's display: Allium cernuum *'Hidcote' and Miss Willmott's ghost furnish the space between roses;* Rosa nutkana *'Plena' hides the border beyond, giving an incentive to explore; its overhanging stems protect* Viola cornuta *in mauve and white from passing feet, allowing it to push forward to soften the edge of the path. Large plants such as this rose and the one opposite, planted towards the front of the borders, give a fuller and more generous appearance to the garden. Two spikes of Madonna lily in the foreground are the sole survivors of a larger group; the lily's basal leaves, which die as the blooms develop, are hidden by surrounding plants. Vita loved Madonna lilies, but despaired of ever growing them successfully. A curtain of handsome fig leaves against the distant wall forms a simple but effective foil for the myriad flowers.*

OPPOSITE ABOVE *In the bed south-west of the Rondel, the spires of* Digitalis purpurea *f.* albiflora *and* D. p. *'Sutton's Apricot' shine against* Sambucus nigra *'Guincho Purple' and the palest lemon-cream Hybrid Musk rose 'Pax'. Devised by the gardeners, this inspired combination remains perfectly within the spirit of Vita's planting.*

OPPOSITE BELOW *North-east of the Rondel, the white standards of the sweet-scented lupin 'Blue Jacket' give sparkle to its richly sombre violet-blue keels; the blooms of the single apricot Hybrid Tea rose 'Mrs Oakley Fisher' unfurl from elegant buds, providing a perfect contrast.*

ABOVE LEFT *Again in the bed north-east of the Rondel,* Lilium *'Attila', one of the most persistent varieties, is placed to harmonize with rose 'Mrs Oakley Fisher' behind, its first flush of bloom now nearly over.* Arctotis *'Apricot', overwintered under glass, is planted in late spring to take the place of pansies.*

ABOVE RIGHT *'Shannopin', bought by Harold, is one of many irises traditionally used to contrast with the roses. This old variety has gracefully drooping falls, found in the species but lacking from many modern hybrids. The split bamboo canes used to support the flower stems are barely visible.*

is relatively new. Pam and Sibylle pruned the elder to encourage bold foliage rather than flowers but Sarah cuts out one-third of the stems of the elder each year; thus a balance is achieved, keeping good foliage but allowing abundant blossom on the two- or three-year-old stems. The foxgloves present a difficulty in that whatever is to be used for late summer bloom in their place must be planted before they have finished flowering. Pam and Sibylle spaced the foxgloves sufficiently far apart to allow interplanting of gentian-blue *Salvia cacaliifolia* and silver *Helichrysum petiolare*. Sarah has opted for more impact, using so many foxgloves that interplanting is impossible but removing them all the moment the peak of their display is over, to be replaced with the silver and sapphire.

Vita and Harold seem to have accepted without question that there would be little to see here after rose time. Such defeatism was excusable in a garden intended only for the family and a few visitors; nor was it easy in Harold and Vita's day to find the few plants that gave the best value at a time when there were no *Plant Finder* guides to help track down scarce varieties. However, Pam and Sibylle had a definite policy to provide something of interest for visitors, most of whom arrived in late summer to find the Rose Garden looking tired and dull. Though they took care to keep the predominant character for which each area was planned, there was a constant quest for worthy and appropriate varieties, a few being tried each year and the most deserving being added to the regular repertoire. Cranesbills, catmints and campanulas all proved valuable and harmonious companions for the roses. But, more significantly, from the 1960s onwards, half-hardy perennials such as salvias came to play an increasing role for their long flowering season and effective show. A few annuals, such as *Nicotiana* 'Lime Green', are similarly useful for their late display.

Among the hardy perennials, agapanthus varieties including 'Loch Hope' and 'Ardernei Hybrid' were added and completely new hybrids such as *Geranium × riversleaianum* 'Mavis Simpson', with pink satin flowers found their way there soon after they had been raised. The gardeners did not share Vita's prejudice against Michaelmas daisies, for the late fifties and early sixties saw the introduction of many excellent new *Aster novi-belgii* varieties invaluable for their late bloom, a number of which are still grown at Sissinghurst, especially the shorter sorts. Other species were also added, among them *Aster × frikartii* hybrids and the vivid carmine *A. novae-angliae* 'Andenken an Alma Pötschke'. However, blooms of the latter occasionally shrivel as they open. This may be caused by a water problem, or perhaps by tarsonemid mite, a common pest of asters which distorts the blooms and stunts their petals.

Like the asters, colchicums are serviceable flowers for extending the floraison into the autumn, *CC. byzantinum, speciosum* and 'Conquest' finding a home here. They have their difficulties, though: borne without leaves, their tight bunches of flowers can look unattractive and ill-furnished against bare earth, especially if nibbled by slugs or spattered with soil. To overcome this, they can be grown through low ground cover such as ajuga or, as at the foot of the Powys Wall, through the lowest leaves of the claret vine, *Vitis vinifera* 'Purpurea'. Another naked-flowered bulb, *Amaryllis belladonna*, did not flourish throughout the border at the foot of the wall; in this shady area the bulbs do not get the summer baking they need if they are to flower well.

Several of Vita's shrubs, such as dipelta, kolkwitzia and various deutzias, were regularly stripped of buds by birds and had to be replaced over the years. Successful substitutes have included shrubby mallows (*Lavatera* 'Rosea' and *L.* 'Barnsley') and *Buddleja davidii* 'Dartmoor'. The buddleja produces enormous panicles of bloom as much as 30cm/12in across; the sheer weight of these can cause the bush to fall apart, particularly after a shower of rain. Severe pruning to about 30cm/12in each spring encourages the sturdiest shoots; once they have made about two-thirds of their growth, the stems are tied to each other to provide mutual support.

In Vita's day the Rose Garden had many more small trees, of which twelve *Malus × purpurea* 'Eleyi' in a row down the middle were perhaps the least satisfactory. By the 1960s they had become elderly and disease-ridden, also casting shade that prevented the roses from performing well. There were two large *Prunus × subhirtella* 'Autumnalis' in the bed at the south-west corner of the garden, shading the plants on the Powys Wall, a large paulownia south-west of the Rondel and a pair each of poplars and Italian cypresses marking the end of the axis from the White Garden. The poplars had been brought from Fez as cuttings in Harold's sponge bag.

Along the eastern vista, the brick edging to the central path makes its scale more intimate, with distant poplars adding welcome accents. Young amelanchiers lurk among the roses, not yet big enough to provide the height the planting requires. Hazel stems have been used as a temporary cordon to protect worn grass near the statue.

Though doubtless attractive in their youth, so many mature trees allowed few opportunities for the roses to flourish. When one by one the trees died of natural causes, they were not mourned; according to Pam Schwerdt: 'It brought back to us, time and time again, the value of light; the moment something goes, something else rips away and says, "How marvellous!" '

Nevertheless, there was a need for some small trees to give height and fullness to the garden. At Graham Thomas's suggestion, *Prunus* 'Okumiyako' was used to replace the crabs but failed, as had so many of Vita's shrubs, stripped of bloom and shoots by birds. Three pairs of *Sorbus cashmiriana* were tried next but suffered from canker, perhaps partly because of the whole garden's high water table. Sarah Cook has planted *Amelanchier lamarckii* along the Rose Garden's axis; its airy canopy should not interfere with the roses beneath, though it too will be at the mercy of the birds.

Vita's description of her garden as 'a tumble of roses and honeysuckle, figs and vines' indicates the importance she attached to generously planted walls. She loved figs for their Mediterranean associations and their luxurious fruits but, with no restriction to their roots, they grew prodigiously and fruited little. Given by Lady Sackville after she had moved from Streatham to Brighton, the Long Border's four figs overtopped the wall considerably and filled the entire width of the section nearest the house. Vita told the gardeners that something must done. To spare her the carnage entailed, they left the pruning until she and Harold had departed on a cruise. After a week of sawing, the Rose Garden was full of fig branches. The remaining supple young shoots were laced in to the wall, providing a curtain of handsome leaves and much more planting space in the border.

Though figs are generally hardy in Kent, the cold winter of 1985 cut them to the ground. The damage to the tips of the shoots is more severe if they are tied close to the wall; to minimize damage, new shoots are left free and not pruned and tied in until mid spring. The gardeners find that other slightly tender wall plants such as *Solanum crispum* are similarly affected, so their pruning and training is also left until the same time.

In Vita's day the Rose Garden contained few clematis varieties save for a *C.* 'Jackmanii' trained on posts in one of the beds and a large *C. montana* var. *rubens* on the Long Border wall, joined by *C. montana* var. *wilsonii* which scrambled over from the wall's other side. Pam and Sibylle feel that in the middle years of this century fewer gardeners appreciated the merits of clematis and it was harder to track down the best varieties. Though they were popular in Victorian times, only William Robinson's gardener, Ernest Markham, had significantly sung their praises in the early twentieth century; Christopher Lloyd's championship of them was yet to come.

Realizing their value for late bloom, the gardeners added more varieties to the walls (*CC.* 'Comtesse de Bouchaud', 'Xerxes', 'Etoile Rose' and 'Etoile Violette'), as well as some trained on tripods (*CC.* × *eriostemon*, 'Ville de Lyon' and 'Victoria'). *C.* × *eriostemon* is not self-clinging and has to be frequently tied to its support. 'Ville de Lyon' and 'Victoria' were each trained on their own tripods but allowed to scramble over adjoining roses. However, this was not an easy combination to manage: the clematis wrapped themselves around rose stems that needed to be removed during deadheading. But by far the most spectacular use of clematis in the whole garden is the planting of five 'Perle d'Azur' on the arc of the Powys Wall.

When in 1969 the level of the soil within the arc was raised by 15cm/ 6in, the gardeners took the opportunity to replace the shabby, trained fruit trees on the wall: *Parthenocissus henryana* was used to provide a backdrop behind the seat; a ceanothus was planted symmetrically on either side of the arc and a *Vitis* 'Brant' on the shady side, echoed by a claret vine on the sunny side opposite. The ceanothus refused to thrive in the shade, and 'Brant' did not produce its annual autumnal blaze of colour. The gardeners removed both and installed *Clematis* 'Perle d'Azur' along the central section of wall where it would intermingle with the vine. The simplicity and panache of this association has proved to be the crowning glory of the Rose Garden. The clematis are cut back hard in late autumn each year, and every ten days or so during May and June they are spread out across the wall and tied in.

The vines are spur pruned at the same time as the clematis, obeying the rule of Miss Havergal at Waterperry that they should be 'cut back to the best bud nearest home' before Christmas; if left later, the wounds would bleed, sapping the vine's strength. The other vine here, *Parthenocissus henryana*, is much less demanding, needing no pruning other than the removal of any dead wood.

Since their arrival in 1959 Pam and Sibylle have made many significant changes, slowly but inexorably improving the Rose Garden's appearance. Many plants were added to extend the season without break from late spring until mid autumn; grass paths, no longer able to withstand the tread of so many thousands of feet, have been replaced with brick or York stone and almost all the hedges have been restored.

In Harold and Vita's day the only hard surface in the Rose Garden was

Allium hollandicum (syn. A. aflatunense of gardens) echoes across the path to the nursery; pots of the old Pelargonium 'Lord Bute' stand by and beyond the gate. This is one of few varieties of Regal pelargonium that can be grown out of doors in southern England.

the York stone path along the front of the Long Border. The main east-west axis and the cross paths were of grass, which by the 1960s scarcely grew in the shade of the trees and hedges and was worn away by the feet of visitors; the ever-widening hedges concentrated the damage. Repairing the turf after the garden closed each year was tried twice but never succeeded: the new turf had not become sufficiently tough to withstand wear when the garden reopened. Furthermore, the disproportionate width of the box hedges and the yew Rondel destroyed the classic proportions of Harold's design; broad hedges made vistas pinched and the walks claustrophobic, as well as narrowing the beds, overshadowing and suppressing the roses and other planting. Drastic remedies were needed.

In 1967, shortly after the National Trust took over, the replanting of hedges began. The box hedges in the Rose Garden had been planted at an unsatisfactory angle, and had layered vigorously along the outside, leaving the centre too weak to regrow if cut back. Within a year they had all been replaced with plants raised from cuttings taken in 1962, those in the east half first, followed by those in the west half.

In 1976, the outside of the Rondel hedge was cut back. By 1981 this had regrown sufficiently to allow the inside to be tackled; the top was also cut to 23cm/9in below the required height. This exposed a broad strip around the central lawn, giving room for a 75cm/30in brick edging to be installed in spring 1981, wide enough to accommodate most pedestrians and diminishing the wear on the grass circle to a level it could tolerate without visible damage. The yews had not been planted in a perfect circle and had been allowed to shoot up too quickly in their formative years, many of them not forming a proper leader; it took some time before the regrowth could be clipped to hide the irregularities and complete symmetry could be achieved. The foot of the yews was furnished by a planting of oak fern (*Gymnocarpium dryopteris*) and grey-green striped *Ornithogalum nutans*, a quietly effective combination that does not detract from the Rondel's classic simplicity.

The replanting of the box hedges exposed anew the full and correct width of the paths, indicating clearly by brick steps where the levels dropped. Paving was installed in the west half of the Rose Garden in 1968–9 in a Greek key pattern using old brick paviors for the cross paths in the centre, with borders of stretchers on edge. Such ambitious and costly work would scarcely have been possible without the backing of the Trust, particularly since most other paths around the garden needed to be replaced or relaid. The gardeners were amused to overhear the verdict of the first visitor the following spring: she said, 'I've always liked these paths so much', proof that the new paths and hedges had blended in almost imperceptibly. The western end of the Rose Garden's main path was deemed too wide to look attractive paved with brick alone and so was flagged with York stone with brick-on-edge margins. York stone alone would have looked monotonous and excessively wide, and an all-brick path here would have emphasized the difference in width between this and the east end of the path beyond the Rondel. Several years later the eastern cross path was replaced. The grass along the main axis in this half of the garden took little wear and could be left as turf, except where the cross path traversed it, where regrettably it had to be paved.

The soil that had to be removed to install paving proved valuable for correcting levels around the garden, nowhere more so than in the small terrace created by the arc of the Powys Wall. The turf here had been 15cm/6in below the level of its retaining wall; by raising it to the level of the wall it grew better and became both more attractive and easier to mow. Mowing was further simplified by paving the standing for the Lutyens bench that terminates the vista here. When the original bench from Lady Sackville's Brighton garden had to be replaced, the new one was left unoiled and unstained, so that it would age to an attractive silvery grey. None of the garden's benches is oiled because oiling makes wood sticky and turns it a blackish colour that is scarcely visible as a focal point.

Other hedges needed attention. The tall and wide holly hedge along the southern edge of the garden prevented anything much from growing in its shade. The lilacs here, brought by Vita as suckers from Hidcote, were crowded, overshadowed and regularly stripped by birds, producing little flower. The gardeners cut back the holly hedge and removed a section of it, opening up the view to the large oak tree and the countryside beyond. This encouraged visitors to explore this far side of the garden, reducing congestion elsewhere, and allowed a seat to be put around the oak. Prestoniae hybrid lilacs were added nearby; flowering late enough to avoid bird damage, they produce elegant panicles of blossom but lack the alluring scent of the common lilacs. The bed beyond the oak was fringed with a large drift of *Symphoricarpos × chenaultii*, an elegant snowberry whose feathery stems of fresh green foliage blend agreeably with the rusticity of distant woods and fields.

Removal of the rough field hedge within the Cottage Garden left a gap behind the seat at the east end of the Long Border path. This was planted with yew; as the new section of hedge grew up, a debate arose about whether a view to the Cottage Garden should be kept open. A broad vista would have revealed colours that clashed with those in the Rose Garden; seen from the other side of the hedge, the roses would have jarred similarly with the surrounding sunset colours. Graham Thomas suggested creating a porthole in the hedge. Through this, only yellow azaleas and bluebells would be seen from the Rose Garden; the gardeners planted *Crambe cordifolia* to supply a haze of white when seen from the opposite Cottage Garden side. This seemed a clever compromise, providing a stronger focal point to the end of the Long Border path than the Lutyens bench and encouraging the visitor to explore the Cottage Garden beyond.

Nigel Nicolson's perception of the merits or otherwise of the porthole was different. Considering whether his parents would have liked it, he felt that it compromised the 'succession of privacies' that they so valued and diminished the surprise of discovering the Cottage Garden. Vita and Harold would not have wanted to peep from one garden to the next and would have thought such a feature altogether too tricksy. Their taste must always be respected, for this is, and must always remain, their garden; and so the porthole is being allowed to fill with shoots of yew.

The garden closes in mid October, a fortnight earlier than many other National Trust gardens, giving essential extra time to complete autumn and winter work. Hardy climbers on the walls are pruned, trained and tied in first so that feet and ladders do not interfere with subsequent planting. This task cannot be started while visitors are walking underneath.

Then follows removal of half-hardies, giving the gardeners welcome standing places where they know they will not be trampling precious plants. The staking, pruning and tying of shrub roses is tackled next and hopefully completed by the turn of the year.

The maintenance of the Rose Garden is fairly labour-intensive. Areas to be replanted are dug thoroughly. As the gardeners work through each bed, frequent treading on the beds is unavoidable, easily compressing the fine particles of Sissinghurst's soil; the ground must be pricked over afterwards with a fork to relieve compaction. Well-rotted compost is used for mulch. Humus from the mulch improves soil structure, lessening the problems of compaction, and helps to retain mineral nutrients. The gardeners put in any plants that need several months to settle before starting growth in spring, often using plants that have been grown in the nursery. The Rose Garden's beds comprise much the largest planted area in the garden; Pam and Sibylle always heaved a sigh of relief when they were finished.

A balanced general fertilizer is applied to all the beds in spring, the formulation occasionally being altered to prevent any excesses of soil nutrients building up. Even so, many plants have shown signs of damage from manganese toxicity, a common though often unrecognized danger in acidic soils or those rich in metal ions such as potash. Sissinghurst's soils show such wide variation in pH, from very acid in some areas to strongly alkaline where influenced by lime mortar from the walls, that it is hard to find a standard treatment that suits them all.

❧

Nowhere is the character of Vita's planting more apparent than in the Rose Garden: its soft abundance and the colours she most loved are here as evident as ever. In the years since her death, many companion plants have been added, making it almost as enchanting before and after the roses as when they bloom. The efforts of the National Trust and the gardeners have restored the crisp geometry of Harold's design and strengthened the garden's fabric so that we all may see Harold and Vita's vision, still in a state of near perfection after almost sixty years.

Spring planting requires substantial groups in several different colours for the interplay between plants to be effective. At the entrance to the Rose Garden from the Lower Courtyard, tulips 'Clara Butt' and 'Maytime', pansies, Clematis alpina *'Ruby' and* Berberis thunbergii *'Rose Glow' are sufficient to initiate the Long Border's spring-to-autumn colour scheme. Silver* Artemisia ludoviciana *softens the edge of the path.*

At the entrance to the Rose Garden, the curved end of the Lime Walk helps mask an awkward change of axis. The bacchante's plinth has been raised on bricks both to make the statue more imposing and to ensure that its full height is visible from the White Garden. The ends of the yew hedges are kept absolutely vertical.

The Lime Walk is the only one of Sissinghurst's garden rooms planted solely by Harold, who called it 'My Life's Work'. The first of the main areas of the garden to be in flower, its strong and simple architecture remains satisfying after the bulbs have finished their display.

Harold realized in 1932 that his plan for a single grand axis uniting the Rose Garden (then the kitchen garden), the Cottage Garden and the Nuttery was thwarted by the geography of the site. Frustrated by the fact that such a scheme would not relate well to existing alignments and would cut angularly across the Cottage Garden, he wrote that this was 'what is such a bore about Sissinghurst. It is magnificent but constantly obtuse.'

His solution that year was to create an axis that ran along the outside of both the Rose and Cottage Gardens, aligning perfectly with the rows of nuts. A pleached allée of common lime was planted and the path between paved in 1936 with concrete slabs in pinkish, greenish and yellowish tones that thankfully weathered to more mellow hues resembling natural stone. The lime was not an ideal choice: it produces suckers that are abundant and unsightly, particularly from the base; regular removal of these entailed much work. In summer everything beneath was covered with sooty mould, which grows on sugary honeydew secreted by the lime aphid.

The extent to which Harold's life's work had reached maturity by the outbreak of war in 1939 is not clear. The war years, with the gardeners away in the forces and Harold preoccupied by parliamentary matters, saw a decline. With the end of the war and the loss of his seat in Parliament in 1945, Harold resolved to concentrate on improving the planting of the walk. In a series of notebooks started in 1946 and continuing to 1962, he mapped the plant content of each side, stated which areas had been successful, which had not and what had to be done during the coming months to enhance it. This proved effective in overcoming the problem of the bulbs not being visible at planting time. Given that labels were not used, had there not been an accurate plan and a detailed analysis of work to be done it would have been almost impossible to fill gaps, correct colour associations, replant crowded groups and reduce those that had grown too large.

The notebooks are a touching record, describing triumphs and failures alike and showing changes in planting:

'12 Anemone blue bonnet planted. But it didn't come up!!'

'Rather a dull section – enliven.'

'Terrible section for celandine. Dig up & replant & refill primroses.'

'Tulips are wrong colour – replace.'

'Same old story – heaps of primroses but tiny & flowerless.'

'A very bad section. It must be entirely redug & filled with yellow daffs. (No tulips).' [Beneath this, a later note: 'Redone & planted with 100 Bandoeng tulips.']

Vita's influence is little in evidence, though there is one entry headed 'Big note for 1955':

'Mar [Lady Sackville's name for Vita] says & she is quite right that the St Bavo [anemones] must be largely extended over part I have hatched where common anemones now are.'

The anemones, ordered by Harold in the thousand and subsequently planted by Pam and Sibylle, though they seldom survived the winter, played an important role, providing enough red to balance roughly equal quantities of blue and yellow. Leavened by white and cream, the primary colours have always predominated, with fewer flowers in purple, mauve or orange. Though red is now provided by tulips and Cowichan polyanthus, one rather misses the grace and Mediterranean associations of the simpler anemones such as *A. × fulgens* and *A. pavonina* var. *ocellata*.

⁓

In the walk's first decades, shrubs such as forsythias, brooms and Rugosa roses were used to give bulk along the back of its borders. When Pam and Sibylle came to Sissinghurst in 1959, only *Cytisus × praecox* and *Prunus tenella* remained. The short-lived broom was not replaced when it died and the showier *Prunus tenella* 'Fire Hill' was substituted for the less satisfactory species, leaving it the only shrub. It is hard to tell whether it was Harold's intention to phase out the shrubs; however, without them an attractive view opens out along the full length of the border; this has the advantage of strengthening the simple architecture of the walk, emphasizing the rhythmic repetition of lime trunks and terracotta pots.

Harold used named primulas such as 'Wanda', 'Guinevere' and 'E.R. Janes', as well as some of the double varieties, which both he and Vita enjoyed. Some came from their near neighbour, 'Cherry' Collingwood Ingram, perhaps including the still extant 'Ingram's Blue'. Most of the primroses lacked a jarring orange-yellow eye and Pam and Sibylle also avoided such sorts, favouring those easily raised from seed such as the

Cowichan strains with their sumptuous velvety flowers and dark foliage.

Harold considered *Narcissus* 'Beryl', one of the first Cyclamineus hybrids, a particular treasure and noted that it should be added for the 1956 season. Creamy white 'Thalia' was another of the few dwarf hybrids available to him, although species such as *NN. asturiensis*, *bulbocodium* and *triandrus* were much used and frequently topped up. Vita also loved small-flowered narcissi such as 'Charity May' and 'Jenny', given to her by the raiser Cyril Coleman, the 'Cyclamineus King'. They were cosseted in pots solely for use in the house, to be added to the walk only after Harold's death. Pam and Sibylle also added the early-flowering Cyclamineus hybrids 'Peeping Tom' and 'February Gold', though both usually started to bloom before the visitors arrived in spring.

Trumpet daffodils were much in evidence from the start. It must be owned that some, such as 'Fortune' and 'Carlton', seem coarse in comparison with other large-flowered sorts, though they are undeniably reliable and colourful. This did not stop Vita from praising them in her *Observer* column in April 1953. 'Mrs R.O. Backhouse', the first popular pink-trumpeted variety, was noted as being very good in 1951 and the original planting also included some old-fashioned doubles such as *N. poeticus* 'Plenus' and *N. × odorus* 'Double Campernelle'.

Harold seems to have been attracted by the old florists' flowers which acquaintances such as Sacheverell Sitwell and Wilfrid Blunt were then championing after a long period of neglect. Auriculas were one such group and were always represented in the walk. Striped tulips such as 'James Wild', 'Habit de Noce', 'Absalom' and Rembrandt varieties are mentioned in the notebooks as being used in pots, three dozen in each. These must have made an astonishing spectacle, though it would be hard today to find enough of each of the named sorts to fill a single pot. The flower paintings of the Dutch masters were doubtless an influence; most of the blooms they painted could be found in the garden: poppies, roses, wallflowers, tulips, narcissi, anemones and many more. In her epic poem *The Garden*, Vita wrote of 'the Dutchman's canvas/Crammed to absurdity' and of tulips 'To charm Van Huysum and the curious Breughel,/And Rachel Ruysch, so nice so leisurely/ That seven years were given to two pictures.'

By 1960, the notebooks contain less analysis and fewer jottings of plants required. It is clear that Harold was becoming less conscientious about his life's work, for many of the sections mapped in the notebook are annotated 'rather sparse' or 'bad gap' without any suggestion of what should be done to rectify the fault. During the fifties, many of the shorter-lived plants such as anemones, tulips and primroses had disappeared; other gems had dwindled to just one or two bulbs. Alpines such as arabis, gentians, dwarf irises, phlox and fine named cultivars of pulsatilla, all plants which benefit from regular replanting or other cosseting, had disappeared.

The latest-flowering tulips include long-blooming 'Red Shine', seen with white forget-me-nots in the far right pot. The lime spurs produce early leaves; if annual shoots were pruned to the knuckle, foliage would not appear until the flowers had faded. Euphorbia polychroma 'Major' is now the walk's dominant plant, its colour echoed by E. characias subsp. wulfenii in the tall pots at either end. The centre of the walk is paved with riven York stone slabs in attractively varied sizes. Harold's concrete paving slabs, their contrasting colours mellowed by time, were once used for the main path but now furnish the sides. The hornbeams for these were grown to full size in the nursery before planting.

Each of the farthest ends of the hedges finishes in a return, suggested by Graham Thomas to enclose the walk and separate it from the Nuttery beyond. One of the returns is just visible at the far end of the right-hand hedge. They were not repeated at the west end of the walk, where they would have emphasized the awkwardly angled axes and separated the apsidal border, an integral part of the ensemble, from the main body of the walk.

In their early years at Sissinghurst, Pam and Sibylle were reluctant to make changes to a part of the garden that was so much Harold's own, though all was kept shipshape and the scarcest plants were encouraged to increase. Harold's own gardener, Sidney Neve, spent two days each week weeding the walk. The use of mulch was not allowed so the soil was stripped away with the weeds, leaving the bulbs high and dry on the surface.

After Harold's death in 1968, some major changes were implemented. The hornbeam hedges, by then so thick that the borders had narrowed to an unsatisfactory ribbon, were cut back to their main branches; the original pots that had stood in the shade and sooty drip beneath the limes were placed at Graham Thomas's suggestion on the borders, increasing their impact and improving their flowering. A thorough replanting was tackled, reducing groups that were overcrowded or too large, expanding those that were too small and adjusting colour combinations so that each group was in harmony with its neighbours, though as today the planting contained almost every colour of the rainbow. Annual mulching became routine, greatly reducing the task of weeding.

Pam and Sibylle devised a new method of planting for the walk, still used today. For new bulb groups or those that need augmenting, bulbs are potted into 9cm/3½in pots or 12.5cm/5in pans, placed in an open frame and covered with 7.5cm/3in of crushed bark mulch. When bulb leaves appear in the walk, the contents of the pots or pans can be planted without disturbance. By using pots and pans of varying sizes containing different numbers of bulbs (from one to four for larger bulbs, up to eight for small varieties), the shape of the group can be accurately amended and the density kept uneven for greater informality.

As the common limes grew older, they became more troublesome to maintain. Ousting the spring flowers, the basal shoots took up most of the bed around each tree and had to be cut several times a year. The limes' main stems had started to lean; knobbly arms had dropped significantly from the horizontal. The paving was dangerously uneven and the slabs at the side of the path had slipped into the border, further narrowing the planting area. The hornbeam hedges had once again grown fat, reducing the borders' effective width. A vigorous overhaul was needed, and Pam and Sibylle planned a concerted attack on all the unsatisfactory aspects of the walk. They reasoned that there was bound to be a period of upheaval but if all were put right at once that period would be kept as short as possible. To remove the limes, the paving had to be lifted. Repaving meant disturbing the edges of the borders and replanting these and the small beds around the trees. The hornbeam hedges would also need to be cut back for a second time, releasing space at the back of the borders for further replanting.

Tilia × euchlora was chosen as a suitable alternative to common lime because of its lack of suckers, glossy leaves, more moderate growth and resistance to aphid attack. Plants were bought to train and grow on in the nursery for a planned replanting in 1972. However, the property's budget had to be spent on more urgent priorities such as roof repairs, and funds were not available until 1976. Old trees were removed in August and the new paving installed on a concrete base incorporating a 15cm/6in steel mesh to prevent the tree roots causing upheaval. Planting trenches were left along the sides for the new limes, by then quite large, to be planted in spring 1977; the trenches also allowed bulbs to be planted in cracks in the paving along the row of trees. The summer of 1977 was exceptionally dry and few of the limes survived the move. Undaunted by this disaster, that autumn the gardeners installed a drainage system along the paving trenches by mining under the paving, and set about replacing the trees.

Shaken by the loss in other gardens of several important avenues of *Tilia × euchlora* to bacterial slime flux disease, the Trust advised that this time *T. platyphyllos* 'Rubra' should be used instead. This is coarser than *T. × euchlora* but has few disease problems, though the gardeners must be vigilant against caterpillars that can defoliate the entire walk in days. Maidens raised from seed were planted, trained against posts with horizontal wires at intervals, the lowest of them at 2.2m/7ft 2in, for training the tiers of the espaliers. The outermost posts were held rigidly upright by guy wires, beyond the extremities of the walk, in the Nuttery at one end and the Rose Garden at the other. When young, laterals were summer pruned and leaders were winter pruned to encourage extension growth. Some notching was needed to stimulate production of a lateral wherever there was a horizontal wire. Where laterals from adjacent trees met, their tips were side-grafted together. Once the framework of branches was complete, Pam and Sibylle envisaged a balance of winter and summer pruning to encourage vigour along the laterals and discourage too much growth at the top of the main stems. However, Sarah Cook finds that by leaving pruning until mid August, there is no significant Lammas growth and yearly winter pruning is not necessary, though the spurs occasionally have to be reduced in winter to prevent the limes becoming too wide.

So many bulbs have blooms in bright primary colours that a good proportion of white and cream flowers is needed to soften the effect. White narcissi, snakeshead fritillaries, wood anemones and Erythronium *'White Beauty' all fill this role, with statuesque crown imperials providing strong yellow or orange accents at intervals. The shorter plants, including erythroniums and many blue muscari and scillas, act as a foil for taller tulips and daffodils and the borders' only remaining shrubs, bright carmine* Prunus tenella *'Fire Hill'. Gold-laced polyanthus are a reminder of the old-fashioned flowers Harold enjoyed, while pink bluebells and* Primula sieboldii *are used to extend the display into late spring.*

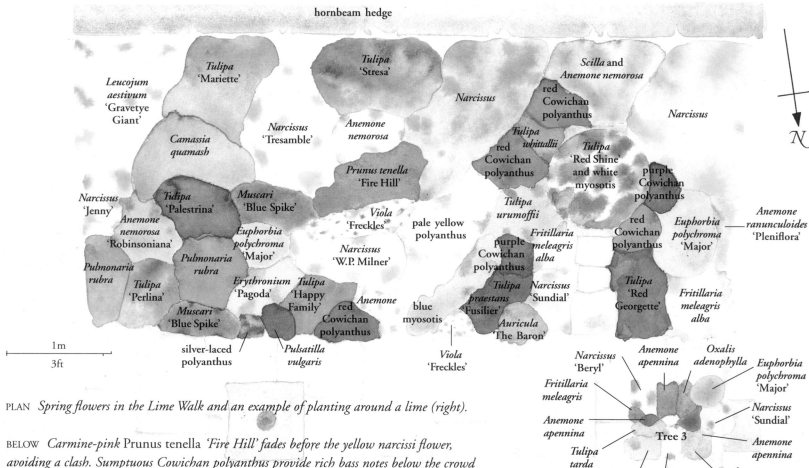

hornbeam hedge

Leucojum aestivum 'Gravetye Giant'

Tulipa 'Mariette'

Tulipa 'Stresa'

Scilla and *Anemone nemorosa*

Narcissus

red Cowichan polyanthus

Narcissus

Camassia quamash

Narcissus 'Tresamble'

Anemone nemorosa

Tulipa whittallii

red Cowichan polyanthus

Tulipa 'Red Shine' and white myosotis

purple Cowichan polyanthus

Narcissus 'Jenny'

Tulipa 'Palestrina'

Muscari 'Blue Spike'

Prunus tenella 'Fire Hill'

Viola 'Freckles'

pale yellow polyanthus

Tulipa urumoffii

Fritillaria meleagris alba

red Cowichan polyanthus

Euphorbia polychroma 'Major'

Anemone ranunculoides 'Pleniflora'

Anemone nemorosa 'Robinsoniana'

Euphorbia polychroma 'Major'

Pulmonaria rubra

Narcissus 'W.P. Milner'

purple Cowichan polyanthus

Pulmonaria rubra

Tulipa 'Perlina'

Erythronium 'Pagoda'

Tulipa 'Happy Family'

Anemone

Tulipa praestans 'Fusilier'

Narcissus 'Sundial'

Tulipa 'Red Georgette'

Fritillaria meleagris alba

Muscari 'Blue Spike'

red Cowichan polyanthus

blue myosotis

Auricula 'The Baron'

1m
3ft

silver-laced polyanthus

Pulsatilla vulgaris

Viola 'Freckles'

N

PLAN *Spring flowers in the Lime Walk and an example of planting around a lime (right).*

BELOW *Carmine-pink* Prunus tenella *'Fire Hill' fades before the yellow narcissi flower, avoiding a clash. Sumptuous Cowichan polyanthus provide rich bass notes below the crowd of bright bulbs.*

Narcissus 'Beryl'

Anemone apennina

Oxalis adenophylla

Euphorbia polychroma 'Major'

Fritillaria meleagris

Narcissus 'Sundial'

Anemone apennina

Tree 3

Anemone apennina

Tulipa tarda

Erythronium dens-canis

Erythronium dens-canis

Fritillaria meleagris alba

Erythronium dens-canis

RIGHT *As filling for a wide and spacious walk, bulbs have the disadvantage of being short, an inevitable consequence of their fleeting growing season, timed to make the most of spring moisture before summer drought. The limes make up for this deficit, their man-made structure providing the perfect architecture for this imposing garden room, a long gallery set with pictures of the most brilliant spring flowers. Were it not for the trees, the broad expanse of York stone paving might seem monotonous. Patterned with the shadows of the limes, its surface glistening after a spring shower, the path becomes a vital element of the design.*

The spurs of the pleached limes are sufficiently branched to produce dense and abundant shoots. The horizontal stems are side-grafted at their tips to those of the adjacent tree, giving greater rigidity.

In addition to the prime objectives of making the paving safe and stable and replacing the limes, there were additional bonuses: the two ends of the walk, dipping below a central hump near the Cottage Garden entrance, were brought up to the same level; two ill-placed trees, one in the middle of the Cottage Garden entrance and one in front of the gate to the field, could be removed, and the spacing of all the limes be adjusted so that no important access was blocked by trunks; the lowest tier of the branches of the new limes was now comfortably above head height; the statue of a bacchante was raised on a plinth to a more commanding position, and the hornbeam hedge on the field side was allowed to grow 30cm/1ft taller to match the hedge on the Cottage Garden side. Concrete paving slabs were replaced down the centre of the walk with hardwearing and attractive York stone, the original slabs being used for the outer edges. Graham Thomas suggested hornbeam buttresses to give more enclosure at the nut end of the walk; these were grown in the kitchen garden until they had reached their final size, having an instant effect on planting.

In spring the terracotta pots are filled with forget-me-nots and Lily-flowered tulips, favoured for their shorter habit and less formal appearance. Tulip 'Red Shine' is usually planted, its late flowers lasting as much as a month, though yellow 'West Point' has occasionally been used. Tulip bulbs for pots and borders need to be treated with a fungicide before planting to lessen damage by tulip fire fungus, *Botrytis tulipae*, and unfolding leaves are sometimes sprayed later to ward off damage.

Summer plants for the pots proved a problem: they had to look attractive from every side. Plants which constantly grew towards the light, with those on the field side facing the hedge, simply would not do. Nasturtiums, geraniums and *Helichrysum petiolare* were used but all were failures. Tried in the early 1970s before they were widely used as bedding plants, busy lizzies proved an outstanding success, growing symmetrically on both sunny and shady sides. The size of plant is important: 'Orange Imp' proved ideal and since its disappearance the Blitz Series has served well. Sadly, this might not be available in future, and the dwarf cultivars that replace it are simply too short.

When bulb leaves appear, showing their positions, gaps are filled with new bulbs and other plants to remedy deficiencies noted the previous year. The borders are at their best during six weeks of mid to late spring, bluebell cultivars and *Euphorbia polychroma* 'Major' being especially valuable for the latter part of the display before the flowers carpeting the Nuttery take over. Sarah Cook feels that the addition of a few herbaceous perennials such as pulmonarias, fortunately no longer stripped by birds, has helped prevent the planting from looking 'too much like a bulb catalogue'.

Weekly deadheading and hand weeding are beneficial while the bulbs flower; provided there is a good mulch, weed control is relatively easy, though slug pellets are sometimes needed to protect the tulips. Diseased bulbs are removed while still showing, and an assessment is made of requirements for the following year. Meanwhile, the busy lizzies for the terracotta pots are being grown from seed sown in mid spring under glass. Then follows a period when the foliage must be left to die back.

Soon after the bulbs' display is finished, new bulbs and other plants are ordered to fill gaps, correct colour associations and remedy any shortcomings of the previous season's display. Daffodils and anemones are potted as soon as they are received to prevent them drying out; tulips and other bulbs are not potted until mid autumn. The pots are then covered with bark mulch to await spring planting. Once the bulb grass has died by early summer, the borders can be cut down and cleared, leaving only perennials such as spurges. The hornbeam hedges are clipped and the pots emptied and planted with busy lizzies. Cutting the hedges so early has the disadvantage that there is a little regrowth which must be cut later in the year. However, the gardeners think the clipping should be left no later if the formal architecture of the walk is to be enjoyed; the second trim is quick to do.

When the limes finish their flush of growth in summer they are pruned. After that, there is little summer work except occasional hoeing, made

easy by the generous mulch. This has to stop when the leaves of the grape hyacinths start to push through in late summer. When the garden closes, the hedges are given a second trim, herbaceous plants are cut back, and the borders are dressed with bonemeal and mulched with crushed bark.

Occasionally a section of border shows signs of a disease such as narcissus eelworm, virus or tulip fire and must then be emptied in late summer, sterilized with dazomet and replanted. Polythene must be laid to keep in the dazomet fumes but it can be covered with bark mulch to improve its appearance. By spring the polythene can be removed, the fumes allowed to escape and the border replanted so that not one season's display is lost.

❧

It is hard to divine the inspiration and sources behind Harold's 'life's work', for it is highly original in the way it combines a dazzlingly intense informal display of spring flowers within a strongly architectural framework. True, exactly the same range of flowers had been used by Victorian and Edwardian gardeners, as seen in such books as *Spring Flowers at Belvoir Castle* by W.H. Divers (1909), but planted in a forced and semi-formal bedding style that would not have appealed to either Harold or Vita. Miss Jekyll's spring garden at Munstead seems to have had some similarities, and Nigel Nicolson believes Italian Renaissance paintings such as Botticelli's *Primavera* to have been an influence. However, there are few examples of directly comparable schemes; the borders beneath the beech avenue at

Keukenhof in the Netherlands, combining a riotous patchwork of bulbs with the formality of the trees, are too new (1949) to have inspired but too old to have been influenced by Harold's work. It is also puzzling that, while the Rose Garden, Cottage Garden and White Garden have had many imitators, the Lime Walk, though it has been a delight and inspiration for thousands of visitors, has seldom been copied. This may, however, be because of the reluctance of modern gardeners to plant for a single season.

It is easy to see why both Harold and Vita so loved spring flowers. The enamelled brilliance of their colours is the harbinger of the garden's new season after the dreary winter. The Lime Walk's rich carpet was associated with places they loved – tulips from Turkey, crown imperials from Persia, *Clematis alpina* from the Dolomites, anemones from the Mediterranean – and its flowers must have brought back a wealth of happy memories.

Probably no other area of the garden has seen so many improvements since the Nicolsons' time. Some considered the old imperfections of the Lime Walk endearing. However, Sissinghurst's change of use from private to public garden brings an expectation that the garden should approach perfection. This paradox, the conflict between public and private, amateur and professional, conservation and improvement, makes for difficult decisions: no solution will satisfy everybody. Would Harold and Vita have liked the changes? Harold would probably have approved wholeheartedly; Vita might have had reservations. Perhaps we should not quibble about such niceties; what matters most is that the garden survives.

Vita and Harold both had their bedrooms in the South Cottage. Here began and ended each gardening day at Sissinghurst. But the name Cottage Garden is misleading. The range of plants far transcends that of the traditional gardens painted by artists such as Helen Allingham: here are tender exotics, hedychiums, salvias and cannas and the bold foliage of ligularias and veratrums. The flowers are restricted to the sunset colours, orange, red and yellow, a more deliberate mix than the riot of the cottager. The display begins early with wallflowers and tulips and ends with the golds and russets of autumn and a blaze of dahlias.

Harold and Vita considered the Cottage Garden 'our own little garden', the innermost and most intimate of what Harold called Sissinghurst's 'succession of privacies'. He is often credited as the inventor of the garden's colour scheme of orange, red and yellow. However, Vita claimed it as her own in an *Observer* article of 1955 in which she wrote that it was:

> '. . . a muddle of flowers but all of them in the range of colours you might find in a sunset. I used to call it the sunset garden in my own mind before I even started to plant it up.'

In that same article Vita called her sunset garden 'a typical cottage garden'. Many have believed her, suggesting that she was following the great gardener William Robinson's exhortation to plant in a traditional country style. This was pure romance: it may have been the garden of a cottage, but it was as much a cottage garden as Marie-Antoinette was a milkmaid. Colours were carefully marshalled, most of them in the orange to scarlet range so rare among the traditional plants of the cottage garden. Even when a typical genus such as aquilegia or iris was used, the varieties were the very latest and most choice, their hues not in the least traditional, most of them being products of the breeder's art during the preceding couple of decades.

It is easy to forget that long-spurred aquilegia hybrids only started to appear in British gardens at about the time of Harold and Vita's marriage in 1913; helianthemum cultivars, important front-rank plants in the Cottage Garden, were then relatively rare and reached the height of their popularity only in the 1920s; irises in clear yellows, ambers and apricots came much later. Such plants are not at all old-fashioned or unsophisticated. True, the plants were and are jumbled but with neither the artlessness nor the repetition of the true cottage garden, whose plants are far more numerously represented in Sissinghurst's White and Rose Gardens.

In recent years, the inclusion of more bold-leaved exotics and tender plants has made the mix even less cottagey, though immeasurably more attractive and longer lasting in its display. During the fifties and sixties, the writings of influential authors such as Margery Fish and Christopher Lloyd heralded an increasing awareness of the value of foliage texture and form. The gardeners here, as elsewhere, made conscious efforts to improve these aspects of the planting, which they considered particularly important in areas with a restricted range of flower colours. Vita would have had sympathy with this: though her own planting favoured soft textures with limited use of form, she reiterated the teaching of her friend Margery Fish in her articles and saw their sense.

Mrs Fish championed plants for their beauty of shape and texture, even if they were not colourful or showy. She was one of the first to encourage gardeners to grow green-flowered plants, to appreciate the subtlety of the tiniest variations of colour and not to demand the brilliant floraison that had dominated gardens of the previous hundred years. She had perhaps unwittingly put her finger on what it was that Vita found so unsatisfactory about the traditional herbaceous border: it was not the plants themselves that she disliked, for almost all found a home somewhere in her

Outside the South Cottage in spring, wallflowers, tulips and Euphorbia griffithii *'Dixter' provide colour among burgeoning foliage. Harold's chair sits by the door (left). Six weeks later (right), as spring moves into summer, columbines, irises, tree lupins and spurge flourish as rose 'Madame Alfred Carrière' fades.*

Garden

garden; it was the fact that too many were amorphous, planted all too often for a showy display of flowers with no consideration for form. Planted *en masse*, the likes of solidago, coreopsis or helianthus are too shapeless to satisfy. In the Cottage Garden, mixed with the contrasting forms of cannas, grasses, crocosmias and veratrum, they help temper the excitement of so many diverse shapes and become an essential element of the design.

Here, more than in any other part of the garden, foliage is used to the full. In spring, a verdant carpet spreads low across the beds, studded with bright groups of wallflowers and tulips. Spears of iris, felted rosettes of verbascum, bold ligularias combine to form a tapestry of pleasing shapes in gently varied shades of green. The appearance changes as the seasons advance: in summer, the beds are no longer flat but generously filled, dominated by cotton-wool candelabra of mullein; by early autumn, parts are jungle-like in their exuberant growth, more Rousseau than Robinson. One expects to see a tiger emerging from between cannas, dahlias and miscanthus, burning bright among the autumnal flowers.

One of Harold and Vita's earliest tasks was to create intimacy by providing enclosure, planting not only hedges but small trees. An ancient laburnum already existed at the garden's south-west corner, with an old mixed farm hedge enclosing the south and west sides. The screen of pleached limes of the Lime Walk, overtopping the farm hedge, gave enclosure along the southern side.

Five *Robinia pseudoacacia* around Sissinghurst Crescent were used to frame the view to the moat; all have since been lost to honey fungus or the 1987 storm. *Cercidiphyllum japonicum* is the only remaining small tree along the southern side of the garden, though this too is suffering from fungal attack. *Koelreuteria paniculata*, planted in 1964 and an important frame for the view of the tower, has also died. Attempts to replace some of the losses with reputedly disease-resistant species have generally met with failure. Coping with a persistent and pernicious sickness like honey fungus is often one of the most vexing problems of an old garden; selecting a new generation of disease-resistant small trees will tax the gardeners' ingenuity in the coming years. The area south of the cottage was thickly filled with a balsam poplar, *Abelia triflora*, *Cytisus battandieri*, three *Philadelphus coronarius* and the Mediterranean strawberry tree, *Arbutus andrachne*. Scent was clearly a major consideration but little underplanting was possible in the dense shade beneath. Of all these, only one philadelphus survives. Although the planting here is now full of interest, it will be some time before the ptelea here and the pear in the Orchard beyond have grown sufficiently to stop the eye straying towards the Orchard, when it would be better drawn down the more important vista to the moat.

Harold and Vita had planted winter-flowering shrubs in the southern part of the garden: a witch hazel, *Hamamelis japonica* 'Arborea', one of the least satisfactory of its genus, was destroyed when an ancient laburnum fell; a large stachyurus died of old age. Both had taken up a good deal of room, flowering when few people saw them, and so were not replaced.

Since the Nicolsons' time there have been numerous refinements to the Cottage Garden. The field hedge along the garden's west side was replaced with yew and another was removed from the south side to reveal the hornbeam hedge of the Lime Walk behind; levels of beds and paths were adjusted, removing some irritating and potentially dangerous steps and giving a better vantage for the vista down the Moat Walk; paths were relaid, making them firm and even but retaining their fanciful mix of brickbats and stone. Countless pairs of visitors' feet already prevented the self-sown flowers Vita loved from seeding themselves in the path: it was no loss to set its stones on a concrete base impenetrable to seedling roots.

There was no border around the outside of the garden and the perimeter path was unnavigable, narrow and overhung by the farm hedge. Removal of this, re-laying the path and planting a narrow border established a comfortable outer route, a vantage for views across the whole Cottage Garden. Weeds such as wild garlic were removed and thuggish perennials such as *Thalictrum flavum* subsp. *glaucum*, *Sinacalia tangutica* and alstroemeria, which had taken over large areas, were much reduced.

❧

The two box bushes standing sentinel at either side of the entrance from the Lime Walk were originally clipped as cubes, serving only to draw attention to the strange alignment of the perimeter path, which was far from parallel with the sides of the cubes. The gardeners' solution was to replace them with box columns.

The tall Irish yews in the centre of the Cottage Garden, intended as vertical accents analogous to Italian cypresses, had, like those in the Top Courtyard, become impossibly large, blotting out the view of the tower and the front of the cottage from most of the garden. Leaving them as they were to keep their craggy and picturesque outline was simply not an option. The Nicolsons had tied them in with 'waistbands', but these no longer contained their inexorable growth.

In the late 1960s, the gardeners decided to remove superfluous wood and to reduce their height considerably. Quite large branches including the main stem were sawn out, leaving other large stems supple enough to be tied into shape and a fringe of younger, softer branches to furnish what remained. All was then wired into the central branches, using radial rather than peripheral ties; this avoids an unnaturally trussed appearance and allows close trimming without cutting the ties. Two quarter-mile reels of government-surplus covered telephone cable were used over the years, the covering preventing the ties from biting into the wood. Thus the yews were kept as slim and as evenly matched as was feasible, the focus of both the Cottage Garden and the westward view along the Moat Walk. They will nevertheless need occasionally to be rebuilt to keep them slim and within reach of the ladder used when they are pruned. Even so, the yews do seem to dominate the Cottage Garden. Sarah Cook feels that their eccentrically large size contributes a lot to the garden's charm; had they remained ideally scaled, the character of the garden would have been diminished; perfect proportions, though theoretically more beautiful, can seem bland and dull. She also points out that looking from the cottage's bedroom windows, as Harold and Vita would have done, the yews seem perfectly in scale.

Here, as elsewhere at Sissinghurst, the choice of plants and their groupings were continually adjusted and reworked in the quest for perfection.

OPPOSITE *An early display of tulips, wallflowers and other spring flowers. Sufficient quantities establish an interplay of colours from group to group, with here, behind tulip 'Georgette', a combination of maroon-purple 'Black Parrot' tulips with* Euphorbia polychroma *'Major' in front of wallflower 'Vulcan',* Trollius × cultorum *'Superbus' and Siberian wallflowers. By the cottage is a border wallflower, 'Fire King', beneath rose 'Helen Knight' and* Paeonia mlokosewitschii *(right); Vita was proud that she raised this from seed, saving 30 shillings a plant, five times the price of more usual varieties.*

ABOVE *The delights of the Cottage Garden in spring do not depend on flowers alone. The low patchwork of foliage is never more attractive than in mid to late spring with its variety of textures and shades of green. In the foreground are felted mulleins, chartreuse spears of crocosmia, bronzed fennel and spurge and fernlike poppies. Beyond lie the grassy glaucous leaves of asphodel and boldly pleated* Veratrum nigrum. *In the background, the sweep of the Sissinghurst Crescent hedge supplies structure and enclosure.*

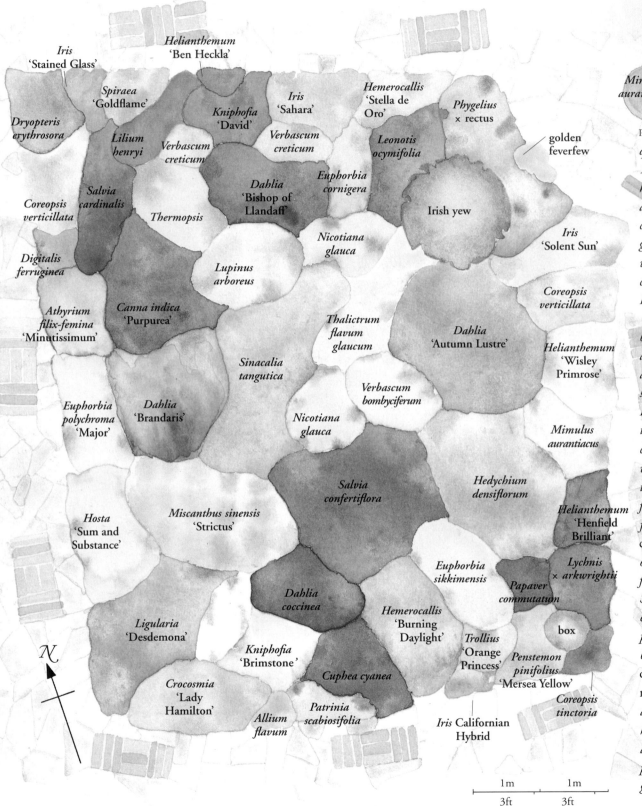

PLAN AND RIGHT *The south-west quarter of the Cottage Garden in 1994. Flower colours here harmonize perfectly with the stone and brick of the paths and the cottage itself.* Mimulus aurantiacus *glows appealingly against the verdigris of the central copper, a combination of colours first used by Harold and Vita.*

A balance between colours must be maintained from spring until autumn, not an easy task as red and orange blooms are relatively scarce among garden plants. Enough of each must be in flower throughout the season to carry the counterpoint of colours, with no wide expanses of green to interrupt the harmonies. Plants with a fleeting season are avoided, except for a few annuals such as Papaver commutatum *(foreground) which obligingly fit into small spaces later filled by the surrounding plants. Some variation in foliage texture is essential: the area shown in the picture would be dull without the bold leaves of* Hedychium densiflorum *and* Crocosmia masoniorum. *Front-rank plants are mostly short but a few medium-height plants such as the crocosmia and phygelius are brought to the path's edge to give a full and generous effect.*

During the 1960s, the incessant seeking out of better plants was no easy task. The gardeners worked on Saturdays; nurseries were usually closed on Sundays; there were no local garden centres, no *Plant Finder* guides and few illustrated catalogues. The search for catalogues listing new plants and assessment of merits or faults of resulting acquisitions was unending.

ᧁ

Wallflowers were introduced by the gardeners shortly after Vita's death to give spring colour, bushy plants being raised in the nursery each year. The gardeners have noticed a decline in quality of the stock over the years, a result of either excessive inbreeding or poor selection by seed producers. 'Ivory White' was generally lacking in vigour, though the other regular varieties, 'Orange Bedder', 'Fire King' and 'Primrose Dame' proved less difficult. In late spring, they have to be removed from the sunny beds at the foot of the cottage wall to make way for the arctotis hybrids 'Flame' and 'Mahogany', brought out from the glasshouse.

Flaming orange Siberian wallflowers are also grown, their later display coinciding agreeably with the spurges. Pam and Sibylle feel that 'you need a few bright things to keep you awake' and are not repentant about their brilliance; nor should they be, for there seems to be nothing to suggest that Vita and Harold excluded such colours. A less startling Siberian variety, 'Apricot', used to be grown but is no longer available.

Though wallflowers have become the mainstay of the early display since the Nicolsons' time, tulips have also come to play a greater role. Harold and Vita had *Tulipa* 'Couleur Cardinal' growing in a copper, not solely because of the richness and depth of its petals but because its blue-green foliage tones with the verdigris of the pot. Now standing at the centre of the Cottage Garden, the copper was found by Vita in a barn once used as a laundry when Sissinghurst was a workhouse. It is usually planted with *Mimulus aurantiacus*, as it was in her time, though sulphur-yellow *Argyranthemum maderense*, exceptional for its blue-green leaves, is sometimes used for a change.

Other varieties of tulip, added to complement the wallflowers, are 'Black Parrot', a persistent variety whose intense maroon-purple also assorts well with spurges and Bowles' golden sedge. *Tulipa viridiflora* 'Praecox', striped yellow and green, chimes perfectly with *Euphorbia polychroma* 'Major' against the wall. The burnt orange blooms of 'Dillenburg' made an effective display next to reddish-bronze-leaved *Ligularia* 'Desdemona', particularly when both were seen glowing against the sun. Other cultivars occasionally used include Lily-flowered 'Aladdin' in vermilion edged with yellow, red Triumph 'Cassini', the large and early yellow Darwin Hybrid 'Flower of Spring', Single Late orange-edged red 'Yuma', the Parrot variety 'Orange Favourite' and flame-flowered *Tulipa gesneriana*. However, few other spring

bulbs are used in the Cottage Garden; the Lime Walk's performance must not be upstaged.

The irises begin their display with the wallflowers, the taller varieties continuing, with columbines and spurges, through the 'June gap'. Most are cultivars raised since World War II and were given by breeders such as Sir Cedric Morris and John Taylor, whose clear yellow Intermediate variety 'Curlew' is perhaps the most commendable of the lot. There are also several Californian Hybrids in soft colours with attractively veined falls.

In 1959, *Euphorbia griffithii* was the only spurge to be found anywhere at Sissinghurst. They are now a recurring theme in the Cottage Garden where their coloured bracts in yellow, gamboge or orange give long-lasting value, often with the added bonus of brilliant autumn colour. Here are *EE. cornigera*, a non-running form of *cyparissias, sikkimensis* (valued for spring foliage), *griffithii* 'Dixter', *palustris, polychroma* 'Major' and *characias* subsp. *wulfenii* Margery Fish Group, a name given to seedlings of 'Lambrook Gold' with handsomely architectural long panicles.

Vita grew columbines in the days when seed of single-colour strains of long-spurred hybrids was available. When these became scarce, the gardeners saved seed of the best plants, growing them in isolation so that most bred true to type. Species such as *Aquilegia formosa* var. *truncata*, *A. skinneri*, *A. canadensis* and *A.* × *longissima* have also been introduced. Though it is a constant battle to prevent them from intermarrying, they are valuable for filling the gap between the spring and summer displays.

ᧁ

Dahlias were Harold's choice for the Cottage Garden and their use has been extended since his time so that the garden remains as colourful in autumn as it is in high summer. The choice of cultivars has been refined over the years, by careful selection of a range of varieties with refined flower colours or good foliage. Some came from E.C.W. Cooper, raiser of the Jescot series, including 'Jescot Buttercup', still to be seen in the garden, and the sumptuous purple-black 'Jescot Nubia', which sadly succumbed to virus and is no longer grown. 'Bishop of Llandaff' was another regular, though its health also declined; 'John Street' was used as a replacement for some years though it lacked the Bishop's dark leaves. Healthy tissue-cultured plants of the Bishop have become available in recent years, making this the most popular variety in British gardens – justly so, for its finely divided dark foliage and dazzling scarlet flowers are outstanding.

Other choice varieties came from John Crutchfield's nursery at Turner's Hill, Sussex. These include 'Yellow Hammer' and bright orange 'East Court', both dark-leaved varieties with single flowers. 'Autumn Lustre' in rich but gentle orange, soft vermilion *D. coccinea*, 'David Howard' with bronze leaves and golden-orange flowers and lemon-yellow 'Glorie van

Heemstede' were other additions still grown in the garden today. The plants are overwintered in frost-free conditions in the nursery and occasionally repropagated from cuttings taken in mid spring.

Tender shrubby salvias are also key plants during the summer, valued for their jewel-box flowers of scarlet or crimson if not always for their leaves. *S. confertiflora* is handsome enough, though its fragrance is not to everyone's taste: some are reminded of roast beef; others recall burning rubber. *S. dombeyi* is included scarcely for show but for its strangely sinister slender scarlet flowers on hanging calyces the colour of congealed blood; tall and lax, it needs careful staking and full sun. Much the best value is *S. fulgens*, early and long flowering, and hardy in mild winters.

Lilies have traditionally had a place in the garden. The tiger lily, *Lilium lancifolium* var. *splendens*, was introduced by Jack Vass and was a success for some years, until its vigour declined. Attempts to reintroduce it met with similar problems, though soft orange *Lilium henryi* and *L.* 'Enchantment' have been more persistent. I find it hard to love the latter; its stiff stems, tightly packed spikes and uncompromisingly bright flowers seem perhaps to lack the charm of most of its kin, though it is undoubtedly a 'good doer'.

ABOVE *Irish yews dominate the Cottage Garden, though the tower, here topped with the Sackville-West flag, also exerts a strong presence. Noisette rose 'Madame Alfred Carrière' approaches the peak of its display.*

PAGES 84–5 *Bringing* Achillea *'Coronation Gold',* Kniphofia *'David' and other medium-sized plants to the path's edge softens its hard lines, enhancing the romantic fullness of the garden. A wisp of canary creeper scrambles insouciantly up the solemn yew. Seemingly the sort of self-sown accident Vita loved, this planting has in fact been contrived by the gardeners.*

Flat heads of achillea provide a distinctive contrast of shape, quite different from any other flower in the garden. Vita grew 'Gold Plate' and the gardeners have experimented with others over the years. Grey-leaved 'Taygetea' was an early addition but was soon replaced by the superior 'Moonshine' when this was introduced by Alan Bloom in the early 1960s. Like 'Taygetea', 'Moonshine' has the disadvantage of becoming shy-flowering, developing a woody and congested base to the plant unless it is regularly repropagated. Another Bloom introduction, 'Anthea', promises to be an improvement, having the grey-green leaves and pale yellow flowers

LEFT ABOVE *Bright candelabra of verbascum shine against the dark yews next to rich red Floribunda rose 'Dusky Maiden'.*

LEFT BELOW *Rousseauesque planting of* Salvia confertiflora, *sunflower and* Miscanthus sinensis *'Strictus'. The miscanthus is usually misidentified as 'Zebrinus', a spreading variety needing more space to display its gracefully arching habit; upright 'Strictus' is much better suited to such close planting.*

RIGHT, FROM LEFT TO RIGHT:
TOP *Iris 'Curlew', an admirable Intermediate hybrid raised by John Taylor, with Siberian wallflowers and columbines; woolly verbascums and columbines;* Kniphofia *'Royal Standard', a reliable poker flowering in mid to late summer.*

CENTRE *Arctotis 'Mahogany', introduced by Harold and regularly used in the border beneath the cottage; ramrod stems of* Canna indica *'Purpurea' rise above bold exotic foliage; persistent pale orange* Lilium henryi.

BOTTOM *Crocosmia 'Lady Hamilton', an elegant Edwardian variety;* Hedychium coccineum *'Tara', introduced in 1972 by Tony Schilling from Nepal and absolutely hardy here;* Dahlia *'David Howard', among the worthiest and most popular of dark-leaved cultivars.*

of its predecessors but needing less frequent replanting and producing a good secondary crop of flowers lasting into the autumn.

Mulleins are planted out in autumn once the existing mullein plants have finished blooming. Raised from seed in the nursery, they produce plants of prodigious size, full of the promise of a spectacular starburst to sparkle against the sombre yews. The verbascums are usually promiscuous: wherever two or more are gathered together, hybrids appear among their offspring. On rare occasions, these are much better than their parents and they are used to produce seed for the next generation. Two strains are used in the Cottage Garden: one is green-leaved, the gardeners' own selection from the Harkness Hybrids; the other is white-felted, derived probably from *V. olympicum* or *V. bombyciferum,* but an improvement chosen for its exceptional whiteness, vigour and generously branched inflorescence. It was originally grown in the White Garden where Harold solemnly used to cut off all its yellow flowers, a task which seemed rather a waste to the gardeners, who felt they would be better appreciated in their present home.

Harold and Vita disagreed about kniphofias. In a letter to her in 1937, he wrote: 'Except for those beastly red-hot pokers which you have a weakness for, there is not an ugly flower in the whole place.' *Kniphofia* 'Royal Standard' survives from her time and the gardeners have added *KK. triangularis,* 'David', 'Samuel's Sensation' and the clear yellow autumn-flowering 'Brimstone'.

Crocosmias are further important additions, for their striking foliage as well as their flowers, particularly the excellent recent hybrids such as 'Lucifer' whose handsome pleated leaves derive from *C. paniculata.* Like the crocosmias, hedychiums such as *HH. densiflorum,* and *H. coccineum* 'Tara' have been added as much for bold foliage as for flower, contributing to the exotic appearance of the planting. *Hedychium gardnerianum* proved scarcely hardy enough; if it survived the winter, it started into growth too late to fulfil its intended role. Now overwintered under glass, it is used elsewhere in the garden as a particularly handsome pot plant.

A small area bounded by the Cottage Garden, the Nuttery and an azalea bank is known as the Triangle. Shady enough for woodlanders and not restricted to the Cottage Garden's sunset colours, this is a useful area to bring on unusual plants until there are enough to stock a group elsewhere in the garden. The magenta-purple hardy orchid *Dactylorhiza × grandis* has proved so vigorous here that it needs regular replanting and has produced enough offspring to populate large swathes in the shade of the Nuttery. The kingfisher-blue Himalayan poppy *Meconopsis betonicifolia* is another inhabitant, its colour making it difficult to place elsewhere in the garden. Sarah Cook thinks it is not likely to prove reliably perennial, for it prefers climates with cooler, wetter summers, such as the west coast of Scotland.

When the garden closes for maintenance in mid autumn, the first job is a quick tidy, removing temporary planting and any plants that are liable to seed, and also cutting down perennials that have died back. However, many of the perennials are much easier to tackle in late winter when their tops have become less sappy.

The dahlias are removed after they have been blackened by the first frost. The high-ladder pruning of climbers on the cottage is another task for late autumn, after the garden closes but before the weather becomes uncomfortably chilly; this is completed first so as not to interfere with the later bedding of wallflowers beneath the wall. There is no rush to plant out wallflowers before the garden closes for the winter; this would cause them to wilt unless they were regularly watered; provided the ground has not cooled down too much, they will still establish well before the turn of the year. The planting positions are varied from season to season to minimize diseases that can accumulate through growing in the same spot for years. However, the bed beneath the cottage wall always contains wallflowers and occasionally needs to be sterilized.

The Cottage Garden is left over Christmas while the gardeners' attention turns to the pruning and staking of roses in the Rose Garden. Once that is finished, the gardeners cut the tall Irish yews in the centre of the Cottage Garden.

In early spring the rest of the herbaceous plants are cut down and the beds pricked over with a fork to open the soil and relieve compaction before mulching. Some division of perennials is needed before the garden opens to the public and the spring flowers start their display in earnest. There is no general rule about the frequency of this: plants such as goldenrod need dividing every two to three years; others such as ligularia and kirengeshoma hardly ever need attention. Kniphofias are occasionally divided in spring. A few plants such as achilleas are replaced with new plants from the nursery, sometimes from pots during the summer and occasionally after flowering in mid autumn. Once the danger of spring frost is past, the wallflowers are removed and dahlias and other tender perennials planted for the summer and autumn display.

❧

The Cottage Garden remains discrete, visually connected to the Moat Walk alone among the rest of the garden rooms. Other areas are so enmeshed together by the matrix of vistas that they become utterly integrated with each other, scarcely capable of being considered in isolation. The relative seclusion and cosiness of the Cottage Garden, its sunset colours harmonizing with the warm brick of the cottage and the generous abundance of its planting, made it a favourite with Vita and particularly with Harold, whose chair still stands by the cottage door.

ABOVE *Looking from the Triangle across Sissinghurst Crescent to the Cottage Garden. Cool woodlanders contrast with hot hues beyond. To the left, behind* Primula sieboldii, *are pale yellow pendent flowers of* Dicentra macrantha; *this rarity, though hardy, is often damaged by late frosts and demands moist soil. To the right is the pure bright blue of* Omphalodes cappadocica.

RIGHT *Also in the Triangle is* Dactylorhiza × grandis, *a remarkable and vigorous hybrid orchid, with fern* Polystichum setiferum.

FAR RIGHT *The striking kingfisher blue of Tibetan poppy,* Meconopsis betonicifolia.

The Nuttery

Nowhere else at Sissinghurst has planting changed so completely since Harold and Vita's day as in the Nuttery. The carpet of polyanthus that astonished visitors in the 1950s and, after a period of decline, again in the 1960s, is no more. A tapestry of woodlanders, flowers, ferns and grasses has been created, more subtle and in many ways more delightful than the bright bedding they replaced. Such plants last in beauty longer than poly-anthus, beginning at the same time as the bulbs of the Lime Walk but at their best as the flowers of the walk fade. The intermingling pattern of foliage, fruits and fewer flowers remains charming and richly varied even throughout summer and autumn. This is ground-cover planting at its best: diverse and suited in character and scale to its setting, with no acres of interminable comfrey, cotoneaster or ivy; it is also easy to maintain.

In April 1930, Harold's diary records: 'We come suddenly upon the nut-walk and that settles it.' Thus a planting of filberts, inseparably associated with the rural life of Kent, clinched their decision to make their home and garden here. Within months, weeds and undergrowth were cleared. Vita lost little time in planting narcissi through the nuts; in 1932, Harold added foxgloves collected from Sissinghurst's woods in an old pram. That same year, he came to realize that the alignment of the nuts would frustrate his plan for a long axis from the Rose Garden through the Nuttery. His solution was to set the Lime Walk at an angle to the Rose and Cottage Gardens, aligned with the middle rows of filberts.

When Harold and Vita added polyanthus to the Nuttery planting, they were probably influenced by Gertrude Jekyll's famed Primrose Garden at Munstead Wood. By the 1870s, the polyanthus had lost much of the popularity it enjoyed in the first half of the nineteenth century. Only two basic sorts were grown: the then-scarce silver- or gold-laced varieties of the florists, and the more common red. Miss Jekyll began to develop her poly-anthus strain (she called them 'bunch-flowered Primroses') from the mid 1870s onwards, using as parents an old cultivar, 'Golden Plover', and a white polyanthus found in a cottage garden. She tried to categorize the varieties but gave up when she had identified sixty different classes, none of them deep enough to be called gold. In choosing to develop strains of pure white or yellow, Miss Jekyll was breaking with tradition. However, in her *Wood and Garden* (1899), she admitted that the recently improved red strain raised by Anthony Waterer and sorts with a contrasting dark eye were more popular in nurseries then than her own. By the time of her death in 1932, her Primrose Garden and Munstead polyanthus were so famous it would have been almost impossible to think of the plants without thinking of their use at Munstead and her writings about them in several of her books. She commented:

'I always think of the Hazel as a kind nurse to Primroses; in the copses they grow together, and the finest Primrose plants are often nestled close in to the base of the nut-stool.'

The polyanthus at Munstead must have looked very fresh and bright beneath the dappled shade of oak, chestnut and hazel. However, when Vita visited Miss Jekyll's garden in late summer 1917, there would have been only foliage to see.

Harold and Vita opted for a wider range of colours than Miss Jekyll; by 1938, the ground beneath the nuts was entirely carpeted. When war came, though, there was no labour to spare for the regular replanting and soil improvement they demanded; the polyanthus dwindled and weeds took over. When Jack Vass returned to Sissinghurst in 1946, the restoration of the Nuttery was one of his first priorities. Harold, who referred to the carpet as 'the loveliest planting scheme in the whole world' and 'the company of the bright and the good', was determined that the planting should

Wood anemones flower early (left) between Bowles' golden grass and white bluebells. The anemones will soon be enveloped by the other plants as the bluebells come into flower. A week later (right), the bluebells have started to bloom; here bronze-flushed sensitive fern (Onoclea sensibilis) *starts to unfurl. The two plants grow happily together, though the fern will shortly form a canopy above the bluebells.*

be restored. For a few years the Nuttery produced a glorious spring display; but by the time Pam and Sibylle arrived, it was clear that all was not well. Symptoms of soil sickness were already apparent; furthermore, the Pacific Hybrids that Vita was then using proved not to be reliably hardy. They were replaced with the Munstead Hybrids to which other colours – flames, tawny oranges, reds and maroons – were added to give an impression of opulent richness. However, the health of the polyanthus declined to such an extent that few remained. Vita discussed the problem in an *Observer* article in autumn 1960.

⁊

The gardeners refused to be daunted. After Vita's death in 1962, they set to work to improve the soil. The arrival of paraquat weedkiller in the late 1960s offered an opportunity to eliminate the more aggressive native subspecies of celandine (*Ranunculus ficaria* subsp. *bulbilifer*) that had smothered the polyanthus. One of the Nuttery's four alleyways was cleared each year and left for a full season, allowing celandine to be killed. By that time, the garden budget allowed for the purchase of substantial quantities of organic matter (spent hops originally) and grit; many tons were barrowed from the opposite end of the garden and dug into the root-congested clay. A prodigious quantity of new polyanthus plants, raised in the garden, could then be planted. For a few years, the polyanthus responded to the massive input of labour and humus and flowered magnificently. But by the early 1970s not even perfect cultural conditions would persuade them to thrive.

Plants were sent to Wisley for the cause to be identified; several fungal diseases were found, including brown root rot (*Thielaviopsis basicola*) and red core (*Phytophthora fragariae*). Wisley pointed out that, as the garden-

ers already knew, it is not possible to continue growing primulas in the same soil in perpetuity. Added to this, the local bird population had developed a taste for polyanthus flowers; in an area far too big to be protected by cotton, all the blooms were stripped. The arrival of dazomet soil sterilant seemed to offer a solution to fungal diseases but it would not kill them without also killing the nuts. By 1974, the gardeners had to accept that the polyanthus would no longer grow here; a different planting scheme was needed.

The new scheme, of 'greenery-yallery', blue and white, was implemented in 1975, aided by the emptiness of the ground after the demise of the polyanthus. Greenish-yellow was supplied by *Euphorbia amygdaloides* var. *robbiae*, Bowles' golden grass and biennial *Smyrnium perfoliatum*. In blue were *Omphalodes cappadocica* and forget-me-nots, the latter used as a temporary filler: covering such a large area with perennials in a single season would have made impossible demands on both labour and the garden's budget. The white form of Spanish bluebell, sweet woodruff, *Cardamine raphanifolia* and *Epimedium × youngianum* 'Niveum' leavened the scheme, with other epimediums contributing fine and long-lasting foliage. The cardamine was a showy success for a while until wood pigeons developed a taste for it, grazing it annually to the ground; it had to go.

Veratrums and ferns such as onoclea and matteuccia provided foliage contrast while natives such as *Viola riviniana, V.r.* Purpurea Group (long misidentified as *V. labradorica*) and, introduced with leaf mould from the woods, *Anemone nemorosa* were allowed to weave among larger plants to complete the tapestry. A few trilliums from the top of the azalea bank proved to like conditions here and were slowly increased by division to make substantial groups. The variegated strawberry *Fragaria × ananassa* 'Variegata' was also added.

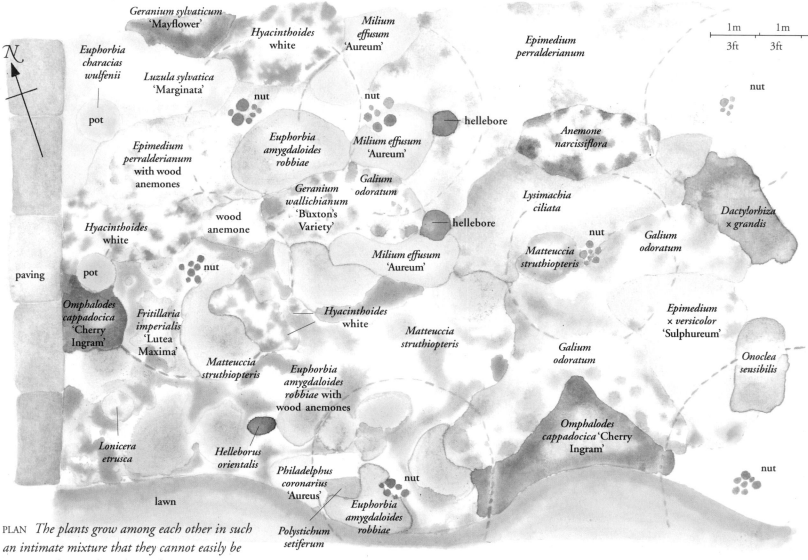

Geranium sylvaticum 'Mayflower'

Hyacinthoides white

Milium effusum 'Aureum'

Epimedium perralderianum

1m   1m
3ft   3ft

Euphorbia characias wulfenii

Luzula sylvatica 'Marginata'

nut

nut

nut

N

pot

Epimedium perralderianum with wood anemones

Euphorbia amygdaloides robbiae

Milium effusum 'Aureum'

hellebore

Anemone narcissiflora

Galium odoratum

Geranium wallichianum 'Buxton's Variety'

Lysimachia ciliata

Dactylorhiza × grandis

Hyacinthoides white

wood anemone

hellebore

nut

Galium odoratum

Matteuccia struthiopteris

paving

pot

Milium effusum 'Aureum'

Matteuccia struthiopteris

Omphalodes cappadocica 'Cherry Ingram'

Fritillaria imperialis 'Lutea Maxima'

nut

Hyacinthoides white

Matteuccia struthiopteris

Epimedium × versicolor 'Sulphureum'

Galium odoratum

Onoclea sensibilis

Matteuccia struthiopteris

Euphorbia amygdaloides robbiae with wood anemones

Omphalodes cappadocica 'Cherry Ingram'

Lonicera etrusca

Helleborus orientalis

Philadelphus coronarius 'Aureus'

nut

nut

lawn

Polystichum setiferum

Euphorbia amygdaloides robbiae

PLAN *The plants grow among each other in such an intimate mixture that they cannot easily be represented on a plan: the predominant species in each area is named, though other plants sow themselves or spread throughout each space.*

RIGHT *Biennial* Smyrnium perfoliatum *with shuttlecock fern,* Matteuccia struthiopteris, *another two plants that coexist happily to create a simple but charming combination.*

OPPOSITE *Pale lavender* Anemone nemorosa *'Robinsoniana' flows through white bluebells and* Geranium sylvaticum *'Mayflower' (above), while wood anemones, oxlips and* Viola riviniana *Purpurea Group appear with emerging shoots of* Polygonatum odoratum *'Variegatum' (below).*

Bold terracotta pots planted with Euphorbia characias *subsp.* wulfenii *at the end of the Lime Walk mark the beginning of the Nuttery. Here a young god gazes stonily from his plinth along an axis that continues behind him and beyond to the Herb Garden's oak bench. At his feet, a miliefleurs carpet, recalling Botticelli's* Primavera *or Burne-Jones, is woven from a thousand wild flowers and woodlanders, some native, some not. All of them are mixed and mingled as though placed by nature. Wild wood anemones, woodruff, violets, cowslips and primroses jostle with Bowles' golden grass, white bluebells, trilliums, epimediums and Mrs Robb's bonnet,* Euphorbia amygdaloides *var.* robbiae.*

The planting is most successful where there is a combination of two or three plants that grow at similar rates, coexist contentedly and complement each other beautifully. Mixtures such as Onoclea sensibilis *with* Smyrnium perfoliatum, *white bluebells with golden grass or* Epimedium × youngianum *'Niveum' with anemones are not happy accidents but carefully contrived and skilfully managed feats of the gardeners' art.*

Also essential is the yearly pruning and thinning of the nuts: the canopy they provide should be sufficient to give dappled but not dense shade and the important central axis must remain uncluttered by errant twigs.

Lathraea clandestina

Trillium sessile

Wood anemones and Epimedium × youngianum *'Niveum'*

Not all the planting was so successful: *Eomecon chionantha* was uncontrollably rampageous, though its glaucous leaves and white flowers were attractive; the gardeners planted what they hoped would be a river of *Geranium procurrens* running down the centre of the nuts. This, too, proved to be an invasive thug, rooting at every one of its far-flung nodes and soon threatening to engulf the whole walk. Graham Thomas had warned that *Smilacina stellata* and *Maianthemum bifolium* were likely to be equally encroaching; however, they proved to be more manageable, their groups remaining in reasonable scale with the broad area beneath the nuts. The white martagon lily, chosen to extend the display into summer, disliked the dry conditions and faded away; *Tiarella cordifolia* was destroyed at one point by vine weevils. The gardeners opted not to struggle with problem plants: there were plenty of suitable subjects that would survive happily without becoming too invasive or dwindling away; there should be no need for cosseting, frequent division or reduction of groups. The planting had to be far less labour-intensive than the polyanthus.

Euphorbia amygdaloides var. *robbiae*, as is its wont, throve for a few years before dying where it was put and moving on elsewhere. This habit makes it unsatisfactory as a ground-cover plant but does not matter in the Nuttery: any spaces it vacates are soon filled by other woodlanders and its handsome rosettes of deep green leaves topped with showy chartreuse inflorescences are welcome wherever they choose to appear.

Many spring visitors to Sissinghurst in the late 1970s were surprised to find the polyanthus gone and wanted to know the reason for what seemed to them to be an unjustifiable change. But though the polyanthus were an undoubted *coup de théâtre*, I do not miss them: such brash bravado, a solid sheet of strong colour, seems too forced and unnatural beneath half-wild nuts in an outer part of the garden and too much akin to parks bedding. Nor do I think Vita would have disliked today's more gently romantic planting with its soft and subtle interminglings of quietly pretty foliage and flowers. Sarah Cook wonders how Vita could possibly have liked the polyanthus and considers the present planting to be infinitely nicer; furthermore, it provides interest after most spring flowers have finished, when the garden is relatively lacking in bloom.

Possibly the Nuttery's most fascinating plant is the parasitic toothwort, *Lathraea clandestina*. Pam had made a spring visit to Guincho, Mrs Mackie's garden near Belfast, in the late 1960s. Here she saw a great sheet of magenta flowers beneath its host, the black-catkined willow *Salix gracilistyla* 'Melanostachys', which flowered at the same time. Pam and Sibylle were determined to try to re-create the combination at Sissinghurst. Both plants were ordered from Hilliers but only the lathraea arrived, to be duly planted on a poplar in the lilac bed at the side of the Rose Garden. When at last the willow arrived, the lathraea refused to grow on its roots, nor would the two flower at the same time, as they had done in Ireland. When the poplar's toothwort produced seed, some was scattered along the Nuttery to grow on the roots of the nuts; after three years the strange flowers were produced.

Of the early summer flowers the most striking is the orchid, *Dactylorhiza* × *grandis*. Sibylle considers that its one fault is its excessive vigour, causing its magenta flowers to become so plentiful that they are positively vulgar unless the corms are regularly thinned. Autumn brings more flowers including *Crocus speciosus* and colchicums and rich foliage colour from

Rheum palmatum *'Atrosanguineum'*   Veratrum album   Xanthorhiza simplicissima

Xanthorhiza simplicissima and *Euonymus alatus* var. *apterus* by the eastern end of the path.

Occasionally new plants are introduced to the Nuttery, though there is no attempt to create a diverse collection of choice woodlanders: too many varieties would make the planting look bitty and diminish its charm. Sarah has added *Lysimachia ciliata* (the plain green-leaved form, not the purple 'Firecracker') to fill a space left by *Euphorbia amygdaloides* var. *robbiae*, and has also created a group of uvularias, a liliaceous plant that bridges the botanical gap between trilliums and smilacinas, and assorts agreeably with them both.

❧

Sarah's policy is to replant large swathes of perennials when necessary, targeting areas in which the balance is least satisfactory or the plants' health poor as a result of congestion. Choice woodlanders that are slow to spread, such as orchids and trilliums, are divided periodically to make impressive drifts of a size seen in few other gardens in the British Isles. The temptation to be greedy with such treasures, making a drift so large and dense that it disturbs the scale and balance of the rest of the planting, must be avoided. Sarah is aware that, because such planting shows negligible deterioration if left, replanting can get pushed down the list of priorities, though it is essential that it should not be left indefinitely. Sarah makes occasional adjustments to the more invasive plants to maintain a balance. Onoclea, matteuccias, violets and anemones are sometimes dug out if they stray beyond their allotted space and self-seeding plants must be prevented from sowing themselves too thickly: for *Smyrnium perfoliatum*, all but one plant

are removed before seed is shed; the seedlings must later be thinned to ensure that large, and therefore longer-flowering, plants are produced. *Milium effusum* 'Aureum' can also become a menace if allowed to seed too profusely. Of the bluebells, only white-flowered seedlings are allowed to remain, though the common blue is favoured beneath the yellow azaleas of the Moat Walk bank below, where they provide an effective contrast.

Since the early 1960s, the Nuttery has been mulched annually, originally with spent hops but more recently, since hops have become scarce and expensive, with crushed bark. Believed to have been planted in about 1900, the nuts are all filberts (*Corylus maxima*), more vigorous than cobnut (*Corylus avellana*) and with a long calyx or husk extending beyond the end of the nut. (Cobs have husks shorter than the nut.) The name is reputedly derived from 'full beard', though others claim that it commemorates St Philibert, whose feast day, 22nd August, falls at the start of the picking season. Though the nuts at the top of the azalea bank are a more vigorous cultivar, most of the planting here is of 'Kentish Cob' (which is paradoxically a filbert). Its synonym, 'Lambert Filbert', is also a matter for debate: tradition insists that it was introduced by a Mr Lambert of nearby Goudhurst in about 1830. However, the great Victorian fruit expert, Dr Hogg, wrote in 1884 that it had only recently been introduced to Kent and that it was Aylmer Bourke Lambert of Wiltshire who first showed it at the Horticultural Society in 1812.

The heavy shade cast by the dense canopy of nuts had been one of the reasons for the decline of the polyanthus; when the polyanthus were replaced, the canopy was thinned, winching out every other row of nuts altogether plus alternate bushes along each row. The nut bushes growing

LEFT *Dionysus seen from the east end of the Nuttery.* Viburnum plicatum *and azaleas take on autumnal tints while* Euonymus alatus *var.* apterus *turns a flaming scarlet.*

RIGHT *Quieter colours at the heart of the Nuttery. The nuts are tinged with russet and gold, though shield fern* (Polystichum setiferum) *in the foreground remains a fresh green. The hornbeam hedge behind will hold cinnamon-coloured leaves throughout the winter.*

in grass on the Nuttery's south side had been cut off at 1.7m/5ft 8in before Pam and Sibylle arrived, giving the bushes an unpleasantly truncated appearance. The gardeners instituted a system of pruning all the bushes each winter, cutting down to the base any unhealthy old stems to encourage a succession of vigorous new growth. The more upright and robust of the picturesquely arching old branches were retained, keeping the predominant gothic arch structure along the rows and allowing visitors to walk between those nuts that were grown in grass. At about the same time, the coarse field hedge was replaced with hornbeam.

Suckering is always a problem with filberts, especially after heavy pruning: far more shoots are produced than are ultimately needed to maintain the structure of the bush; all the excess shoots must be cut off each year, a tiresome job for the winter months, to help the occasional strong sucker, chosen to remain, to develop vigorously. Pruning is intended to keep the proportion of old stems in balance with that of younger developing ones which will succeed them. However, a series of unfavourable seasons followed the introduction of this regime, with either late frost, destroying new leaves and shoots, or blistering heat; by the mid 1980s, it was clear

that too few replacement shoots were being produced. In consequence, the nuts' canopy initially gave little shade to the plants beneath, leaving them scorched and dry. Nevertheless, in spite of the sparseness of the stems, Pam and Sibylle decided that more severe pruning would be needed if a succession of healthy young shoots was to be achieved.

❧

It is only in the last few years that the canopy has become dense enough for the woodlanders beneath and the balance of old and new stems has at last been achieved. The badly pruned bushes along the south side of the Nuttery have lost their stubby and inelegant appearance, and match the other trees in their tall and gracefully arching habit.

The planting now is perhaps less formal than any other in the garden, with woodlanders weaving amongst each other in a way that imitates nature. The gardeners' art is scarcely seen, though without it both balance and beauty would be lost. Such a charming and romantic tapestry maintains perfectly the traditions of Sissinghurst, proof that the spirit of a garden need not depart with its creators.

The Moat Walk

Lead urns, swathed with wisteria and Viticella clematis, ornament the top of the medieval wall, with Corydalis ochroleuca and native ferns growing in the brickwork. The effect is both formal and romantic. The wisteria, its flower buds protected from birds by threads of black cotton, and other climbers are held by wires along the top of the wall, allowing them to loll gracefully beneath.

The simplest of Sissinghurst's garden rooms, the Moat Walk combines elements from medieval times to the present in a formal framework furnished with the most restrained planting. The flanking borders, glorious in late spring and again in autumn, need little labour, though the walk's turf presents constant challenges of cultivation.

Of all the features Harold and Vita discovered in their new garden, perhaps no other fascinated them as much as the moat wall, unearthed during the late months of 1930. Its scale clearly demanded bold treatment: Harold's diary for 12th September records their decision to 'make the bowling-green longer and to reach right down to the moat. Our general line is to keep the whole thing as green and quite as simple as we can.' A month later, Vita wrote to Harold: 'Hayter has cleared the Moat Walk and a lovely wall has come into view . . . the east end is perfect but the west end is very bitty.' Her excitement was such that another report followed the next day: 'The moat wall is going to be very superb. They have uncovered its foot a bit and I think there is no doubt that there was originally water there too. There are lovely big stones at the foot of the piers. The piers are going to be lovely . . .'

Believed to be as old as any of Sissinghurst's surviving structures, the moat wall was probably part of the medieval manor house predating the Tudor buildings. When Sir Richard Baker built the house, its timber-framed servants' quarters probably stood in the orchard above the wall, a third arm of the moat perhaps lying where the Moat Walk is today.

In 1932 the walk was turfed and the paved semicircle, nicknamed Sissinghurst Crescent by Harold, was built to his design with its flanking bastions and steps. Lutyens, then a close companion of Vita's mother Lady

Sackville and a friend of both Harold and Vita, often used a semicircle or circle to mask an awkward change of axis, perhaps most memorably at Hestercombe, and the whole ensemble is strongly reminiscent of him. The Crescent not only succeeds in resolving the oddly angled entrances from the Cottage Garden, Lime Walk and Nuttery, but also presents a skilful and dramatic use of levels. A copy of a Lutyens seat originally made for Miss Jekyll was placed to command a view along the walk and make a focal point when seen from below. Five acacias were planted around the Crescent, adding height and dramatizing the view while helping to enclose the Cottage Garden behind; two poplars were added to terminate the moat end of the walk.

Lady Sackville's move from Streatham to Brighton that year occasioned a gift of wisterias from her garden that still survive along the walk, plus six magnificent bronze vases originally from the garden at Bagatelle in Paris. Some of these were used to top alternate piers of the wall, though it was soon apparent that their scale and grandeur did not match the wall's modest rusticity. The vases were moved to ornament the area outside the main entrance, to be replaced along the wall by five Adam-style lead urns.

The focal point from the Moat Walk provided by the Lutyens seat was strengthened by the planting of four Irish yews, a hardy alternative to Italian cypresses, in the adjacent Cottage Garden. Vita and Harold might have been thinking of Italian gardens where spiky conifers crown the head of a grand vista; perhaps those they saw in Tuscany when visiting friends such as Harold Acton, Geoffrey Scott and the eminent garden designer Cecil Pinsent.

Very little is recorded of the walk during the war years, when new

developments had to be postponed for lack of staff. The grass of the walk grew long and lupins and bluebells seeded themselves in it; Vita insisted they be left. But 1946 saw the arrival of more gardeners, a new sense of purpose and further improvements. The statue of Dionysus was installed in March, cleverly terminating the view along the Moat Walk and also the vista through the tower and across the Orchard. The planting of the moat bank occupied both their minds, as Harold's diary for 29th December 1946 records:

'In the afternoon I moon about with Vita trying to persuade her that planning is an element in gardening. I want to show her that the top of the moat-walk bank must be planted with forethought and design. She just wishes to jab in the things which she has left over. The tragedy of the romantic temperament is that it dislikes form so much that it ignores the effect of the masses. She wants to put in stuff which will "give a lovely red colour in autumn". I wish to put in stuff which will furnish shape to the perspective. In the end we part not as friends.'

In July 1947, Harold and Vita's conflict over the planting was still not resolved. Harold wrote to Vita:

'No, darling – I do not agree about the azaleas. And why is that? First because I don't feel that azaleas are very Sissinghurst in any case. They are Ascot, Sunningdale sort of plants. Not our lovely romantic Saxon, Roman, Tudor Kent. I know you will say, and rightly, that nor are magnolias. But you know what I mean. Anything with the suggestion of suburbia should be excluded. But secondly because I think we want something formal. You have the wall; you have Dionysus; you have the strip of mown grass; you have then the bank; and along the top I want

something different from the bank and different from the nuttery. Something dividing the formality of the moat walk from the comparative informality of the nuttery. I should rather have a row of stiff Irish yews than a flurry of azaleas. But we may find something different. It is a very important site.'

Vita got her way: the suburban azaleas were planted. And yet for all Harold's exasperation at her unwillingness to remove plants that he felt spoilt the design, we find him writing to Vita a few years later that he believes she would 'be ruthless enough to remove anything that does not look well or do well'. Was this wishful thinking, or diplomatic flattery calculated to encourage more discriminating planting?

One can sympathize with Harold: the young plants must have looked irritatingly spotty when small, never more so than when their jarring flowers appeared, in carmine, orange, salmon, yellow, scarlet and apricot. But perhaps Vita was looking further ahead to the time when the bushes would be big enough to mask the Nuttery from the Moat Walk, providing also spectacular autumn colour and alluring scent in spring. Certainly, one feels no lack of structure here today, though the intense colour of the azaleas in spring does come as a shock.

It has been suggested that Vita chose mainly late-nineteenth-century varieties because of their patina of age. However, these were generally selected to extend the range of colours available beyond those of the parent species; they are usually even more brash than their ancestors and lack the subtlety of more recent hybrids such as those from Knap Hill or Exbury. Mainly flame and yellow sorts survive today, most bushes having reverted to their gold-flowered *Rhododendron luteum* rootstock by 1959. Still much

the brightest of Sissinghurst's planting, the original colours would have been even gaudier and more discordant. Was this Vita's original intention? Did she change her mind and decide to let the suckering rootstock take over, to simplify the colour scheme and form a more effective contrast with the wild bluebells? Why did she not chose a more restrained range of colours from the first, perhaps leavening gold and flame with softer yellows and a dash of cream?

The bluebells found their way to the walk in the leaf mould mulch brought from the woods nearby and were allowed to stay, coinciding exactly in flowering time with the azaleas. It is essential to deadhead them to prevent them self-sowing, ousting the improved varieties in the adjacent Nuttery. Groups of the leopard lily, *Lilium pardalinum*, were added between the azaleas for the summer.

By the early 1970s, the azaleas had become crowded and unhealthy as well as being suppressed by the nuts and a large belt of *Cotoneaster horizontalis* along the front of the bank. Covered with lichen and by now shy-flowering, the azaleas needed rejuvenation. Pam and Sibylle embarked on an 'Azalea Improvement Scheme', restoring them to a state of floriferous good health over about five years. The cotoneasters were removed and the azaleas cut back in stages, removing old and unhealthy stems and encouraging renewal growth, further aided by foliar feed given about three times during the summer season. Where azaleas were overcrowded some were removed, favouring varieties in golden-yellow and orange over those in clashing pink.

It is preferable to deadhead the azaleas immediately after flowering to give more bloom the following season, but this is not always possible because of the pressure of other work. However, their seedheads are removed in winter so that they do not detract from the plants' appearance when in flower. The azaleas still need some pruning each winter to prevent them becoming too large and to encourage continuous renewal of healthy young flowering wood.

Planting bays were created along the front of the border, allowing spurges, hostas and a few other choice woodlanders to be added and preventing the azaleas from towering too close to the lawn. At the head of the walk where the bank cut forward in front of the side of the steps, the gardeners reshaped it so that the walk was centred on the steps and its sides were straight; *Houttuynia cordata* was used to hold the now-steep slope together, to Graham Thomas's dismay, for it is a notoriously invasive thug. Fortunately its presence here has not been a problem and it has succeeded admirably in preventing the bank from slipping back across the inviolable edge of the walk.

The underplanting of herbaceous plants is of species ecologically suited to their rather dry site in the dappled shade of the azaleas. Thus they coexist in happy equilibrium for many years, neither overwhelming each other nor being forced into a miserable decline. As in the Nuttery, there is none of the desperately dull planting that has given ground cover a bad name, seemingly endless stretches of symphytum, pulmonaria or *Hypericum calycinum* totally out of scale with their site. At Sissinghurst, replanting of ground cover is rarely needed but when necessary is tackled in late summer or early autumn while the ground is still warm and plants can re-establish quickly.

A mulch of crushed bark each autumn retains moisture and minimizes weeding, but it can have disadvantages: some shallow-rooting plants root only into the mulch and suffer in summer when the bark becomes as dry as dust. Saxifrage relatives such as tellima and tiarella fall into this category and can also suffer from vine weevil, though this has not yet been such a problem that nematodes have had to be used as biological control.

❧

In the Nicolsons' time the moat wall was much as we see it today, lightly clad with wisterias and native ferns growing in its brickwork. The gardeners subsequently added Viticella clematis and *Corydalis ochroleuca*. 'Bowles' Mauve' wallflower, a variety of mysterious provenance probably not grown by Bowles himself, was added later by Pam and Sibylle on its appearance in the 1970s. Cuttings rooted in Jiffy pots (small peat blocks held in a plastic mesh) are pressed into holes in the wall every year, using twice the quantity that will ultimately be needed to allow for some losses from theft, drought or winter cold. Relatively short-lived, the plants will survive for about four seasons provided they escape severe winters. There was general dismay among the gardeners when told that the wall had to be repointed. Once done, it was sufficiently unpointed and holes were chiselled out to accommodate once more wallflowers and resident pairs of nesting tits.

Vita liked to grow zinnias in the border at the foot of the wall, sown there every year by one of the gardeners, Sidney Neve. Pam and Sibylle remember the zinnias succeeding only about one year in four: drainage was poor and there were occasional floods that washed all into the moat. However, their shape, size and flowering season, through late summer into autumn, were ideal; any replacement needed to match these. Graham Thomas's suggestion of *Aster × frikartii* 'Mönch' fitted all the requirements admirably without the need to sow seed annually. For many years it has been a great success, though its habit of flopping forward across the walk has necessitated both staking and a paved edging.

After such a long tenure, the soil is now sick of asters and, although they still look spectacular from a distance, close inspection shows them to be spindly and lacking in vigour. Sarah Cook finds that healthy asters planted to fill gaps here soon become as sick as the older tenants; any

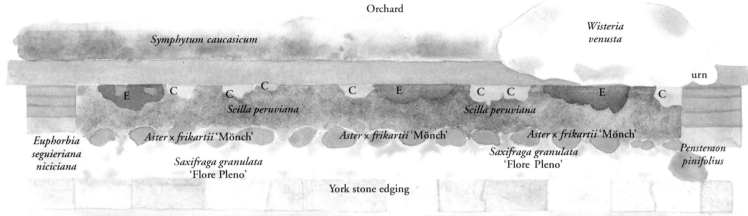

Orchard

Symphytum caucasicum

Wisteria
venusta

urn

E C C C C E C C E C

Scilla peruviana

Scilla peruviana

Euphorbia
seguieriana
niciciana

Aster x frikartii 'Mönch'

Aster x frikartii 'Mönch'

Aster x frikartii 'Mönch'

Penstemon
pinifolius

Saxifraga granulata
'Flore Pleno'

Saxifraga granulata
'Flore Pleno'

York stone edging

turf

E = Erysimum 'Bowles' Mauve'
C = Corydalis lutea

PAGES 102–3 AND RIGHT *The Moat Walk in late spring. 'Bowles' Mauve' wallflowers in the wall and saxifrages beneath contrast with the bank of azaleas and bluebells across the lawn, seen here (right) in close up.*

FAR RIGHT Scilla peruviana *at the foot of the wall. Eighteenth-century gardener Philip Miller advised siting it to receive only the morning sun; in hotter situations it can fade in less than a week.*

PLANS *The linear planting (above) of the border's three main subjects allows the scilla and saxifrage to fill the space in spring and early summer; the aster spreads to occupy the whole width in late summer and autumn. The azalea bank planting (below) is by contrast informal, the smaller plants at the front mingling with each other and with the larger plants.*

1 m

3 ft

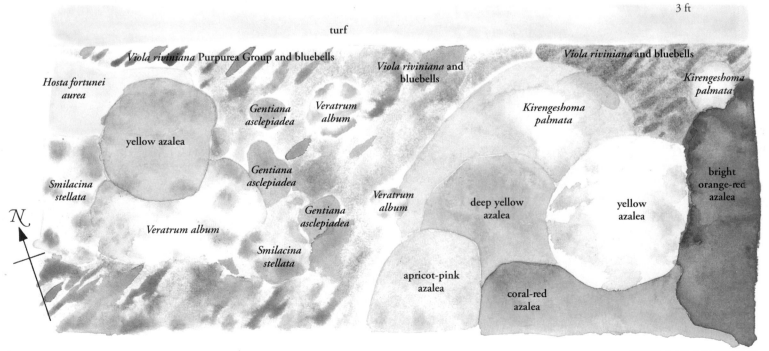

turf

Viola riviniana Purpurea Group and bluebells

Viola riviniana and
bluebells

Viola riviniana and bluebells

Hosta fortunei
aurea

Kirengeshoma
palmata

Gentiana
asclepiadea

Veratrum
album

Kirengeshoma
palmata

yellow azalea

bright
orange-red
azalea

Smilacina
stellata

Gentiana
asclepiadea

Veratrum
album

deep yellow
azalea

yellow
azalea

N

Veratrum album

Gentiana
asclepiadea

Smilacina
stellata

apricot-pink
azalea

coral-red
azalea

LEFT *In late summer* Aster × frikartii '*Mönch*' *spills across the border's stone edging at the start of almost three months' display. The continuous band of asters is interrupted only by a cascade of Japanese glory vine,* Vitis coignetiae. *The stone edging allows the asters to lean gracefully forwards, giving a softer and more romantic effect. Above the wall, the trumpet vine* Campsis radicans *contrasts with* Elaeagnus '*Quicksilver*'. *The wall is the garden's most historic feature: there is no attempt to cover it completely with climbers.*

RIGHT *The view from the Orchard across the Moat Walk to Dionysus. A border of azure* Symphytum caucasicum, *added by the gardeners, contrasts with Vita's original plant of glistening white* Wisteria venusta. *Buds of later-flowering* W. floribunda '*Alba*' *promise a spectacular display of 45cm/18in-long racemes. Nigel Nicolson considers this the most beautiful of the plants in the garden.*

attempt to replant or disturb the existing stock causes heavy losses. The plants are left alone, only adding new plants where gaps have appeared. Soil sterilization was tried once without success, perhaps because the sickness re-invaded from the adjacent lawn or wall; soil replacement is likely to be equally ineffective and even more laborious. A different plant seems to be needed soon. Unfortunately, few hardy perennials could match 'Mönch' for its long and splendid display, except other asters and near relatives that would suffer from the same soil sickness. A tender perennial or annual might do the job, though it would need more work.

The border's other denizens, *Scilla peruviana* and *Saxifraga granulata* 'Flore Pleno', have mutually opposite requirements, though each gets what it needs: the scilla enjoys being baked at the foot of this sunny wall through the dry summer months and flowers profusely though fleetingly as a result; the saxifrage, an inhabitant of riverside meadows, enjoys the high water table created by the nearby moat throughout its spring growing season. Both need occasional replanting to maintain optimum spacing without overcrowding. The scilla, a Mediterranean plant reputedly so named because it was brought to Bristol on a ship called the *Peru*, once grew in the Lime Walk where its moment of glory came when all other bulbs were dying back untidily.

Large matching pots are traditionally used to flank the Lutyens seat. Various plants have been used here over the years such as the incense plant, *Calomeria amaranthoides* (formerly *Humea elegans*), a favourite of Vita. She wrote of its far-carrying fragrance reminiscent of an Italian cathedral and its tall and elegant cedarwood-coloured plumes. However, its leaves and copiously produced pollen cause violent allergic reactions and it is exceptionally dangerous to asthmatics; it is simply not safe in a much-visited garden. *Abutilon* 'Canary Bird', with its bold, dark, glossy leaves among the most handsome of its genus, and standards of glaucous feathery-leaved *Argyranthemum foeniculaceum* of gardens have served well here recently. In autumn the flowers of the aster are complemented by brilliant colour from vines, euonymus, cotinus and especially azaleas. Trees of *Prunus sargentii* along the top of the wall added spectacularly to the display but, weakened by birds which continually stripped the growth buds, they were finally killed by honey fungus in the late 1970s.

The vines need to be pruned annually by New Year's Day. Once a framework of main branches and flowering spurs has been established on the wisteria, Sarah finds that they need only be pruned once each year, in the last week of July or the first week of August. New stems, cut back to two or three nodes at this time, produce virtually no later growth; there is no necessity for pruning later on, except to remove any dead wood in winter. This is a much simpler routine than traditional methods that insist on pruning two or even three times during the course of a year. Sarah finds

there is no shortage of bloom as a result, provided that the flower buds are protected from birds by threads of black cotton. Wires along the top of the wall are used to train out the wisterias and the Viticella clematis, which can then drape themselves elegantly from the top of the wall.

The Moat Walk turf is trodden by almost every visitor and would not survive without exemplary cultivation. It is spiked regularly and checked for excessive wear; any bald areas are cordoned off and patched with 2cm/1in-square cells of newly raised turf from the nursery. When the garden closes in autumn, the turf is scarified and spiked to remove thatch and improve surface aeration. Worn areas are oversown with a mix of hard-wearing dwarf ryegrasses with creeping red fescue and a little browntop bent. Every few years, a hollow tine aerator and a dressing of sand are used to improve surface drainage, making the turf more resistant to wear.

Soil analysis has shown that, as in many old gardens, the ground is too rich in phosphate but deficient in potash, encouraging coarse and ugly soft-grasses such as Yorkshire fog (*Holcus lanatus*). Conventional lawn fertilizers are not ideal: they contain too much phosphate and would need to be applied in spring and again in summer; the combination of bruising by feet and concentrated salts would cause unsightly scorching. The present policy is to apply a potash fertilizer in late autumn, a slow-release nitrogenous fertilizer in spring and a top-up feed of potash, a liquid formulation derived from seaweed, in summer.

❧

The Moat Walk is a feature full of delicious paradoxes: it is absolutely formal, yet its two sides are utterly dissimilar; it combines a medieval wall with a classical statue, Georgian urns and a twentieth-century seat in the style of the early 1700s. It is hard to imagine gardeners nowadays having the courage to mix their styles so thoroughly; we are all too self-conscious, overawed by decades of garden history, to allow ourselves to be led purely by beauty. When the garden was made, there was no Garden History Society, nor had the subject been invented. Vita and Harold would not have worried for a moment about what ornamentation and planting ought to go with a medieval wall, any more than they would have bothered about using Georgian furniture in a Tudor house. Beauty alone was paramount. The garden at Sissinghurst is no essay in historic pedantry but a synthesis of all that is beautiful in the twentieth-century garden.

In mid autumn, the asters still bloom bravely, though the Japanese glory vine has lost all but a few flaming leaves. Argyranthemums still flank the Lutyens bench but must be taken into the glasshouses when frost threatens. Deep blood-red azalea leaves will turn to blazing scarlet before they fall.

The Herb

Vita was fascinated by herbs, their wealth of history, folklore and fragrance. But to incorporate them with other planting risked overwhelming their quiet charms among showier neighbours. By planting them together in this strangely far-flung formal outpost of the garden, she created an enclave where the romance of herbs, their associations, literary, historical, medical and culinary, and their beauty and scent, could be enjoyed.

It is not easy to make a herb garden that is beautiful throughout the year. Many herbs are annuals or biennials, leaving gaps that demand to be filled by midsummer; others from the sunny Mediterranean can languish miserably in the cool damp winters of Kent. The gardener's skill has been used here to overcome all these problems and to make the Herb Garden attractive from spring to autumn.

Vita's Long Barn garden notebook for 1925–9 shows that she was by then becoming increasingly interested in herbs and acquiring more and more varieties. Her inspiration might well have been Eleanour Sinclair Rohde's *Garden of Herbs*, published in 1920, the first English book on the subject for decades. Miss Rohde was a prolific author, writing for *The Times, Country Life, The Field* and *The Countryman,* and was at one time President of the Society of Women Journalists. Vita's curiosity and sympathy must have been aroused, for many of their interests coincided: herbs, old herbals, garden history, Shakespeare's plants, scent in the garden, epicurean vegetables and old roses.

In 1934 the yew hedges of Sissinghurst's Herb Garden were planted. Eleanour Rohde's *Herbs and Herb Gardening* appeared in 1936, stimulating once again a widespread interest in the subject. In 1938, Vita planted the first herbs, three varieties in each of the four beds. The war prevented further developments and by the time Jack Vass returned to Sissinghurst in 1946, the Herb Garden had been overrun by ground elder. The weeds

were cleared and a crop of early potatoes planted, purifying the ground and allowing the pattern of paths and twenty beds to be created as we see it today, though the main axes were paved with concrete slabs and the side paths were of turf. Thyme grew in cracks between the paving, withstanding the few feet that passed by and releasing its refreshing aroma. The chauffeur, Jack Copper, created the camomile seat, christened Edward the Confessor's chair by Harold and Vita, from fragments of masonry from the old house. At about the same time, Eleanour Rohde was making the largest and most ambitious herb garden in England at Lullingstone Castle, a few miles north of Vita's beloved Knole, for Lady Hart Dyke.

It comes as a surprise to find such a formal enclosure so far from the heart of the garden, so close to the near-wildness of the Orchard and Nuttery. Nor were the herbs conveniently placed for the kitchen. But then Sissinghurst's cook was not Vita but Mrs Staples (who later married the butler George Hayter, though Vita continued to call her Mrs Staples). Essential culinary herbs had been given a home by the door of the Priest's House, where they could easily be gathered for the sort of simple recipes that Vita preferred. Vita felt compelled to grow more herbs and there was simply nowhere else in the garden to put them. By 1948, she had gathered together over sixty different herbs here. As at Lullingstone, a formal system of many beds divided by paths allowed each herb to be picked and enjoyed without the soil being trampled.

Vita had tried to grow hollyhocks outside the north entrance to the Herb Garden but in this windy site they were perpetually flattened, no matter how hard she tried to stake them. In 1948 she implemented her idea of planting two beds here entirely with creeping thymes, a patchwork of purple, red and white 'like a Persian carpet laid flat on the ground out of doors'. This proved a triumph, so much so that Vita proclaimed:

Edward the Confessor's chair (left) in spring with spurge laurel and parsley pots and (right) the chair in summer, well-upholstered with non-flowering 'Treneague' camomile, behind white borage and biennial clary.

Garden

'It really is a lovely sight; I do not want to boast, but I cannot help being pleased with it; it is so seldom that one's experiments in gardening are wholly successful.'

Vita also included crocuses, miniature narcissi and pink cyclamen. These proved less successful; returning to the subject of thyme lawns in 1959, she admitted her error:

'They grew all right and loved being where they were, but they made the thyme lawn look untidy by breaking the flatness. They have now been eliminated and replanted elsewhere. The thyme lawn looks much better without them.'

She also regretted including white thyme ('red and purple and mauve would have been more homogeneous') and not giving them a thoroughly prepared sharp-draining soil from the first.

❧

When Pam and Sibylle arrived, little remained but a few plants of thyme among weedy grass: as always with turf abutting thyme, the grass continually invaded the beds and was troublesome to remove. Surrounding the lawns with paving in 1969 was not a complete solution, for visitors continued to walk on the thyme. As visitor numbers increased, the thyme suffered more. A raised brick edge proved sufficient to deter errant feet as well as helping the drainage of the beds.

The thyme needed continual work if it was to thrive on ground that was predominantly Kentish clay. The gardeners found that only the most prostrate varieties performed satisfactorily; taller varieties, when clipped over after flowering to maintain a perfect carpet, did not always regrow well. Even relatively short *Thymus serpyllum* var. *coccineus* 'Major' is left with twiggy bristles in a bare and dying centre after clipping, but this is its

nature: it always moves on from its epicentre to colonize new areas.

Every five or six years it is necessary to replant the beds using cuttings rooted in cells. Pam and Sibylle found that drifts of single colours looked more effective than the very jumbled mixture that Vita had grown. Apart from low-growing cultivars of *Thymus serpyllum* and the British native *T. praecox* subsp. *britannicus*, the woolly thyme, *T. pseudolanuginosus*, is used, though it is occasionally lost in severe winters. Thorough weed control is essential; it is quite useless planting into ground containing weed seeds and any weeds that blow in must be regularly removed as part of the 'Friday tidy'. An invasion of the tiny prostrate *Oxalis corniculata* could only be controlled by emptying the beds and sterilizing them. Pam says the lawn is 'quite fun when it is really flowering and wobbling with bees but it is not a labour-saving idea'.

At the centre of the garden sits the marble bowl, supported by three lions, which Harold and Vita had brought back in 1914 from Cospoli in Turkey. It has held various herbs over the years, not always successfully. Thyme suffered sullenly there in 1959, resenting its tiny volume of hot dry soil. The gardeners planted saffron (*Crocus sativus*) through it; this grew leaves but never flowered, in spite of its summer baking. Houseleeks replaced the thyme and grew here until 1994, thriving as well as looking attractive in this inhospitable position. However, attempts to grow five different varieties only encouraged light-fingered visitors to take one of each. Even with a single variety, theft can destroy the effect, and the gardeners used to keep a replacement set of plants.

Since Vita's time, the gardeners have continually added to the herbs, looking particularly for attractive ones but also for those that have the most interesting uses or folklore. Pam and Sibylle acquired with great difficulty a mandrake and were most disappointed when it refused to shriek, as tradition insists it should, when uprooted and moved to a new site.

Teasels had been grown in the garden for many years before Pam and Sibylle discovered they were not the fuller's teasel, *Dipsacus sativus*, whose hooks point in the opposite direction, and introduced the true variety. However, they admit that this isn't as decorative as the native wild teasel, *D. fullonum*, which is altogether more imposing and easier to stake. The fuller's teasel has paler washy mauve flowers and brittle foliage that clasps the stem, holding a pool of water that can fill with rotting vegetation.

Sarah Cook continues the tradition of enhancing the range of herbs, her additions including the nasturtium 'Empress of India' with rich red flowers and deep blue-green leaves, and lemon-scented *Monarda citriodora.*

❧

Although many of the one hundred or more herbs are annuals and biennials, few are grown in situ. The gardeners find they get better results by growing them in the nursery, either in pots or nursery rows, and transplanting them to the Herb Garden at the appropriate time. Angelica will sow itself if left but the seedlings seldom put themselves in the right place. Furthermore, two generations are needed, one of flowering size and the other growing on for the following season; the younger generation must always be growing somewhere else behind the scenes because the mature plants cast too much shade to coexist happily with them. Plants are either raised in the nursery from seed or self-sown ones lifted from the Herb Garden and transplanted. When the Herb Garden's angelicas have finished flowering and their foliage has started to die back, the new generation is ready to replace them.

Teasels, biennial clary, woad and caraway are sown with other biennials at the same time as the wallflowers and lined out in nursery rows. Borage and pot marigolds are sometimes sown in autumn or alternatively raised early under glass.

Not all herbs are a success at Sissinghurst, the Kent summers proving too cool for the likes of sesame, cumin and basil. The purple basil 'Dark Opal' is still grown but thrives only in hot summers. Pam and Sibylle aimed primarily to make the Herb Garden attractive and were not fond of the many 'rotten little white umbels' such as chervil and coriander that had to be replaced as often as three times a year and contributed little to the garden's beauty. Nor was caraway a blessing, for its seeds, its herbal *raison d'être*, sowed themselves with a vengeance if left on the plant. Some less rotten umbels, particularly dill, were occasionally smitten with a plague of carrot root fly. Pesticides are seldom used in the Herb Garden lest any visitors taste or rub the leaves.

The gardeners found it was essential to keep cutting back sages to prevent them from getting lanky and susceptible to breakage. 'Icterina' proved

to be much the longest lasting because it seldom flowers. Mints were once grown all in the same bed, useful for comparison but hazardous if they were left for more than a season and their groups started to coalesce. Now they are treated as annuals and are moved round in individual groups into one of the newly planted beds each year. New plants are raised either from cuttings or by division. Cuttings are easier and usually preferable, giving plants that are free of root diseases. However, some mints, particularly ginger mint, *Mentha* × *gracilis* 'Variegata', occasionally suffer from rust and must then be propagated by division of the roots.

Herbs are far from being the easiest plants to grow and many have troublesome ailments. Sub-shrubby labiates such as hyssop, lavender, thyme and sage can suffer from fungal diseases that cause the branchlets to die, known in lavender as shab. Where many such labiates are grown together, they seem to be even more prone to attack and can only be encouraged to thrive by periodically sterilizing or replacing the soil.

Some herbs that are not labiates, such as woad, suffer from similar soil-borne diseases and need similar treatment. At Sissinghurst, Pam and Sibylle devised a rotation whereby two of the twenty beds were cultivated each year for growing annual and biennial herbs. After a period, the two beds were planted with perennials for a few years and another two beds were cultivated. Periodic sterilization with dazomet was necessary and the gardeners also worked hard to incorporate humus, essential for improvement of soil structure on Sissinghurst's heavy clay. To minimize the risk of a build-up of disease, the annuals and biennials were never grown in the same place two years running.

❧

The concrete slabs that formed the main paths of the Herb Garden were originally laid with 10cm/4in gaps, allowing camomile and thyme to grow in between. This was not a success, for the gaps were wide enough to accommodate visitors' feet, causing them to stumble. In spite of being returfed each year, the grass side paths were reduced by wear to whiskers along the sides.

In 1970 the decision was taken to pave all the Herb Garden paths. The gardeners had hoped to take this opportunity to improve the levels but this did not prove possible, although the more disturbing slopes, particularly a deep dip at the south-west corner, were reduced. Nigel Nicolson devised the present paving plan, making minor refinements to the old plan and using York stone for the two main axes. Some small chinks were left between some of the slabs in the hope that thyme and camomile could again be encouraged to sprawl there. The side paths were to be of brick. Nigel's design for the marble bowl, following one of Lutyens', was to place it on a millstone, surrounded by a sunburst of tiles on edge.

ABOVE *Dyer's greenweed* (Genista tinctoria, *left*) *is one of the showiest herbs in early summer; white-flowered shoo fly* (Nicandra physaloides) *can be seen behind. Camphor plant* (Tanacetum balsamita *subsp.* balsamitoides) *appears in bloom to the right; the thyme lawn is glimpsed beyond the entrance.*

RIGHT *'Cambridge Scarlet' bergamot, variegated applemint and fennel.*

FAR RIGHT *In autumn, the shoo fly is hung with paper-covered fruits behind annual lemon mint* (Monarda citriodora), *a recent addition here.*

LEFT AND PLAN *The bed shown to the right of the plan, with arnica, old man, birthwort, foxgloves and the seedheads of Pasque flower. Nigel Nicolson's design for the tile-on-edge paving in the centre follows one by Lutyens, used at Goddards and Papillon Hall among other gardens. The seat, made by Andrew Skelton in the early 1980s, is based on a seventeenth-century wainscot chair. Oak was used, as for all wooden benches at Sissinghurst, so that it would age to an attractive silver. Because a straight top would draw attention to the sloping hedge behind, the gardeners specified that it must be wavy. The plan shows a considerable proportion of short-lived annuals (coriander, nasturtium and flax), as well as several biennials (silybum, foxgloves and feverfew). The labour involved in propagating these once a year, even two or three times a year for the annuals, makes such gardening very labour-intensive, though it is essential if the planting is to remain flourishing throughout the year. Dating from 1882, nasturtium 'Empress of India' is remarkable for its deep blue-green leaves and rich vermilion flowers.*

PAGES 114-15 *The Herb Garden in spring with pink* Persicaria bistorta *'Superba' and attractively varied brick and stone paths. The far left corner is filled with the handsome foliage of angelica, with the American mandrake (*Podophyllum peltatum*) in front.*

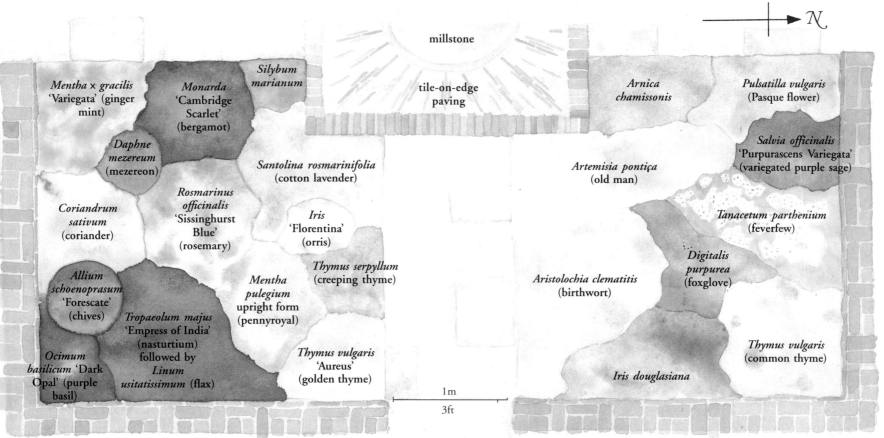

millstone

tile-on-edge paving

N

Mentha × *gracilis* 'Variegata' (ginger mint)

Monarda 'Cambridge Scarlet' (bergamot)

Silybum marianum

Daphne mezereum (mezereon)

Santolina rosmarinifolia (cotton lavender)

Coriandrum sativum (coriander)

Rosmarinus officinalis 'Sissinghurst Blue' (rosemary)

Iris 'Florentina' (orris)

Allium schoenoprasum 'Forescate' (chives)

Mentha pulegium upright form (pennyroyal)

Thymus serpyllum (creeping thyme)

Tropaeolum majus 'Empress of India' (nasturtium) followed by *Linum usitatissimum* (flax)

Ocimum basilicum 'Dark Opal' (purple basil)

Thymus vulgaris 'Aureus' (golden thyme)

Arnica chamissonis

Pulsatilla vulgaris (Pasque flower)

Artemisia pontica (old man)

Salvia officinalis 'Purpurascens Variegata' (variegated purple sage)

Tanacetum parthenium (feverfew)

Aristolochia clematitis (birthwort)

Digitalis purpurea (foxglove)

Thymus vulgaris (common thyme)

Iris douglasiana

1m
3ft

Good drainage is essential for many herbs, especially labiates from dry Mediterranean climates. When the paving was being installed, an elaborate system of drains was laid within the garden, and the main problem, the occasional overflowing of the moat, was solved by supplying the moat with an outlet, a 15cm/6in drain from the corner of the moat down to the lower lake.

Restoration of the yew hedge was a gradual and continuous process, beginning when the paving was installed. The entrance from the thyme lawn was barely wide enough to squeeze through and the hedges here had to be cut back beyond the width of the new paving. Next came the cutting back of the outside of the hedge. The gardeners preferred this to cutting the inside first, which would have looked more unsightly from within the Herb Garden; leaving the inside until the outside had regrown and the centres of the yews were well furnished with young green shoots meant that the hedges would be bare for as short a time as possible. As Pam Schwerdt says: 'The second cut-back is much less agony than the first.' Removal of a field hedge around the outside of the garden also helped: letting light in encouraged the yews to sprout and long shoots of elder and bramble no longer peered impudently above them.

When the inside of the hedge was cut the top was also removed, pruning to below the height that would ultimately be needed, to allow for the upward growth of the hedge. The next stage of restoration was to rationalize the yew buttresses, some of which were positioned in a way that bore little relation to the paths. The least logically placed buttresses were simply removed and new buttresses were grown to full height in the nursery to be placed where the design seemed to demand. Buttresses that nearly blocked the entrance from the Nuttery were removed and later replaced farther apart in this way.

The sloping levels of the Herb Garden are still a problem when clipping the hedges: the gardeners must take their levels from the garden's two diagonals, for none of the hedges has a level top. Thus the hedge follows roughly the lie of the land, a different approach from that adopted in the White Garden.

☙

The Herb Garden is charming for its apparent simplicity. But this is an illusion, for its management is as complex, sophisticated and laborious as any at Sissinghurst. Full of the romance of the herbalists and poets of old and of faraway places, it is perhaps especially reminiscent of the Mediterranean, with, as Anne Scott-James has remarked, the scent of the maquis country of Corsica or the thyme-clothed mountains of Greece hanging in the summer air.

The Orchard

The richly perfumed rose 'Félicité Perpétue', a hybrid of Rosa sempervirens, *growing into a pear tree; raised in 1827 by Monsieur Jacques, gardener to the Duc d'Orléans, this sweetly scented variety commemorates Jacques' two daughters.*

Though nature has conspired to strip it of the bosky trees that held its roses, the Orchard still has much to offer. Its naturalized bulbs, wild flowers, shimmering grasses and the encircling moat all provide informal and charming elements not found elsewhere in the garden; the success of each of these depends on precisely judged and carefully timed maintenance, and on tackling the problems of poor drainage and plant diseases, which beset so many gardens though they are often not addressed.

When Harold and Vita came to Sissinghurst, the Orchard was occupied by rather elderly and unproductive apples and pears, full of character but seldom laden with fruit. They could have opted to replant with the finest varieties, chosen to give exquisite flavour throughout most of the year, as their friend Edward Ashdown Bunyard, as much an expert on choice fruit as he was on old roses, might have advised. Instead they spared the trees, festooned them with fragrant swags of rambling roses and studded the grass at their feet with daffodils, crocuses and wild flowers.

Harold did not impose a formal design on the Orchard: its irregular shape would have challenged even his skills with a ruler; there seems to be no evidence that either he or Vita felt the need to replace its romantic confusion with a more logical geometry. And so this part of the garden came to be an effective contrast to the formality and complex planting of the rest of the garden. His letter to Vita in October 1937 shows that it was still then evolving:

> 'I think your idea of following the path Hayter has made while duck feeding i.e. round the edge, is right, edged with musk roses and iris and winding paths in the middle with dells, boskies, tangles – in fact, scope for everything but not garden flowers – wild roses, white foxgloves in droves, narcissus in regiments . . . .'

This sounds rather self-contradictory: what are most of these if not garden flowers? Harold seems to have been hinting at a mixture of rather more highly bred plants than we find today, perhaps Hybrid Musk roses and fancy irises as well as the plainer species, a sort of English Ninfa in its mixture of sophisticated plants and tumbledown rusticity. But perhaps through the intervention of the war, the Orchard planting remained agreeably restrained and sufficiently simple to give the contrast in style that the garden so needs.

Miss Jekyll had recommended growing roses into fruit trees, but she never suggested, and perhaps never envisaged, the extravagant exploitation of the technique as at Sissinghurst, where not merely one or two trees but almost every one dripped and tumbled roses. In his book, *The Old Shrub Roses*, Graham Thomas commented on the 3.6m/12ft high 'Madame Plantier' roses, a photograph of three of them engulfing the trunks of adjacent trees bearing testament to the extraordinary success of this method. However, Pam and Sibylle consider it has limitations: the demise of picturesque old trees can be hastened by the roses, which themselves are almost impossible to prune and thus relatively short-lived.

Vita wrote of 'Madame Plantier':

'it is 15 feet [4.5m] high and with a girth of 15 yards [14m], tapering towards the top like the waist of a Victorian beauty and pouring down in a vast crinoline stitched all over with its white sweet-scented clusters of flowers. . . . I go out to look at her in the moonlight: she gleams, a pear-shaped ghost, contriving to look both matronly and virginal. She has to be tied up round her tree, in long strands, otherwise she would make a big straggly bush; we have found that the best method is to fix a sort of tripod of bean-poles against the tree and tie the strands to that.'

Such felicitous, though rather jolting, juxtapositions of the poetic with the prosaically practical make her gardening articles both inspiring and as useful to gardeners today as they were forty years ago.

Most of the roses used were white, *RR. filipes* 'Kiftsgate', sweet-scented *multiflora*, *sericea* subsp. *omeiensis* f. *pteracantha* with broad red translucent thorns and 'Félicité Perpétue'. Coloured varieties were muted, slatey violet 'Améthyste' and peach 'Auguste Gervais', or tempered with abundant green foliage, as for rich pink 'Hollandica' and *Rosa virginiana*. Many were lost when their host trees fell in the great storm of 1987, leaving the Orchard bare, devoid of its dells and tangles. A few roses remain, some as sprawling mounds, a handful climbing the trees that are left and some trained up tripods of rustic poles; but it will be decades before the boskiness of the Orchard and its lavish drapery of roses is restored.

The Orchard also proved a convenient home for many of the gifts of plants presented to the Nicolsons, particularly the small trees that could not be accommodated elsewhere in the garden. Some, such as the cherries from near neighbour Captain 'Cherry' Collingwood Ingram, were welcome. One of them, *Prunus* 'Taihaku', still survives; unaccountably lost to cultivation in Japan, it was found by Ingram in a Surrey garden in 1923. Greenish-white 'Ukon' was another favourite, as was the now all too fa-

miliar 'Amanogawa', but perhaps the most striking use of cherries in the Orchard was the row of *Prunus sargentii* above the Moat Walk, aflame in early autumn. A less satisfactory survivor is 'that wickedly vulgar Kansan ['Kanzan' or 'Kwanzan'], so strong and crude that it will spread like measles in an infectious rash'; Vita's opinion of this sickly pink and stiffly branched variety was shared by 'Cherry' Ingram. It would undoubtedly have galled her to see that of all the trees in the Orchard 'Kanzan' is one of the most flourishing today. One wonders why she planted it at all, unless it was wrongly supplied, as was often the case, for *Prunus* 'Chôshû-hizakura'.

Vita would choose planting sites for gifts of plants with the gardeners; they, knowing that any holes dug in the Orchard would instantly fill with water, drowning the unfortunate specimen, would often stall for time, hoping to find a more propitious site. In spite of continual efforts to improve drainage, the high water table in the Orchard continued to contribute to the poor health of the fruit trees. Some suffered from honey fungus and many original trees were gradually lost throughout the seventies and eighties. The gardeners replanted wherever possible, only to lose many of their replacements in the 1987 storm.

The first temptation after such a catastrophe is to fill all the gaps with new trees but the gardeners wisely decided this would be a bad policy: if all the trees were the same age, they might once again all die at about the same time, leaving the Orchard relatively bare for ten or twenty years. The plan now is to fill several gaps every few years, avoiding the exact places where trees once were to minimize the risk of replant disease, which seriously inhibits the growth of both roses and fruit trees. Soil sterilization is not an option here because of rubble, roots and the foundations of old buildings that prevent the essential preparation of a deep and even tilth. There remains a worry that trees will again be attacked by honey fungus: all young trees are treated annually with a phenolic contact fungicide and soil sterilant in the hope that this will at least enable the trees to compete successfully against the omnipresent disease.

New trees are chosen for attractive flower or fruit and are mostly apples (such as 'Kentish Quarrenden' and 'Flower of Kent') and pears (such as 'Catillac'), grafted on to non-dwarfing rootstocks (seedling pear or, for apples, MM111) to give the appearance of a traditional orchard and to

PAGES 120–21 *The Orchard in spring with daffodils and the great white cherry of Japan,* Prunus *'Taihaku'. The dovecote, no longer inhabited by the white pigeons that were a feature of the garden in Vita's time, is near the centre of the picture. The gazebo hides behind a haze of young bronze leaves of amelanchier. Turf is never more vulnerable than in spring when heavy rain and thousands of feet can turn it into a quagmire; hazel hoops are used temporarily to preserve grass at risk and to protect emerging bulbs.*

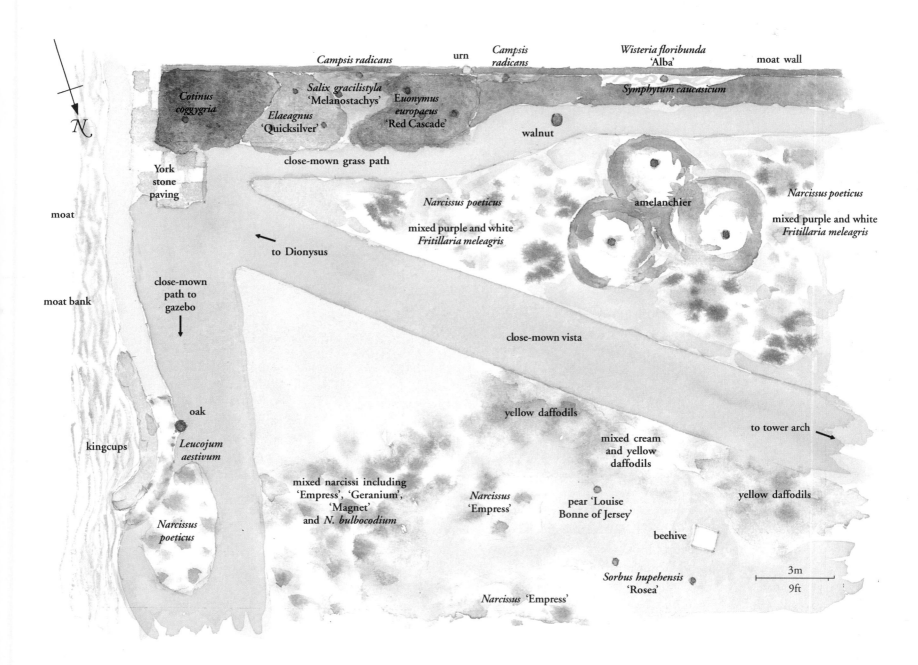

Campsis radicans   urn   Campsis radicans   Wisteria floribunda 'Alba'   moat wall

N

Cotinus coggygria

Salix gracilistyla 'Melanostachys'

Elaeagnus 'Quicksilver'

Euonymus europaeus 'Red Cascade'

Symphytum caucasicum

walnut

York stone paving

close-mown grass path

moat

Narcissus poeticus

amelanchier

Narcissus poeticus

mixed purple and white Fritillaria meleagris

mixed purple and white Fritillaria meleagris

to Dionysus

moat bank

close-mown path to gazebo

close-mown vista

oak

kingcups

Leucojum aestivum

yellow daffodils

to tower arch

mixed cream and yellow daffodils

Narcissus poeticus

mixed narcissi including 'Empress', 'Geranium', 'Magnet' and N. bulbocodium

Narcissus 'Empress'

pear 'Louise Bonne of Jersey'

yellow daffodils

beehive

3m

9ft

Sorbus hupehensis 'Rosea'

Narcissus 'Empress'

LEFT ABOVE   *The view along the tower vista to Dionysus in late spring, showing the area towards the top of the plan. Pheasant's eye narcissi bloom, along with azure* Symphytum caucasicum *and misty leaves of* Elaeagnus *'Quicksilver', after other daffodils .*

LEFT BELOW   *A view of Dionysus from the moat bank framed in the autumnal leaves of the oak tree on the plan. The revetment of the sweet-chestnut poles can be seen at the water's edge.*

PLAN   *The south-east corner of the Orchard, showing close-mown paths and longer grass with naturalized bulbs. Shrubs planted along the top of the moat wall help separate the Orchard from the Moat Walk below; the climbers here can tumble down the wall to furnish it. Late cutting of the grass lets bulbs die back naturally, giving them time to build up reserves for flowering the next year, and allows snakeshead fritillaries to sow themselves. Numerous varieties of narcissi give a long flowering season, starting before the visitors arrive with lenten lilies and slightly tender 'Soleil d'Or' and finishing with single and double* N. poeticus.

provide supports for the roses. Other rosaceous trees have been included such as amelanchiers, in the past stripped of blossom by bullfinches but now more successful; however, *Sorbus* species seem reluctant to grow.

Trees are often planted on a hump rather than in a prepared hole that would act as a fatal sump; this is effectively a return to eighteenth-century mound planting, popular for parkland specimen trees because it obviated digging and draining. A stake was driven into the undug ground, the tree, sitting on the surface, was tied to it and the roots were covered with good soil. Although the Sissinghurst technique involves more soil preparation, it does have something of the pragmatism of the earlier technique: because of the abundant rubble in the ground from the old buildings, thorough digging is difficult.

The gardeners first attempted to improve drainage here in the early seventies, employing Fred Judge, an expert with years of experience of low-lying fenland soils. He commented that he had 'never met such a lazy soil as this – the water won't pass through it at all'. The distances between drains, normally one chain (20m/66ft), had to be halved and the depth reduced from the usual 90cm/3ft to 60cm/2ft. This was before the days of

In 1937 Harold brought the Shanganagh column from Ireland, where it had once been a feature at his uncle Lord Dufferin's home. It was tried in several places around the garden before finally being installed in the Orchard. The Greek column base is set on a plinth with an inscription commemorating the Reform Act of 1832; a later plaque on the plinth adds 'Alas, to this date a humbug'. It was once encircled with Rosa pimpinellifolia *'Irish Marbled', so tall that it hid the inscription. The gardeners, who refer to the memorial as 'the humbug', have surrounded it with low-growing* Persicaria affinis *'Superba'.*

perforated plastic drainage pipes, and earthenware pipes, 7.5cm/3in for side drains or 10cm/4in for main drains, were covered with straw followed by a generous layer at least 15cm/6in deep of large pebbles, backfilled to surface level with soil.

Drains had to link with those serving other parts of the garden such as the Yew Walk and it was particularly important to achieve good drainage along the grass paths to help them withstand heavy wear in wet seasons. The network has been augmented with more drains from time to time.

One suspects that some of the original drains are approaching the end of their useful life for they can easily become clogged by tree roots, particularly those of cherries. In wet weather when standing water appears, the gardeners ease the surface of the ground with a fork along the line of drains. If there is a grateful gurgle as the water runs away, it is clear that the drains are not blocked and surface compaction is to blame.

Vita began planting bulbs in the Orchard's turf in the early years after she and Harold moved to Sissinghurst. Snowdrops, most of them added by the gardeners since 1959, and *Crocus tommasinianus* still thrive, though they flower before the garden opens to the public. The crocus seeds itself freely and is much more plentiful than in Vita's day. However, the snowdrops do not increase unless they are regularly divided, perhaps because they prefer conditions more alkaline than the fairly acid soil of Sissinghurst.

Snakeshead fritillaries and colchicums also date back to the Nicolsons' time, as do the narcissi, most of them grown originally in bowls for the house. The daffodils are now almost too abundant, the beauty of the individuals in peril of being lost through the sheer density of their flowers. This will cease to be a problem once the canopy of trees is restored, for the narcissi will then flower less profusely. Fortunately there are enough cream and white varieties to leaven the many yellows and to avoid the all-too-even carpet of yellow, sometimes christened 'scrambled egg syndrome'.

Vita wrote in *More for Your Garden* about her favourite varieties: 'Among the yellow trumpets, I remain faithful to Fortune, Carlton, Golden Harvest, King Alfred, and even the old Winter Gold. Among the pure white trumpets, Beersheba still seems the best, at a reasonable price. Tunis, a creamy white, is a good doer. John Evelyn, white and yellow, increases so rapidly that I can scarcely keep pace with digging up lumps of bulbs when the foliage is turning yellow and replanting them in the neighbourhood of the original dozen I bought years ago, and what a wealth of flowers he throws up without fail every year! Then among the flat faces I like Medusa, so sweet scented; and among the thick-headed sorts I like Cheerfulness and Abundance and Soleil d'Or, now so charmingly turned into the vernacular as Sally Door by our English gardeners who don't know French: it suggests a clump growing beside a cottage door, as though Sally in a sunbonnet might emerge at any moment, carrying a pail.'

Most of these varieties survive today, though Sally's winter emergence is often thwarted by frost, for she is a tender soul. There have been few additions, save for some unnamed Cyclamineus varieties given by their raiser, Cyril Coleman, and single and, latest-flowering of all, double poeticus narcissi, added to extend the display into early summer. There were others not mentioned by Vita: 'Mrs R.O. Backhouse', the first popular pink-trumpeted variety, was raised before 1921 and used by Harold in the Lime

A charming if puzzling small-scale formal feature surrounded by large-scale informality: against the outside of the Yew Walk hedge, Iris *'Quaker Lady' is planted around the brick paving that marks the foundations of the old house.*

Walk where it disliked the dry conditions, preferring the abundant spring moisture of the Orchard; 'Camellia' (pre-1930), a formally double pale yellow quite unlike a traditional daffodil, which Pam found useful for picking; 'Irene Copeland', a double white narcissus with yellow petals in its muddled centre; Large-cupped 'Scarlet Elegance' (pre-1938), yellow with a red trumpet; yellow 'Brunswick' (pre-1931), also Large-cupped; Tazetta 'Geranium' (pre-1930) and Small-cupped 'La Riante' (pre-1933), both in white and orange. All these were popular varieties during the Nicolsons' early years at Sissinghurst. There are also many Barrii types, with elegant narrow petals and short cups, widely grown from late-Victorian to Edwardian times, and which perhaps grew there when Vita and Harold first came. Tiny *Narcissus bulbocodium* was tried but proved unable to compete with the vigorous grass. Pam and Sibylle thought the Orchard's glory was not the braying trumpets of daffodils but the misty blue haze of *Veronica filiformis*, studded with golden stars of celandines and dandelions.

❧

The mowing regime is timed to accommodate all the flowering plants growing in the turf, allowing bulb foliage to die back and wild flowers to seed themselves. The grass is cut as late as possible in autumn or early winter just as the daffodils start to nose through the ground. This ensures that their clumps of blooms will stand clear above a tidy sward for maximum effect. Thereafter only the paths are mown until late July, when a rear-discharge rotary mower is used over the whole Orchard; this also picks up the long grass, a great saving in labour over mowers which leave it to be raked by hand. As for all wildflower meadows, it is essential to remove the grass clippings, otherwise the ground would be too rich and grasses would oust the less competitive flowers. This system differs from that used when the Orchard was generously planted with roses: then, the gardeners felt that, to be seen at their best, the roses should be complemented by a green and tidy sward; thus mowing was usually tackled in the third week of June, before abundant grass and wildflower seeds had been shed to become weeds throughout the rest of the garden and giving time for the turf to reassume its verdant colour.

The new system of later mowing allows the intricate tapestry of grass flowers to be enjoyed to the full, with waving heads in shades of fawn, soft sage green, russet and dusky purple. This is as subtle and delightful a display as any at Sissinghurst. Though wet weather in late spring or early summer can make the grasses lodge into a jumbled tangle, the gardeners are prepared to take this risk, particularly as late mowing also gives time for flowers such as ox-eye daisies and perhaps even wild orchids to seed.

The sward is mown to about 5cm/2in, high enough to discourage visitors from walking across it, and needs a further cut on 19th August, about two days before the first flowers of *Colchicum byzantinum* appear. Some colchicums planted by Vita survive though many have been added over the years, different sorts being chosen to give a succession of bloom from late summer into autumn. Stocks of new varieties are cosseted in the borders until there are sufficient for naturalizing. Thereafter, as the leaves die back, occasional division is necessary to prevent the bulbs producing a series of tight and evenly sized blobs of blossom. The varieties include 'Prinses Astrid', 'Autumn Queen', *agrippinum*, 'The Giant', *tenorei*, 'Conquest', double 'Waterlily' (which Vita hated for its muddled flopping flowers), *speciosum* and *s.* 'Album', the latter two particularly late-flowering. There are also naturalized autumn-flowering *Crocus speciosus*, though marauding mice have left scarcely enough to make an impact.

It was Graham Thomas who suggested close-mown paths to encourage visitors to use the Orchard more without treading on the bulbs or flattening leaves and grass, making mowing difficult. This has worked well, though the paths require some additional work to keep them both tidy and serviceable. Selective weedkiller is occasionally used to remove the most unsightly lawn weeds and worn patches sometimes have to be oversown or rotovated and resown with a grass seed mixture designed for racecourses. This contains mostly dwarf ryegrasses that remain hardwearing and green throughout the summer.

The moat needs maintenance from time to time. It was dredged and provided with a new revetment of chestnut poles in 1970. The Sissinghurst clay is sufficiently retentive for it to need no other lining. Its resident goldfish and carp are scarcely decorative, rarely surfacing from its darkest depths and tending to muddy the waters as they feed along the bottom. Golden orfe do not share these habits and are more ornamental, often to be seen darting near the surface.

Algae are sometimes a problem, turning the water green in late spring, to the consternation of those short-sighted visitors who mistake it for grass and stride out boldly into its midst. An occasional application of algicide is necessary to restore the water's reflective surface, an important part of the Orchard's appeal. A low dose is used when the water outflow from the moat is low, to minimize any pollution to the lakes downstream. This seems not to harm the moat's fish and keeps the water free of algae for about two years.

The banks of the moat are strimmed twice each summer to keep them tidy but not unduly manicured. Another routine job is checking the oak trees by the moat which enclose the north and east sides of the Orchard to ensure that they remain sound. The magnificent oak framing the view of Dionysus along the moat is a particular worry: already showing signs of rot, it is inspected every six months and has been sensitively pruned to ensure that it can withstand gales. The shelter belt was further thickened in 1970 by planting more oaks east of the moat to give shelter to the garden and ensure that this screen of splendid trees would survive.

The belt of oaks has one gap at the north-east corner of the moat. Here stands the gazebo, Harold's memorial. Encouraging visitors to this outermost reach of the garden, it offers a fine view across rolling Kent countryside that is a particular favourite of Nigel Nicolson.

⁊

The Orchard is one of the few suitable areas of the garden in which to position a number of seats for visitors. The existing benches, rather decrepit and a little municipal in design, may well need to be replaced in the coming years. Sarah Cook is undecided about the best policy for replacement: should they be rustic, or perhaps in Georgian-style reeded metal? Maybe they should be commissioned specially? What would Harold and Vita have chosen? Such decisions are sensitive, but there is general agreement that the Nicolsons would not have been swayed by pedantic historicism but solely by what they considered to be beautiful and useful.

The design of the gazebo, planned by Nigel Nicolson and the architect Francis Pym, met with Harold's approval during his lifetime. When completed in 1969, the year after Harold died, his sons dedicated it to his memory. Its conical roof echoes the shape of the oast houses that dominate Kent rural architecture.

The White Garden

The most renowned of all of Sissinghurst's component areas, the White Garden is an essay in the use of flowers and foliage among a feast of fragrances. Our attention is focused primarily on these while colour, provided by the subtle interplay of leaves in shades of green, is relegated to a secondary role. This famous planting scheme had to wait until several years after World War II ended to be implemented.

At the end of the moat's northern limb, the Priest's House had always been a separate dwelling, probably built in the seventeenth century for the family chaplain. Its garden was enclosed by the planting of the Yew Walk shortly after Vita bought Sissinghurst. For its first two decades, however, it was primarily a rose garden. Paths were laid in September 1931 and the beds were planted mostly with shrub roses that November. The design is curious in consisting of two dissimilar halves, the north a parterre of box-edged L-shaped beds surrounding box cubes, reminiscent of the design devised by Harold and Sir Edwin Lutyens for the garden at Long Barn; the southern half comprising two deep borders on either side of the north-south path, which was lined by an avenue of almonds.

This and the Cottage Garden quickly became the most abundantly planted areas of Sissinghurst. It is no wonder that in 1933 Harold and Vita chose this place, heavy with the summer scent of roses, to make the Erechtheum, a trellis-covered colonnade used as an outdoor dining area, named after one of the temples of the Acropolis. Here they dined in the fading light of summer days. The vine planted in 1935 supplied dappled shade and a Mediterranean touch, as did the figs sent by Lady Sackville. The north–south path was edged with lavender, softening its edge and breaking the severe formality of the box design.

In 1937, the Chinese jar, bought by Harold in Egypt, was placed in the centre of the garden. Graham Thomas has commented on the striking similarity of this to the Martabani jars at Morville Hall, Shropshire. These were used to export commodities such as oil and ginger from China via the Burmese port of Martaban in the seventeenth century.

The shrub roses burgeoned and with them Vita's interest in yet more old varieties. By 1937, the collection had outgrown its home and was transferred to the Rondel garden so that this soon assumed the character of the Rose Garden we know today. The deep borders of the Priest's House garden continued to be dominated in high summer by stately delphiniums, while the box-edged beds held bush roses. One of these, a Hybrid Tea, was first exhibited by McGredy's in 1921 as 'Lady Sackville'. Slow to propagate, it was not offered for sale until 1930, and from then was known as 'Night'. In its day it was the deepest, most sumptuous of all crimson-black roses and its velvety tones would have appealed to Vita. Sadly, though still available in American nurseries, it is no longer grown in Britain.

On 12th December 1939, Vita first began to formulate ideas of all-white planting, but in a different part of the garden. She wrote to Harold:

'The Lion pond [in the Lower Courtyard] is being drained. I have got what I hope will be a really lovely scheme for it: all white flowers, with some clumps of very pale pink. White clematis, white lavender, white agapanthus, white double primroses, white anemones, white camellias, white lilies including *giganteum* in one corner, and the pale peach-coloured *Primula pulverulenta*.'

In his reply the next day, Harold was gently sceptical:

'I love your idea about the Lion pond. Only of course it gets no sun. You know that. You are a horticulturalist. It is impudence on my part to remind you that the Lion pond gets almost no sun. Just a beam at dawn is all it gets. We have the Japanese anemones which do well. We know that the blue Agapanthus flowers, so why not the white? But

what about the clematis, the camellia, the lily, and the *giganteum* ditto? But you know. Only it is such a good idea that I want it to succeed. I like the *Campanula pyramidalis* there, don't you? Of course there is not much room. Then we have the *Clematis montana* above. Yes, it is certainly a good idea.'

Vita was not to be so easily dissuaded. The following day she replied:

'*Of course* I realised the Lion pond was in the shade, and I chose the things accordingly. Primulas and Giant Himalayan lily simply revel in a north aspect. I have been rather extravagant, I fear, on the principle of "Let us plant and be merry, for next autumn we may all be ruined." After all, if I spend £20 on plants now, they will go on increasing in beauty for years, and we may never be able to afford it again.'

Both had been pessimistic about the outcome of the war: fearing that Kent would be the first part of England to be invaded, Vita seemed determined to make the most of her garden while she could. Though this plan for the Lion Pond was never implemented, perhaps because of the shortage of gardeners in wartime England, neither she nor Harold abandoned the idea of an all-white colour scheme.

It must be owned that Vita's initial idea was flawed. There was simply not enough room around the former Lion Pond to accommodate so many varieties if they were to be used with panache, in sufficiently generous quantities and furnished with companion plants to relate them to each other. Harold was probably right in suggesting that shade would be a limitation. But it is interesting that she should have conceived such an idea at all: white gardens were rare at the time, though they seem to have been popular around the turn of the century; in her book *A Garden of Herbs* (1920), Eleanour Sinclair Rohde wrote: 'The fashion for "blue", "grey", "white" or Japanese gardens has died out.'

Miss Jekyll believed that the beauty of white flowers was heightened by the addition of a little blue or lemon-yellow and did not approve of white flowers and silver foliage used alone. Lawrence Johnston had made a small white garden at Hidcote, which Vita and Harold must already have known. Initially called the Phlox Garden, this is but a small *étude* compared with the full-scale symphony of Sissinghurst's White Garden today; neither Harold nor Vita seems to have left any mention of it, suggesting that it did not make a strong impression on them. However, an interesting parallel is Johnston's use of the blush-pink rose 'Gruss an Aachen', analogous to Vita's use of peach *Primula pulverulenta*: few latter-day devotees of white gardens would choose to taint the purity of their schemes with this tone, so it is interesting that two such eminent gardeners should do so.

Another early white garden was Phyllis Reiss's Fountain Garden at Tintinhull in Somerset; in Mrs Reiss's time the whites were complemented with a touch of blue and yellow as Miss Jekyll had decreed. Along with Margery Fish's garden at nearby East Lambrook, Tintinhull was a regular place of pilgrimage for Vita. Mrs Reiss had made her first garden at Dowdeswell near Cheltenham and was influenced by nearby Hidcote. Lady Burnett's White Border at Crathes Castle, Grampian, also predates Sissinghurst's White Garden, but there seems to be nothing to indicate that Harold and Vita knew it or were influenced by it. However, it shows that they were not alone in wanting to use white flowers with silver foliage. Perhaps with the Crathes border in mind, Constance Spry's *Flowers in House and Garden* of 1937 gives a list for such a planting.

It has been suggested that the idea for a white garden might have been generated via Sissinghurst's curious geography. No matter what the weather, Harold and Vita had to cross the garden every night to get from the Priest's House, where the family dined, to the South Cottage, where the bedrooms were. On these nightly walks, perhaps the luminosity of white flowers in the blackness, glimmering ghostly as moon replaced sun, was the inspiration.

It was not until 1949 that Vita and Harold started to discuss the implementation of their white and silver scheme. By early June 1949, Vita had decided that the delphiniums that predominated in the two deep borders in the southern half of the Priest's House garden should be replaced with white and silver planting. Harold wrote enthusiastically to her:

'I think of it as *Cineraria* in masses, Rabbit's Ears in masses, Lad's Love a good deal, some *Santolina* – the whole background . . . predominantly grey. Then out of this jungle growth I wish regale to rise . . . although I would welcome a fid or two of *Anchusa* or something else blue among these white or silver objects, I hope you will keep the main colour scheme firm. Otherwise it may all look just like a flower-border anywhere.'

Harold's letter to Vita three weeks later shows that matters were still not completely decided:

'I am not happy about the Erechtheum garden, I think it is such a lovely shape and we see so much of it that it ought to be turned into a July garden. When the rest have declined – I believe that when we scrap the delphiniums we shall find the grey and white garden very beautiful and then we shall regret the scraggy, unhappy "Night" roses. I want the garden as a whole to be superb for 1951 for the British Fair or Festival, with heaps of overseas visitors and many will come down by car . . . I should like to concentrate on having at least the Erechtheum lovely for July – with regale and silver we shall do that.'

In the following January, Vita's article in the *Observer* describes the proposed planting for one of the two deep borders:

'My grey, green, and white garden will have the advantage of a high yew hedge behind it, a wall along one side, and a path of old brick along the fourth side. It is, in fact, nothing more than a fairly large bed, which has now been divided into halves by a short path of grey flagstones terminating in a rough wooden seat. When you sit on this seat, you will be turning your backs to the yew hedge, and from there I hope you will survey a low sea of grey clumps of foliage, pierced here and there with tall white flowers.'

It is the closing sentence of this first article on the White Garden that most potently captures its romance:

'All the same, I cannot help hoping that the great ghostly barn-owl will sweep silently across a pale garden, next summer, in the twilight – the pale garden that I am now planting, under the first flakes of snow.'

It is not clear how long it took before the whole of the White Garden was planted in this style but by 1954 most of the key plants were in place and the new garden had started to mature. Plants mentioned as being in the White Garden in Vita's articles for the *Observer* in the early 1950s included *Dianthus* 'Mrs Sinkins', pansies, peonies, irises with grey leaves, cistus, delphiniums, tree peonies, campanulas, sea buckthorn, *Buddleja nivea*, white *Platycodon grandiflorus mariesii*, *Hydrangea paniculata* 'Grandiflora', Japanese anemones and Pompon dahlias. Clearly such a mix consisted mainly of early summer flowers with too few to continue the show into the autumn. This shortcoming is illustrated by Vita's pessimistic view of the passing of the seasons, included in another *Observer* article:

'I do not like to think of later on. It is bad enough to have turned over into July, with the freshness of another May and June gone for ever.'

༒

Among the plants that would continue into July were delphiniums, which seem to have played a greater role in the garden in Vita's day than they do now. She particularly liked the contrast of the spire of the delphinium coming up between the rounded shapes of the shrub roses. Writing as President of the Delphinium Society in 1956, and referring to the White Garden, she commented:

'How beautiful the white Delphinium looks rising among the grey foliage of artemisia, with some clouds of gypsophila and clumps of *Lilium regale*, in a separate garden enclosed if possible by yew hedges.'

By 1959, no delphiniums remained in the entire garden; Vita blamed the errant feet of gardeners for destroying the tender young shoots but this was probably unfair; slugs were more likely culprits. Shortly before her death, Vita reordered seed of the Pacific Giant strain, using, as in the early 1950s, the Galahad Group, raised in California by Frank Reinelt; today this is still a highlight of the garden's planting. Vita found Reinelt's strains easy, uniform and reliably perennial, more so than highly bred British clones. In hot Californian summers the British delphiniums can be grown only as biennials, which is why Reinelt developed his own strains. Though these seem not to be so rigorously selected as they once were, Sissinghurst's gardeners still find them more satisfactory than clonal cultivars; though they are not exceptionally long-lived, they are easy to replace. Another of Reinelt's varieties, Black Knight Group, is a regular feature of both the Purple Border and the Rose Garden.

Cotton lavender replaced the lavender along the north–south path but

As Rosa mulliganii *on the arbour fades, many of the White Garden's flowers reach their peak. To the left, rose 'Iceberg', macleaya and zantedeschia fill the box compartments; beyond the path from the arbour to the Orchard,* Galega × hartlandii *'Alba' and towering onopordums dominate. At the foot of the arbour, cosmos, planted late after the removal of white rocket, is beginning to flower. Silvery* Artemisia arborescens *and the floriferous feverfew 'Rowallane' fill the box-edged beds to the right.*

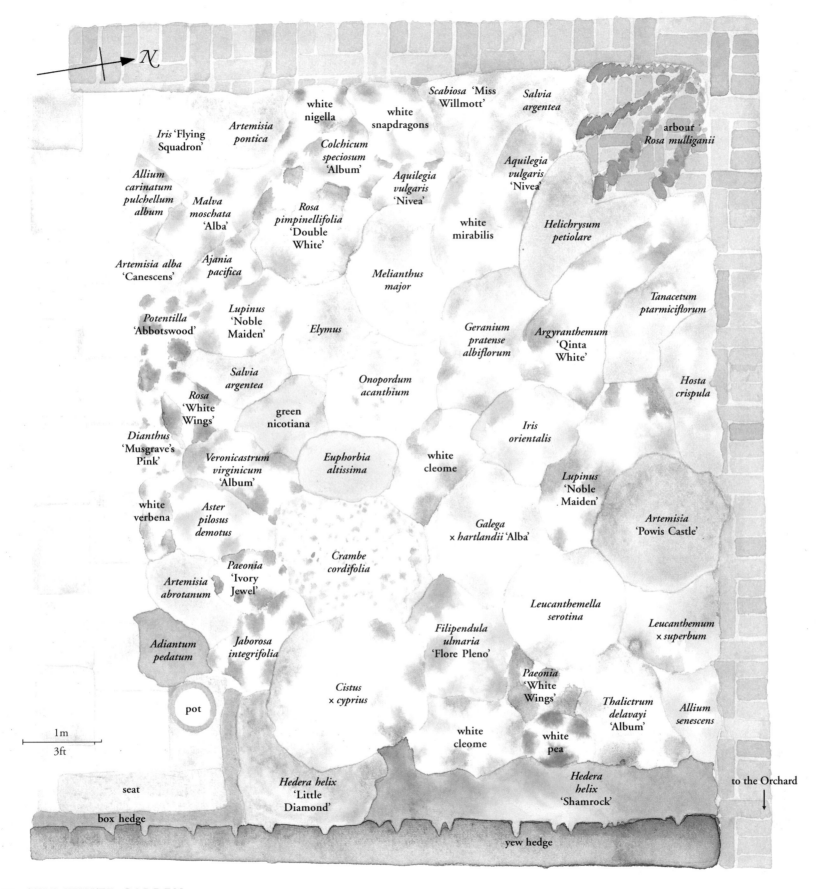

N

Scabiosa 'Miss Willmott'

Salvia argentea

white nigella

white snapdragons

arbour *Rosa mulliganii*

Iris 'Flying Squadron'

Artemisia pontica

Colchicum speciosum 'Album'

Aquilegia vulgaris 'Nivea'

Allium carinatum pulchellum album

Aquilegia vulgaris 'Nivea'

Malva moschata 'Alba'

Rosa pimpinellifolia 'Double White'

white mirabilis

Helichrysum petiolare

Artemisia alba 'Canescens'

Ajania pacifica

Melianthus major

Tanacetum ptarmiciflorum

Potentilla 'Abbotswood'

Lupinus 'Noble Maiden'

Elymus

Geranium pratense albiflorum

Argyranthemum 'Qinta White'

Hosta crispula

Salvia argentea

Onopordum acanthium

Rosa 'White Wings'

green nicotiana

Iris orientalis

Dianthus 'Musgrave's Pink'

Veronicastrum virginicum 'Album'

Euphorbia altissima

white cleome

Lupinus 'Noble Maiden'

white verbena

Aster pilosus demotus

Galega x *hartlandii* 'Alba'

Artemisia 'Powis Castle'

Crambe cordifolia

Paeonia 'Ivory Jewel'

Artemisia abrotanum

Leucanthemella serotina

Leucanthemum x *superbum*

Adiantum pedatum

Jaborosa integrifolia

Filipendula ulmaria 'Flore Pleno'

Paeonia 'White Wings'

Thalictrum delavayi 'Album'

Allium senescens

pot

Cistus x *cyprius*

white cleome

white pea

1m

3ft

seat

Hedera helix 'Little Diamond'

Hedera helix 'Shamrock'

to the Orchard

box hedge

yew hedge

ABOVE AND PLAN *The deep beds south of the arbour contain some of the garden's most symphonic planting: foliage and flowers harmonize with each of their neighbours in a continuous succession of satisfying associations, contributing to the large-scale concerted effect. In both beds, onopordum, leucanthemella and, later in the season, cleome provide height to give this half of the garden a separate sense of enclosure. The biennial eryngium Miss Willmott's ghost seeds itself between the perennials, and a few annuals, such as white nigella, double opium poppies and white and green nicotiana, are added. Some flower early, their spaces being filled by later perennials, while others lengthen the season into autumn. The effect depends as much on the subtle interplay of foliage in shades of green as it does on the flowers. Here are the greys of thistles, artemisia and ajania, glaucous lyme grass and melianthus and the puckered glossy leaves of crambe in the deepest green. This photograph was taken from the wooden seat, with arms and back of box, which provides a view to the statue of the little virgin and the weeping silver pear. Carpeting ivies beneath the hedge allow easy access for clipping.*

Looking from the Bishops' Gate towards the entrance to the Orchard. The path from the statue of the virgin to the seat lies hidden behind Hosta 'Royal Standard', Paeonia lactiflora 'Cheddar Gold', Artemisia absinthium 'Lambrook Silver', Gillenia trifoliata, Iris sibirica 'White Swirl' and Thalictrum aquilegiifolium 'White Cloud'. The peony came from Roy Klehm's nursery in Illinois; it is seldom seen in British gardens.

Throughout the planting there is a balance between flower shapes and sizes and foliage colours and textures. Beyond, in the bed shown in the plan on page 132, are Rosa pimpinellifolia 'Double White', spires of lupin 'Noble Maiden', onopordums, the single rose 'White Wings', clouds of Crambe cordifolia, Cistus × cyprius and a wigwam of hazel twigs supporting the white everlasting pea Lathyrus latifolius 'Albus'.

did not thrive in the shade of the almonds. The gardeners chose not to replace it when it became gappy, thus allowing them easier access to the box-edged beds. This has an effect that is pleasing and worrying in equal measure: on the one hand, the severe formality of the box beds is softened by plants that can spill over on to the path; conversely, the viewer is likely to feel that the edging of the beds looks not altogether complete. Two roses, the larger of which was *Rosa mulliganii*, in those days universally misidentified as *R. longicuspis*, were trained into the almond trees at the centre of the garden. This was a great success, so much so that the roses in time starved the almonds of light, hastening their demise.

The little virgin, cast in lead from Tomas Rosandic's wooden original in 1935, had been placed beyond the gate to the north of the Priest's House garden and several feet below its level. The long vista to the statue from the Bishops' Gate was unsatisfactory, for the virgin's legs were hidden from view. When the White Garden was created, the statue was moved to its present more suitable site at the southern end, where it is canopied by a weeping silver pear.

Before the making of the White Garden, there had been some similarity between the planting of the Priest's House garden and the Rose Garden. Through the creation of the White Garden, Harold and Vita were able to give each of these its own individuality and distinctive ranges of colours and plants. In the process the Rose Garden had lost most of its white-flowered plants, for even in a garden the size of Sissinghurst there is seldom room for duplication of varieties. Removal of most of the white from the Rose Garden has increased its richness of colour, although some silver foliage and pastel flowers remain.

❧

The winter of 1962–3, the first after Vita's death, was one of unusual severity and many of Harold and Vita's original plants, such as cistus species, succumbed. (Some visitors unfairly suspected the gardeners of being guilty of the devastation actually caused by the cold.) In that same year, Hilda Murrell sent the gardeners a bundle of 'Iceberg' roses that are still among the highlights of the garden. Famed for her knowledge of old roses, Miss Murrell recognized the quality of this new variety, and the plants she sent were used to replace 'White Wings', a choice but sparsely flowered single, and 'Pascali', which was too creamy. Though 'Iceberg' is classed as a Floribunda, with lighter pruning it will perform well as a shrub rose. At Sissinghurst, the bushes are not pruned to the ground each year but a substantial framework of branches is left so that they achieve an imposing size. 'Iceberg' is more prone to black spot now than it was when new but merits the extra effort of spraying with fungicide. The ground cover under the roses, *Pulmonaria officinalis* 'Sissinghurst White', is cut to the ground

immediately after flowering to encourage a second flush of young leaves.

Aware that the ever-increasing numbers of visitors wanted to see more flowers, the gardeners constantly strove to improve their quality and lengthen their season of display, which also helped spread the visitors throughout the garden. *Spiraea* 'Arguta' was added for spring, Decorative dahlias for late summer and *Zephyranthes candida* along the base of the house for autumn. A *Rubus* 'Benenden' given to Vita by its raiser, 'Cherry' Collingwood Ingram, was stripped of blossom by birds every year and so abandoned, but the bush of *Paeonia suffruticosa* subsp. *rockii* continued to thrive. Vita used to count its flowers on her morning walk and report the daily tally excitedly to the gardeners. However, by the late 1970s its vigour had declined alarmingly. The gardeners tried to persuade it to set seed but it proved to be self-sterile. Pollen from a different clone was sent from Hampshire by John Newell, the pioneer of John Innes composts, but the resulting seed was stolen by visitors. In spite of the gardeners' best efforts, it died of old age. Replacement plants were not available from British nurseries but were sent by Roy Klehm from the United States. *Stipa barbata*, a grass with astonishingly long feathery awns twisting and twirling from the tips of its seeds, is another plant that suffers from the theft of seeds, a particular shame as they are the plant's horticultural *raison d'être*.

The almond trees planted by Vita, that had cast the beds into shade, died one by one. By 1970 the last four at the centre of the garden also succumbed, their demise hastened by the overexuberant roses they supported. This meant that a drastic remedy was needed. It was agreed that all the trees should be removed and an arbour constructed. Nigel Nicolson's model, made from unfolded paperclips, was followed and the arbour was made in wrought iron by a local blacksmith. The design is a remarkable success, both as a focal point for the garden and to give enclosure to both of its halves. Based on the Perpendicular arches that are such a feature of Sissinghurst's buildings, its understated elegance is perfectly in the tradition of Harold and Vita. It was planned with practical considerations in mind: it was essential that its arches should be high enough to walk beneath without becoming entangled in roses, yet the whole should be low enough for the roses to be easily trained from step ladders. Some extra struts had to be incorporated into its roof to give adequate support to the rose stems and, because of the difficulty of removing the roses, it was left unpainted from the start. Relieved of the competition of the almonds, the two roses throve so well that they turned the arbour into a dark and dismal tunnel; one was removed leaving just *Rosa mulliganii*.

Pruning of the arbour is tackled in midwinter, on an overcast day so that the gardeners are not dazzled by the sun. Two gardeners work solidly and extremely quickly for two days, starting by removing two or three large old pieces from the base, almost at random but avoiding the most

LEFT *Looking from the White Garden's north-east corner towards the Bishops' Gate. Silvery thistles and arum lilies shine in the setting sun. The cosmos are supported by short stout stakes, soon to be hidden as the plants grow.* Argyranthemum *'Qinta White' (in the centre, below the thistles) needs similar stakes to support its sappy stems and heavy flowers; a translaminar or systemic insecticide must sometimes be used to combat the leaf miner that can mar its feathery foliage. The burgeoning buds of 'Iceberg' roses (on the left) promise a sparkling display. Lupin 'Noble Maiden' is raised from seed every five years or so. Regular deadheading encourages prolonged flowering, or even a second flush of bloom in late summer and early autumn.*

RIGHT *The White Garden is at its most glorious in early summer, when* Rosa mulliganii *casts a canopy of fragrant bloom over the gothic arbour. Designed by Nigel Nicolson, the arbour replaces the almond trees that grew here in Vita and Harold's time. In the distance, pink martagon lilies bloom in Delos.*

Zantedeschia aethiopica *'Crowborough'*   Rosa *'Iceberg'*   Tanacetum parthenium *'Rowallane'*

vigorous stems. The gardeners then prune quite hard at various levels, removing as much old wood as possible as they work up and across; this encourages new growth, not just from the base but all over the surface of the arbour. Some of the longest new basal shoots are trained right over to the far side of the arbour while others are shortened to varying lengths, ensuring that the whole structure will be covered with bloom. The rose's annual floraison, traditionally beginning on 1st July each year, is a *tour de force*, spectacular for the simple beauty of the flowers, their persuasive fragrance and their astonishing abundance.

The lack of the almonds made the two halves of the garden, particularly the box parterre, seem relatively flat. Graham Thomas's suggestion of arches to either side of the north–south path was adopted, giving height without the disadvantages of tree roots. However, clothing them with white-flowered climbers has proved difficult: *Rosa wichuraiana* flowered little and waved wands of prickles at passers-by, ensnaring them on its thorns; *Solanum jasminoides* 'Album' was lost in cold winters and slow to reach a telling size each summer. The clematis now used have been reluctant to establish, perhaps because of the eternal problem of iron garden structures: in summer sun they become so hot that they can scorch and kill stems, while in winter they can thoroughly chill them, a particular problem for plants like the solanum that are less than fully hardy.

Though gradual improvements have always been and continue to be made throughout the garden, the late 1960s and early 1970s were a time when much major work was tackled. In the White Garden, the grille at the north end of its axis was installed and white *Clematis* 'Alba Luxurians'

planted to drape itself around. Some impossibly awkward stone steps beyond the grille were removed, to make, along with other stone from Delos, the foundations of the gazebo in the Orchard. All the White Garden's paths were relaid at the same time that the rose arbour was erected.

The box-edged beds are filled with either permanent planting or bedding. The latter usually consists of biennial or spring bedding plants followed by annuals or tender perennials. The biennials are grown at a wide spacing in the nursery in full sun, achieving a generous size for long and copious bloom. For spring, the gardeners had used wallflowers but abandoned them because they were too creamy. Arabis, raised in the nursery from seed sown at the same time as the other biennials, was used instead, although care is needed: it rots if planted too deep. A very pure white, it remains in bloom until all danger of frost has past, when tender *Helichrysum petiolare* can take its place. White foxgloves are also grown in the nursery from Sissinghurst seed. This usually breeds true, there being few other foxgloves nearby; any purple-flowered seedlings show a reddish flush in their leaf stems and can be rogued out. The foxgloves are used in the south-facing border between the Erechtheum and the yew hedge, to be replaced with *Nicotiana sylvestris* after they have flowered in early summer.

White rocket, added to the repertoire in the late 1970s, would have appealed to Vita for its rich and pervasive fragrance in early evening, had she had a nursery to raise it. Sown there in early summer, plants are put in the beds in mid autumn. The rocket is removed the moment it finishes flowering in early summer, to be followed immediately by *Cosmos bipinnatus* 'White Sensation'. Since most modern varieties are too short and seed of

Cosmos bipinnatus *'White Sensation'*   Macleaya cordata *and* Clematis *'John Huxtable'*   Galega × hartlandii *'Alba'*

'White Sensation' is hard to find, the gardeners save their own. The plants must be grown quite late, in large pots so that they are big enough to fill their space quickly. Like many other flowers here, if it is to remain attractive and flower continuously, cosmos needs regular deadheading, a task that forms part of the 'Friday tidy'.

Omphalodes linifolia is a charming biennial relative of the forget-me-not, producing glaucous leaves and pure white flowers in late spring. It is sown next to satin-silver *Salix alba* var. *sericea*, which must be stooled every winter to prevent it getting too big. Some tender silvers are planted out each spring: one, *Artemisia arborescens*, is set over bulbs of *Ornithogalum pyramidale* whose grey-white spires weave gracefully through the feathery leaves of the wormwood. Sarah has tried to introduce some different silvers such as *Anthemis punctata* subsp. *cupaniana* and *Senecio viravira* (syn. *S. leucostachys*) to allow her to ring the changes, lessening the risk of soil disease from growing the same plants in the same beds over many years.

Marguerites have been a useful addition since Vita and Harold's time, their continuous blooming helping to make the garden attractive from late spring until the first frosts. The glaucous-leaved plant generally grown as *Argyranthemum foeniculaceum* (though it is not the true species) flowers profusely over fine foliage, while 'Qinta White' produces fewer, larger anemone-centred daisies over grass-green leaves. Its broader leaf lobes make it more susceptible to damage from leaf miner, which can disfigure the whole group unless a systemic insecticide is used at the first sign of attack. Another long-flowering double daisy, *Tanacetum parthenium* 'Rowallane', introduced by the gardeners, became so much associated with the garden that it was widely known as 'Sissinghurst'. The most floriferous but most miffy of feverfews, it must be cut hard back in August if it is to produce

both cuttings for next year's plants and an autumn show.

Perennials such as *Zantedeschia aethiopica* 'Crowborough' and macleaya seldom need attention; however, the macleaya occasionally runs out of steam and needs moving to another bed, a headache for the gardeners for few of the beds will accommodate such a tall plant. *Clematis* 'John Huxtable' grown on a pillar in the same bed has been a great success; cut back hard each spring, it always produces abundant late flower. It took the place of earlier-flowering 'Marie Boisselot' whose blooms were felt to be disproportionately large.

The Erechtheum is draped with vines and wisteria, originally supported by a roof of 15cm/6in squared trellis. Training the climbers proved difficult until trellis with 35cm/14in squares was substituted, allowing easier access. The wall of the Priest's House is also clothed with climbers, principally the Cherokee rose, *R. laevigata*, and the Noisette 'Madame Alfred Carrière', which Harold and Vita insisted on calling 'Mrs Alfonso's Career'. The Cherokee rose surprisingly survived the cold 1962–3 winter though it succumbed to frost in 1985 and had to be replaced.

Tall candelabra of onopordum tower over the beds to the south of the arbour for much of the summer, their tops lit gold and silver by the setting sun. In Vita's day, they were left to self-sow but seldom placed themselves to advantage: spiny brutes, they advanced menacingly to the edge of the path. Sown in the nursery in early summer, the plants are now placed with precision in late autumn where their great height will be most effective.

Contrasts of form are provided not only by foliage but also by inflorescences – mounds and fluffs, globes and spires – in a variety of sizes. The tallest spires are the eremurus and delphiniums but those in the next size

down such as lupins are scarcely less important. Raised occasionally from seed, lupin 'Noble Maiden' is slightly variable in shape of spike, flower colour and branching: ideally there should be a long central spike with plenty of substantial secondary spikes for lengthy and continuous flowering, with blooms as close to pure white as possible; seedlings are allowed to flower in the nursery and the best ones selected.

There is no fixed rule for the frequency of replanting of herbaceous plants; thugs like some artemisias and lysimachias are often replanted, sedate aristocrats such as dictamnus, daylilies, veratrum and herbaceous peonies very seldom. *Lilium regale*, always a key plant, needs regular topping up if its numbers are to remain sufficient to make an impact; the bold clean lines of its flowers are yet another example of the importance of floral form in the overall design. *Galega* × *hartlandii* 'Alba' is prized both for the purity of its flowers and its good foliage. Like other × *hartlandii* clones it does not set seed; however, it is not inclined to produce more flowers unless it is regularly deadheaded.

Though most flowers here are of the purest white, there are several exceptions. One is *Campanula* 'Burghaltii' in ghostly greyish lilac-pink, a plant the gardeners got from Margery Fish after Vita's death. Lime-green tobacco flowers are also allowed, for shades of green are as important in the scheme as white itself. *Papaver* 'Perry's White' was banished to the Rose Garden because its flowers contained a hint of pink, to be replaced by *P. orientale* 'Black and White'.

Melianthus major is a plant of such splendour that it is accorded the rare distinction of being used here in two magnificent groups. With sawtoothed pinnate leaves in sea green, it has a refreshing pungency likened

LEFT ABOVE *Rosa mulliganii at the peak of its display. The long awns of the grass* Stipa barbata *can be seen to the right of the path. To the left, seedheads of white nigella remain attractive after its flowers fade.*

LEFT BELOW *In winter the geometric precision of clipped box and the neatly trained, evenly spaced rose stems bear witness to the gardeners' skill. All pots and statuary are protected by tarpaulins in winter.*

PAGES 142–3 *An autumn view northwards from the arbour in 1992, with different planting in the box parterre beds. The iron arches are lightly clad with the potato vine,* Solanum jasminoides *'Album'. To the right, graceful* Spiraea *'Arguta' is grey with dew behind silver* Artemisia arborescens. *The pot at the centre of the arbour contains greenish-cream* Clematis forsteri*, a New Zealand species not fully hardy in Kent, with a strong, sweet but synthetic scent. Dwarf white antirrhinums remain in flower thanks to continual deadheading.*

by some to roast beef, while others are reminded of a new mackintosh. The gardeners prided themselves on having recognized its merit before it came to public notice; this occurred when it was shown by Christopher Lloyd at the Royal Horticultural Society in 1975 and awarded a First Class Certificate. Though it is not fully hardy, mild winters occasionally allow it to become a large and gawky shrub. Sissinghurst's gardeners prefer to cut it down each year, though if it is chilled to the roots it is slow to reach a telling size. The solution is to protect the base of the plant with a thick bracken mulch, which is also worked between the stems. This is removed in early spring, encouraging the formation of sturdy basal shoots. Superfluous branches are cut away in mid spring leaving the woody stem bases plus vigorous new growth.

છ

With such a wide variety of plants in the White Garden, a number of methods of support are used. Sarah Cook feels that staking is an art that requires both skill and patience. There are temptations to stake too soon, to use stakes that are too long, or to wait until, weighed down by a heavy shower, the stems have already collapsed into a tangled heap. Pam and Sibylle's rules for staking are a model of clarity. Firstly, it is axiomatic that stakes should be firm and pushed deep enough into the ground, watering the group first if necessary. The group should be staked first through its centre so that the middle does not flop. Then stakes are worked through the fringes. It may be necessary to tie in some outermost stems to prevent them falling out. Stakes should be tall enough to support the flower spikes but be concealed by foliage. This means they must be about two-thirds of the ultimate height of the plant; it is therefore important to know how high the plant will grow. The gardeners try to avoid staking too early so that the garden is only briefly disfigured. The plants soon grow through the stakes and look perfectly natural so that the viewer remains blissfully unaware that the flowers hide a forest of brushwood.

Bamboo canes and dahlia stakes are not used. The gardeners prefer peasticks, sticks of stripped sweet chestnut, or tall, well-branched stems of hazel which are grown at Sissinghurst for the purpose. Hazel is perhaps the most useful staking material, providing a variety of supports with twigs arranged on a single plane. Sometimes very twiggy stems are needed, sometimes slightly less branched ones and occasionally the more woody bases without twiggy 'feathers'. Much of the skill lies in choosing the right material for each plant. For example, if turning the tops of hazel stakes over to form a supporting cage for the plant to grow through, it is essential to use stakes that have been recently cut (that is, in midwinter before the catkins appear). Chestnut is used for a range of plants such as crambes. The plants are tied no higher than they need to be and the stake cut off

above the tie. This means that plants such as onopordum that tend to topple from the base need only to be held by the ankles, using 1m/3½ft chestnut stakes driven 60cm/24in into the ground close to the plant.

Tall branching peasticks about 1.2m/4ft long are used to stake plants such as boltonias, working the brushwood through the group once the plants have reached about 75cm/30in. The value of boltonias for late bloom is generally overlooked in British gardens, partly due to the national reluctance to garden for autumn but also because they demand such skilled staking, looking hideous if allowed to sprawl or if trussed. Artemisias such as *AA. pontica* and *ludoviciana* are held in place by many lighter twigs.

Delphiniums are staked with fairly light, branching stems of hazel. A little of this remains visible at the base of the flower spikes but these can sway gently to and fro and look perfectly natural. The staking method for most plants is to bend over the tops to make an interlocking grid through which the stems grow. For delphiniums, however, the tops are not bent, allowing the flower spikes a degree of movement within their supports. If tied rigidly to bamboo canes, the spikes tend to break off at the top of the cane unless this reaches right to the top of the plant, but staking in this

Autumnal tints of red and fawn add interest: the tiny hips of Rosa mulliganii *echo the scarlet-flushed leaves of* Rosa pimpinellifolia 'Double White'. Glaucous Melianthus major *has perhaps the most handsome late-season foliage. Beyond it,* Leucanthemella serotina (syn. Chrysanthemum uliginosum) *is invaluable for its late flowers.*

way would destroy any natural grace the plant has been left by the hybridist. A wigwam of tall hazel is used to support a perennial white sweet pea.

Once all twiggy material has been pruned off the hazel, the stout pieces that remain are ideal for staking a variety of other plants such as dahlias. Scarcely branched hazel from parts of the coppice growing in shade may also be used for these. Lupins do not need feathery support to the top of the stem in the same way as delphiniums but are well served by stubbier material hidden beneath the foliage. Short stubby stakes, branched but without fine twigs, can be used on plants that need support at the base, including biennials such as sweet rocket. The stakes can be reused later for summer plants like cosmos, working the sticks evenly through the whole group as though it were a single plant.

Although so-called *Argyranthemum foeniculaceum* needs no support, the ungainly *A.* 'Qinta White' is inclined to flop and split apart under the weight of rain on its heavy flowers. Stubby stakes worked throughout the group can assist here and can be used for another Sissinghurst dodge, easing the whole group over if there happens to be any empty space nearby.

Link-Stakes are used for plants such as peonies, putting the stakes in the middle of the group beneath the cover of the foliage and tying stems to the outside so that the stakes are invisible. They can be used for a discrete clump or for an extended group, interlinked throughout its centre. The gardeners find that the longer stakes are generally more useful.

ↄ৩

Also important to the White Garden's management is the maintenance of box edging, executed to exemplary standards here despite major difficulties. The wall at the north end of the garden is at an angle considerably more than the 90 degrees that the formality of the box parterre would seem to demand. Harold's solution was to lose this deviation little by little as the beds approach the centre of the garden, where the paths cross at

By autumn, Helichrysum petiolare *and* Artemisia arborescens *billow above the box, with white cosmos flowering bravely until the frost. Rose 'Iceberg' continues to flower, while the leaves of* Hydrangea quercifolia *beyond turn a rusty red.*

exact right angles. Thus none of the beds is exactly rectilinear. But the site also sloped, further marring the formality of the design. The irregular beds and the slipping levels were worryingly apparent, as disturbing as an Escher print in which superficial normality is geometrically impossible.

The gardeners took the opportunity of the repaving of the White Garden in 1970 to correct the hedge levels as far as was possible, although the site is still not absolutely flat. Keeping the tops of the hedges perfectly level hides the slope of the garden, so where the ground dips, the edgings are taller. Because all hedges here have a batter of about 15 degrees from vertical, the tallest edgings are wider at their base, for the flat tops must remain exactly the same width throughout the parterre.

When the hedge levels were corrected, it was necessary to replace about a quarter of the edging in the White Garden with box propagated by the gardeners. (Apart from the remaining three-quarters, and Sissinghurst Crescent hedge, all the box hedges have had to be replaced.)

This work was planned well in advance, and cuttings were taken in September 1962 from a number of clones of good habit and bluish leaf. The use of several clones gives a slight but pleasing variation in colour; this is a more satisfactory method than using seedling box which can give plants with foliage too yellow, too blue or too grubby in hue for a particular colour scheme, or with too fastigiate a habit to knit together well. The cuttings were bushy, three-to-four-year-old stems about 15cm/6in long with a woody base. After being dipped in hormone rooting solution, the cuttings were set in a channel about 10cm/4in deep in a shady part of the kitchen garden (now the nursery). Grit was placed along the bottom, the channel was filled with soil and the cuttings firmly heeled in, checking occasionally after frost during their first winter to ensure that they had not been loosened but remained firmly in the ground.

After a year almost all had rooted. They were spaced out to about 15cm/6in apart and grown on for five years. The tops were cut only after three years, but the sides received a yearly cut with a batter. Unlike yew, box breaks most readily from side branches and should not be cut back to the main stems. If the main stems remain in the centre of the bush, the resulting hedge can successfully be clipped to regrow in later life. When finally planted at a distance of 25–30cm/10–12in between their centres, the new plants already gave the appearance of a neat hedge.

Replanting was also necessary for the two box cubes at the head of the Moat Walk, which had become far too large and loose, with bare main stems in the centres. Drastic reduction was not an option, as they would have taken too long to recover. Each cube required twenty plants in a grid of five plants by four. If box hedging becomes too wide, it tends to be flattened every year by snow. This is a common problem with box, which is more lax than yew and so less suitable for broad hedges or large topiary pieces. Indeed, Sissinghurst Crescent hedge was so badly damaged during the winter of 1962–3 that severe measures were needed to repair it. Not then knowing how it would respond to cutting back, the gardeners risked a kill-or-cure policy of severe pruning, cutting the Cottage Garden side first. To their relief, this grew back very vigorously and quickly. Within four years, it had filled out and the top and Moat Walk side could also be cut back to regrow. This robust and rapid regrowth does not always occur with box hedges that are under stress from drought, poor soil or heavy shade; severe reduction should not be attempted unless they are in the best of health. Generally, cutting back the top and sunny side first gives the best results, pruning the remaining side after these have regrown.

Sarah Cook prefers to cut box in late summer or early autumn but, because the White Garden hedges cannot be cut while visitors are around,

this is done soon after the garden closes. They are best trimmed before the weather gets very cold because severe frosts shortly after clipping can damage them, scorching the remaining leaves and causing patchy growth the following spring. Electric trimmers are used and give good results, provided they are kept absolutely sharp. There is inevitably browning of the cut edges of the leaves, more so than for hand clipping, for which there is simply neither the time nor the labour available. Sarah considers the 120V Little Wonder single-sided clippers, used with a generator, to be flexible, safe, light, compact, less noisy and smelly than most machines and the easiest method altogether for this type of work.

To keep the edgings in the White Garden as regular as possible, the box must be trimmed to a line the full length of each of the parterre's five sub-axes. The line must be kept absolutely taut so that it is perfectly straight and does not dip in the centre. The gardeners keep a 'hedge book' which notes the exact dimensions of all the hedges and their many idiosyncrasies; these include bulges that must be reduced little by little or hollows that must be allowed to fill. The aim each autumn is to cut off the annual growth increment, although inevitably the hedges become a little larger each year; if too little is removed, the hedges would soon need to be reduced; if too much, only sparse and yellow old foliage would be left.

All hedges in the garden are fed in mid spring with fish, blood and bone fertilizer, in effect a slow-release organic feed. Pests and diseases are not usually a problem on box, although the Sissinghurst Crescent hedge sometimes suffers from box sucker, which can be treated by spraying with a systemic (or translaminar) pesticide in early summer.

❧

Why is the White Garden so successful, the most memorable and most copied area of Sissinghurst? It seems to disprove Miss Jekyll's precept that the beauty of white must be seasoned by a suspicion of blue and yellow. When compared with other single colour themes, white emerges as a clear favourite: yellow and blue are too near to green, red and orange too restless, purple too sullen, pure black too scarce among foliage and flowers. However, this is no reason not to attempt such schemes, for each has its own opportunities, its own range of plants and its individual mood.

The comparison with schemes based on a range or mixture of colours is more difficult. Random use of colour can produce a joyous overall effect but the beauty of individual plants, particularly if they are in soft or subtle tones, can be impaired by more vibrant neighbours. No photographer would present a picture of a delicate mauve flower with vivid magenta, chrome yellow, orange or even bright blue nearby distracting attention from the subject; there is always the risk that gentler tones will be overwhelmed by stronger ones. True, careful design or colour theming can eliminate most of such clashes. Nevertheless, we are likely to be most immediately attracted by colour, while form, texture and scent are able to give deeper and more lasting pleasure. We might even ignore the subtle beauty of foliage, which is used here to such wonderful effect.

Thus white gardens remove the distraction of colour and make us see most clearly the other factors that are fundamental to our enjoyment of gardens. Sissinghurst's White Garden might not have been the first of its genre but it was the most ambitious and successful of its time; enhanced by superlative technique and constantly refined planting, it is still probably the finest, the most entrancing of its type. Though most of us cannot see it as Vita did, gleaming magically in the twilight, it remains a garden of powerful and inspiring romance.

❧

Delos, the area to the west of the White Garden, has always been the most perplexing and least satisfactory part of Sissinghurst, lacking integration with either the White Garden or the Top Courtyard, which it adjoins. Vita explained in her *Country Life* article of 1942 that 'the plan was inspired by the island of Delos, where the ruins of houses have left precisely this kind of little terrace, smothered there by mats of the wild flowers of Greece'. Planted with plums, cherries, myrobalans, alpines such as saxifrages, thyme and aubrieta, and bulbs including irises and muscari, the area was strewn with fragments of masonry so that it resembled the remnants of ruins on an Aegean island. However, as boys, not long after Delos was first made, Ben and Nigel Nicolson were given the task of removing most of the masonry by wheelbarrow, so that it no longer looked like a stone-strewn site of Mediterranean antiquity. The stone edgings to the beds remained until 1970, when they were removed to make the footings for the Orchard's gazebo. At the same time, the maze of small and impractical paths was removed, and numerous choice shrubs, bulbs and ground cover were added; these helped furnish the area and added interest, particularly spring flowers and autumn colour. The gardeners also added shelter and screening in the form of large shrubs such as phillyrea and *Corylus maxima* 'Purpurea', which helped protect both Delos and the White Garden from chilly winds, and blocked the view through to the White Garden from the lane outside the garden gate.

Delos contains some fascinating and choice plants, such as the tender bromeliad *Fascicularia bicolor*, its rosette of pale turquoise flowers surrounded by the brilliant scarlet bases of prickly strap-shaped leaves. (Of all the plants in the garden, this is the only one that is deadheaded using a hammer and chisel and tough leather gloves.) But Delos still rather lacks its own identity and needs to relate more convincingly to the rest of the garden, a challenge the gardeners still hope to confront and resolve.

An oblique view across Delos from the Top Courtyard entrance to the White Garden. Sissinghurst's oast houses appear in the distance, behind the screen of shrubs which helps enclose this outer corner of the garden. Lenten roses bloom unseen by visitors as winter passes into spring. Beyond the path is a phlomis variously known as P. anatolica or P. 'Lloyd's Variety', though neither of these is a valid name. An intermediate between P. fruticosa and P. grandiflora, or possibly a hybrid between the two species, it is perhaps the most handsome foliage plant of its genus, its leaves almost white for much of the year; however, it produces few flowers.

Behind
the Scenes

The border west of the Powys Wall where new plants are trialled before introduction to the garden. The west façade, with the twin gables flanking the entrance arch, can be seen beyond.

Much of the success of any garden, public or private, derives from the skill, artistry and devotion of its gardeners. In this respect Sissinghurst has been and remains immensely fortunate: its fame, wide range of plants and sophisticated techniques of maintenance have ensured that it is always able to attract good gardeners. The present scarcity of training in high standards of gardencraft, comparable to those instilled in Pam and Sibylle by Miss Havergal at Waterperry, has made a spell working at Sissinghurst all the more valued.

Highly esteemed throughout the horticultural world, gardeners from Sissinghurst have over the last thirty years gone on to take distinguished posts throughout the British Isles and overseas. However, the garden cannot be run primarily as a training establishment. Sarah Cook admits that 'to some extent the Trust has to be self-interested. If it's going to train anybody, it should train people who are likely to stay in the Trust'; she must aim to employ gardeners who will not merely spend a short time in the garden to further their own careers, but will stay long enough to be of real value to Sissinghurst. A certain amount of altruism beyond Sissinghurst is desirable: a selfish attitude towards training can never lead to high national or international standards in horticulture; if the garden employed only those who would stay until retirement, there would be no spreading of horticultural knowledge and no cross-fertilization of ideas. In practice, Sarah finds that the garden's employees tend to fall into two categories: those who are content to stay for five to eight years and those, often younger people, who want to make more rapid progress in a horticultural career and tend to stay a shorter time, perhaps three or four years. A balance of these two types ensures the optimum mix of continuity, interest, motivation and efficiency.

Though Sissinghurst's garden staff changes from year to year, some brief details of those employed at the time of writing give an indication of their calibre and the sort of experience and qualifications needed to work here.

At present the staff consists of the Head Gardener plus six full-time gardeners and one trainee. A part-time gardener is also employed and volunteers help with deadheading. All the gardeners have horticultural qualifications and wide experience before they come to the garden. Alexis Datta, Assistant Head Gardener, started work as a parks apprentice before taking a three-year National Certificate in Horticulture at Pershore in Worcestershire followed by eight years at Cliveden. Troy Smith took a three-year National Diploma in Horticulture course at Askham Bryan College near York, including a 'sandwich' year at Bodnant in North Wales immediately before joining the staff; he also had experience in parks and has worked in a private garden in France. Jacqui Ruthven took a two-year course in the United States and worked for the National Trust at Cliveden and Dorneywood, both in Buckinghamshire. Andrew Eddy started in agriculture and in 1987 changed to a career in gardening, working in the arboretum at Kew; while there he took a City & Guilds course in horticulture, followed by a period at Finsbury Park Training Centre, London, as a member of staff before coming to Sissinghurst. Philip Norton took the three-year National Diploma in Horticulture at Pershore and, during his year out of college, the Royal Horticultural Society's Wisley student course. Cornelia Rapp attended horticultural college in Germany before working in parks and then on a private estate in England.

Until recently, before Compulsory Competitive Tendering became government policy and local authority services, such as the maintenance of parks and gardens, became in most cases 'contracted out', many local authorities ran excellent apprenticeship schemes. These provided a pool of skilled labour, not only for their own but for all the country's gardens, including those of the National Trust. The loss of such schemes and the use by contractors of relatively untrained staff diminished drastically the provision of training in gardencraft and threatened the availability of skilled labour. The National Trust's response was to institute their Careership Scheme, whereby young gardeners are able to work for three years in a local Trust garden where varied skills are practised to a high standard. The training equips them for work in similar gardens, within the Trust or elsewhere. The scheme includes a succession of block releases to Cannington College, Somerset, and the resulting qualification is the equivalent of the National Diploma in Horticulture. The current trainee, Kevin Mountford, has a horticultural background (his father grows exhibition chrysanthemums), and he knew when he left school that he wanted to garden; he has taken a one-year first diploma BTEC in horticulture at Brinsbury College, West Sussex. Sarah also hopes to join in with the Trust's exchange scheme whereby gardeners would go away for two to three weeks to work in another garden to widen their experience and achieve a cross-fertilization of ideas.

As Head Gardener and Assistant, Sarah and Alexis plan the next month's work together and carefully prioritize longer-term projects, to be tackled over the coming five to ten winters. They also have a roving responsibility, tackling an assortment of jobs around the garden. For most maintenance, the gardeners are not allocated to any one area and often work together. The beauty of the garden, its balance and proportions, depend most directly on such work, including replanting, pruning and major winter projects. However, weekly tidying is also important and each gardener is allotted one garden area which they must keep spick and span. They are encouraged to make constructive comments about 'their' parts of the garden, but the choice of planting remains the responsibility of Sarah and Alexis: there should be a single style throughout the garden, not seven different ones. Nor should the gardeners ever adopt a competitive attitude: Sarah is keen to foster a team spirit that encourages high standards in all areas; once any gardener has completed the routine tidying of his or her own patch, he or she must help with areas where yet more work is needed. The gardeners are encouraged to widen their knowledge of plants and attend sessions in the early evening after work when they go around the garden discussing each plant of interest and sharing their knowledge.

❧

Though this may change from year to year, the gardeners now work from 7.30am to 4.30pm each weekday, with a one-hour break for lunch. One gardener is responsible for weekend duty, principally looking after the glasshouses. Most lawns are mown on Wednesdays, to allow two days for the grass to grow to withstand weekend wear. In the 'Friday tidy', each gardener sweeps, deadheads and weeds his or her own area; these responsibilities are much better dealt with weekly than on a more random basis.

At the time of writing, the garden does not open on weekday mornings and is shut on all Mondays. These hours and the gardeners' early start were chosen partly to overcome the difficulty of working when the garden is full of visitors. When in the early 1980s visiting numbers reached 100,000, Pam and Sibylle found that it could take them fifteen minutes to dispose of rubbish, shuffling in a queue of visitors towards the tip; gardeners would be engaged in endless conversations; tasks such as mowing were simply not possible if lawns were teeming with people. It became important to choose staff who were not excessively talkative and were able to continue working while the public chatted to them. Jobs in the most popular garden rooms had to be completed before opening time; thereafter some of the gardeners could retreat to the nursery or to less populous parts of the garden. However, Pam always felt that some gardeners had to be on hand, not only to ensure the security of the garden and its plants, but also because 'people are tremendously interested; it's very nice, if they do have a genuine question, to answer it. I think it's part of the service.'

Many of the secrets of Sissinghurst's success can be found in the area west of the Rose Garden, once Harold and Vita's kitchen garden, which contains the nursery beds, frames, glasshouses, tool and machinery sheds. Here it is that new plants are trialled, biennials and tender plants propagated and a constant stock of hardy perennials is kept in pots for the planned renewal of groups and also for any gaps that might arise; cut flowers such as sweet peas are grown for the house here and there is also a plunge bed for growing on pots of bulbs to fill gaps in the Lime Walk. The policy for propagation is always to have enough plants to meet any eventuality but never to produce plants with plant sales primarily in mind: propagation for sale on this scale can seldom be cost-effective and is outside the prime purpose of the gardeners and the Trust, which is to conserve a beautiful and historically important garden. Only plants that are surplus to the garden's requirements are sold through the shop. However, propagation is an effective use of time during rainy or freezing weather; some clumps of hardy perennials can be found waiting in the nursery between autumn and spring, ready to be divided and potted when inclement weather prevents outdoor work.

A large border west of the Powys Wall is used to trial any new and promising plants that might be used in the garden in the future. Sarah, as did Pam and Sibylle before her, collects together suitable plants here for a few years' assessment. If they pass muster, there will by then be enough to stock a group of suitable size. Here is a splendid yellow kniphofia, raised by Gardens Adviser Jim Marshall's father-in-law, and several attractive penstemons. Sarah is less enthusiastic about a dwarf hemerocallis with inelegant flowers buried among its leaves. Though she does not object to breeders making diminutive versions, to rob plants of their natural grace is inexcusable; the daylily will be discarded. Some plants, though attractive, just do not suit any of the garden areas and so cannot be used.

New hardy perennials that prove their worth will be propagated and potted, to occupy the row of frames south of the entrance range, along with replacement plants from the garden's established repertoire. Of the Michaelmas daisies, Sarah finds that most can be replanted directly into their border patch, though *Aster ericoides* cultivars are slower to produce floriferous plants from divisions and benefit from a spell in pots in the nursery. Pam and Sibylle used to rejuvenate irises by potting the most vigorous rhizomes for a few weeks and holding the pots in the nursery. This produced good root action before replanting in the same or another site and ensured some flower the following year, not generally the case after direct replanting. Sarah finds it useful to grow plants such as aquilegias to flowering size in pots so that the balance of colours can be adjusted and the best individuals selected.

South of the row of frames is a large bed used for the production of biennials such as wallflowers, onopordums, sweet rocket, sweet William, mulleins and herbs including teasels, biennial clary and caraway. Seed of most of the biennials is sown in trays in mid June in a dark shed; by this time of year, the glasshouses are so hot that germination would be inhibited. The latest-flowering biennials such as sweet rocket and Siberian wallflowers are sown about a month later. However, mulleins need light to germinate and are sown in trays outside. As soon as they germinate, the seedlings are brought into the light to be pricked out when large enough into plugs; within a few weeks they are ready to be planted in nursery rows. Any earlier sowing would produce plants so big by planting time that they would be unmanageable and would not transplant so well. This method is quicker than the traditional one of sowing in nursery rows in late May and then transplanting the seedlings, which would check their growth, take an extra fortnight to produce the required size of plant and waste much seed. Spacing between rows and between adjacent seedlings is wide enough for them to grow to maximum size; such vigorous plants guarantee plentiful and tall flower spikes, and thus prolonged flowering.

The grass patch between the nursery rows and the hedge down to the field was grandly titled the Turf Nursery by Pam and Sibylle. The grass here is grown from the same seed mix used throughout the garden, a combination of Mommersteeg MM50 racecourse mix and MM14 tennis court mix; the former consists of mixed hard-wearing dwarf ryegrasses, the latter mainly of Chewing's fescue with some mixed ryegrasses plus a little browntop and smooth-stalked meadow grass. Thus there is always matching turf available to repair worn areas. If ever soil-borne diseases became a problem in the nursery rows, this area could be ploughed and used for production of biennials. For smaller repairs, MM50 and MM14 mixes are sown in plugs which can be inserted in threadbare patches.

~

Most propagation of plants from seed and cuttings takes place in the large Cambridge glasshouse, provided in 1967 by the National Trust to replace Harold and Vita's greenhouses. It then had a capillary watering system with pots standing on a layer of silver sand to conduct the water. This was later replaced by capillary matting, but Pam and Sibylle still found that the system was not entirely successful for production of such a mixed range of plants: much hand-watering was still needed to ensure that all the plants were sufficiently moist. The glasshouse is divided by a partition into two sections. The smaller east end of the house is kept at a minimum winter temperature of 10C/50°F and contains the polythene-covered bench where cuttings are rooted; this is equipped with heating cables to warm the rooting medium (peat and vermiculite) to 20–21C/68–70°F. The larger

The gardeners standing by their machines at the entrance to the nursery. From the left: Andrew Eddy with the Graveley 5465 mower; a Little Wonder edger appears in front; Philip Norton, responsible for machinery maintenance, on the Etesia 91cm/36in ride-on rotary mower; in front are two 40cm/16in Little Wonder electric hedge trimmers and a trug, an onion hoe and a hessian sheet; behind him are the Kubota B7100 tractor and its trailer; Jacqui Ruthven with the Ransomes Marquis 53cm/21in cylinder mower; Assistant Head Gardener Alexis Datta with the Kees scarifier; Troy Smith with the Ransomes Matador 60cm/24in mower; Head Gardener Sarah Cook beside the Sisis Auto Turfman spiker and slitter; a fertilizer spreader appears in front.

west end is kept at a winter minimum of 5–6C/41–43°F, with an alarm to warn if the temperature drops below 4C/39°F. Fans in both ends assist air circulation and maintain an even temperature. Most plants will develop well in the cooler end of the house, but for faster growth or with more tender plants such as streptocarpus, heliotropes and busy lizzies, only the warmer end gives satisfactory results.

The yearly routine in the propagation house begins after the contents have been planted out in early summer. Then all surfaces can be cleaned and the floors treated with Jeyes fluid, a mild phenolic disinfectant. In June and July biennials are sown and dianthus cuttings inserted in the polythene-covered cuttings bed. Cuttings of most tender perennials are taken in early September and the resulting plants held outside in frames until frost threatens. Some of these early-propagated plants such as *Cuphea cyanea*, penstemons, salvias and *Felicia amelloides* 'Variegata' will be held right through the winter to be used as large plants in the garden the following year; others, including argyranthemums, verbenas, osteospermums and arctotis hybrids will be used as stock plants for more cuttings to be taken from mid January onwards. Some annuals, such as nicotianas, impatiens, *Cuphea viscosissima*, *Coreopsis* 'Mahogany Midget', *Malva sylvestris* var.

mauritiana, *Anoda cristata*, *Omphalodes linifolia*, *Lupinus texensis*, heliophila and *Brachyscome iberidifolia* are raised from seed that is sown in January.

Suitable potting composts have proved a problem over the years and have had to be changed from time to time. Pam and Sibylle used to make their own John Innes compost from Sissinghurst loam laboriously sieved by hand; to this they added the base fertilizer and, if they felt their plants required it, a little leaf mould or well-rotted manure. However, they had

OPPOSITE *The lean-to glasshouse used primarily for producing large specimen plants. On the right are* Alyogyne hakeifolia, Hechtia argentea, Coronilla valentina *subsp.* glauca *and* Astelia chathamica. *Sprigs of choice plants in bottles on the bench are for the education of the gardeners.*

RIGHT *The cool end of the Cambridge glasshouse in spring. The warm end can be seen beyond, with the polythene-covered cuttings bench to the left.*

BELOW LEFT *One of the cold frames in spring, shortly before arctotis hybrids,* Verbena *'Kemerton',* argyranthemums *and* Alonsoa warscewiczii *'Peachy-Keen' are planted out.*

BELOW RIGHT *The plunge bed with pots of bulbs covered by bark mulch.*

no facilities for sterilizing the loam. By the late 1970s they took the easier option of buying in peat-based compost, though it was sometimes difficult to maintain correct nutrient availability in peat composts if plants were kept in pots for more than a couple of months. For many years peat-based compost with extra grit and slow-release fertilizer added has been used for the outside containers. Because peat is not an ecologically sustainable resource in the British Isles, Sarah would like to be able to use it less, but she has not been able to find a satisfactory alternative, though a compost based on loam with added grit and vermiculite might be preferable.

Cocofibre composts have proved satisfactory for plants, including some herbaceous perennials, that spend only a short time in their pots, but they have been difficult to water: the top of the pot looks dry even when most of the compost is thoroughly wet; as with the peat-based composts, nutrient-holding capabilities over more than a couple of months do not seem to be adequate. A mixture of peat and vermiculite is used for cuttings. By rooting cuttings and growing seedlings in trays of expanded polystyrene cells, the gardeners have found they can produce plants without causing them any check on transplanting.

Pam and Sibylle originally used clay pots but, with no room to store large numbers of them, changed to black polythene sleeves which take up little space. However, in these it is hard to water plants such as nicotianas which form a low rosette of leaves; for such plants, rigid plastic pots are used. Large annuals, like *Cosmos bipinnatus,* require a 2 litre/½ gallon pot if they are to grow without check until planting time.

Sarah finds the serried ranks of cold frames east of the glasshouses extremely useful, allowing her to move plants out of the main glasshouse, which can start to become congested by early spring. Reasonably hardy perennials such as violas and dianthus which have been propagated under glass can be moved out to the frames in February, followed by slightly tender perennials such as penstemons, verbenas, felicias and *Argyranthemum foeniculaceum* (of gardens, not the more shy-flowering true species) in early April. Once the risk of severe frosts has passed, usually in mid April, the tougher tender perennials can be removed from the frames and planted out. Diascias also fall into this category: though they will survive most winters in Kent, they are generally more vigorous and floriferous if treated like other tender perennials and repropagated every year. Sarah thinks it is best to plant out tender perennials as soon as weather permits and chooses the planting time by checking that the long-range weather forecast is for a whole week of mild weather without frost. This is sufficient to harden off the plants; their early start will give them ample time to make a good root system for the summer and reduce the need for watering later on.

The smaller of Sissinghurst's glasshouses is a lean-to used for larger and longer-lived plants such as the hedychiums and puyas used on the tower steps and by the Bishops' Gate, and the standard argyranthemums used at the head of the Moat Walk. Kept just frost-free, this house is also used to ensure the survival of any near-hardy plants that can be lost in very severe winters, such as one of each crocosmia, two of each *Lobelia* × *speciosa* cultivar and dormant tubers of tender *Mirabilis jalapa*. The near-hardy plants can be moved to the cold frames as winter passes into spring, giving more room for the larger specimen plants to develop.

Sarah produces standard argyranthemums on an eighteen-month cycle, starting with cuttings taken in September. The main stem grows straight up until a flush of flower is produced, resulting in a rosette of lateral stems. One of these must be selected as the new leader and trained vertically against a cane; the other laterals are cut back to the main stem. After about a year, a woody main stem of sufficient length has developed and the head of stems starts to form. These stems are regularly pinched out to create a bushy head and cut back in February, so that new flowering stems grow and are about to blossom by April when the plants are ready to go outside. Such plants can be occasionally pruned back so that they remain vigorous and can be reused for two to three seasons. Pam and Sibylle preferred to use a ten-month cycle, starting with cuttings in July, and to keep their plants just for a single season.

Pelargonium 'Lord Bute', trained as a tall bushy plant, is also produced on a long cycle starting with cuttings in August; nineteen to twenty months later a specimen plant for a large pot is ready to go outside. Pam and Sibylle also preferred a shorter cycle, of some nine or ten months, for this. Two or three plants of the tender Chilean bromeliad *Puya alpestris* are held here in winter because they cannot be relied upon to flower each year: if one fails to flower, the other generally obliges. The plants die after flowering but usually produce offsets which can be used for propagation. However, it is easier and almost as quick to grow them from seed; this is only occasionally produced but can be stored for several years. *Phlox divaricata* subsp. *laphamii* 'Chattahoochee' also lends itself to pot culture. Overwintered without heat in a cold frame, in the open border it seldom produces such a spectacular dome of powder-blue violet-eyed flowers as does a two-year-old potted plant. *Tweedia caerulea* does not produce a big enough plant in a single season and is sown in March and grown for a whole year to produce a plant capable of a stunning display.

❧

When Pam and Sibylle first came to Sissinghurst the garden had only the most basic equipment: a pre-war 43cm/17in Atco mower, two wooden wheelbarrows with iron-shod wooden wheels and a very heavy brass knapsack sprayer. Since those days, garden machinery has become much more sophisticated, enabling many tasks to be tackled to a higher standard and with greater efficiency. After an Allen mini tractor and trailer were provided in 1966, the gardeners created a 'highway' around the perimeter of the garden, making it easy for the first time to move heavy or bulky loads such as mulch to the farthest limits. The Allen was chosen partly because it was in those days one of very few machines narrow enough to pass through the archway from the nursery into the Rose Garden, and the width of the arch still determines the choice of machinery, though the steps into the Orchard from the Moat Walk and the narrow path around the nuts are yet more obstacles preventing the use of wider machines.

Although the Allen tractor was equipped with a mid-mounted rotary mower, it was not powerful enough to cut long grass in the Orchard. Pam and Sibylle used to hire a reciprocating-blade Oxford Allen Autoscythe just for this job until the Allen tractor was replaced with a more powerful Kubota with rear-mounted mower. The present Kubota B7100 replaced this machine. However, it is an Etesia 91cm/36in ride-on rotary mower with rear-discharge pickup that is used for Orchard mowing today; this can collect long grass, eliminating the laborious job of raking and picking it all up by hand. Sarah is very pleased with this Etesia and finds it gives a good finish wherever it is used, though it will be some years before it has repaid its considerable cost. A trailed Wessex 1.5m/60in rotary mower is used with the Kubota tractor to tackle large areas of mowing such as the car park and the grass outside the entrance and the garden also has a Graveley 5465 machine with its own trailer. This can be fitted with a rotary deck or, for the roughest areas, a flail deck; it was used for the Orchard before the Etesia was bought and is still often useful, particularly if trailers are needed in two parts of the garden at the same time. A pedestrian-operated Kubota rotary mower with a grassbox has proved satisfactory for cutting smaller areas of coarser grass; it is also used for cutting finer turf in very wet conditions when a heavy mower would cause unacceptable compaction and for trimming off bents if these grow too long to be cut by one of the cylinder mowers.

Cylinder mowers for the fine lawns are also limited by the width of the Rose Garden arch, the largest being a Ransomes Matador 60cm/24in machine; there is also a Ransomes Marquis 53cm/21in machine, the third or fourth of this model provided since 1967; both give good service. But there is much more to fine turf culture than simply mowing: fertilizing and top-dressing are also needed and it is essential to remove dead thatch and improve surface aeration. For these, a Kees scarifier and a Sisis Auto Turfman are used. Sarah would like to be able to scarify regularly throughout the season but the grass has to take too much wear for this to be possible; the job must wait until the garden closes. The Auto Turfman will spike or slit but slitting is not effective on the heavy clay soils of Sissinghurst.

A Little Wonder edger is used to trim lawn edges, saving time and

Troy using the Kees Powerake scarifier on the Top Courtyard lawn shortly after the end of the visiting season. Removal of large quantities of thatch reinvigorates the grass and minimizes the risk of fungal disease in warm, damp autumns.

giving a straighter and more regular cut than edging shears; Sarah considers it particularly effective for cutting down the side of hard edges between paving slabs and grass, though she warns that when it is used for grass-edged beds it is easy little by little to shave away the edges and slowly but inexorably make the bed bigger. A Walkover selective weedkiller applicator is effective, though with low weed populations in the garden, few weeds seed themselves into the lawns and it is seldom used.

The garden has two knapsack sprayers, one a Cooper Pegler reserved for insecticides and fungicides and the other a KEF used for herbicides. Sarah uses them as little as possible, preferring to cut weeds with a cord trimmer wherever she can. However, there are some pests and diseases that must be treated if the appearance of the garden is not to be marred; it is especially important to prevent crippling diseases like black spot or rose rust that can destroy the roses' display. For wall plants, including roses, an air-assisted Solo knapsack sprayer that can reach the top of the wall is used.

Pam and Sibylle found that the longest-bladed hedge trimmers did not give the quickest or most polished results: it was difficult to keep an eye

both ends of a 75cm/30in or longer blade at the same time, and they were tiring to use. The gardeners use 40cm/16in Little Wonder electric trimmers, lighter than petrol-powered machines; three of them can be run from a single Honda generator.

All Sissinghurst's gardeners have their own set of the most important hand tools – spade, border spade, fork, border fork, Dutch hoe, onion or baby hoe, trowel, secateurs and bast broom – each set stored on their own pegs in the large toolshed. Pam, Sibylle and Sarah all feel that the choice of tools is immensely important if gardeners are to work comfortably and efficiently: handles must be the right length for the individual and blades be correctly angled. Mass-produced hand tools seldom meet these criteria; replacing worn-out tools with well-designed new equipment is not easy. Pam and Sibylle are considerable connoisseurs of such tools and collect new and old examples of good design avidly. They prefer spades and forks to have D-handles and flat treads; this is contrary to my own preference deriving from northern England where D-handles are held to be too restricting and uncomfortable for the large hands of labourers, while flat treads hinder the scraping of boots, a frequent activity if lawns and paths are not to be smeared with mud. However, a flat tread is undoubtedly more comfortable on the foot unless the thickest-soled boots are worn.

Smaller border forks and spades are held to be much more useful for the intimate scale of work in Sissinghurst's beds and borders, fitting easily between the fairly closely planted groups of plants; border spades are also the perfect size for most planting and quicker than taking out innumerable trowelfuls of soil. Two large forks are admirable used back to back to divide clumps of plants. Pam and Sibylle do not generally like stainless steel tools: usually heavier and with a blunter edge, they are more tiring to use continually. Muck forks do not have the tines too hooked so that manure can easily be thrown off. Mattocks or grub axes are other digging tools that occasionally prove useful for removal of stumps or roots.

Sibylle does not like modern trowels moulded from steel sheet: they are never correctly angled and have a hollow beneath the stem which collects mud; trowels with a solid neck are preferable by far. The weight of stainless steel trowels is less of a disadvantage and the ease of keeping them clean a substantial boon. However, the handle must be shaped to fit comfortably in the hand and the blade should be curved just enough to produce an average planting hole, but not too much. The kink in the neck of the trowel is also critical and should be sufficiently bent to deliver pressure on the handle directly to the tip of the blade.

Though Dutch hoes are used in wide-open spaces of beds and borders and along nursery rows, small onion hoes are found to be much more useful for working among close planting, especially just before staking, often the last opportunity to be able to get in among the plants before gaps between them close. This is not an implement for those who dislike

Troy using a template to regulate the batter on the Yew Walk hedges; Jacqui using a line to trim the box hedge around the old toolshed bed; Andrew cutting a hornbeam hedge in the Lime Walk. All the gardeners wear ear protectors while clipping.

RIGHT *The new toolshed is roomy enough for wet-weather work such as division of clumps of perennials. Hessian squares hang up to dry. As each plant comes into flower, its label is selected from the rack. Black plastic laminate labels, though not beautiful, are legible, long-lasting and relatively cheap; thefts of labels can be a problem unless stems are too long to fit into a handbag.*

bending but, because hoed weeds between close planting are less likely to shrivel and die, gardeners must in any case bend down to pick them off.

Pam and Sibylle used to favour Rolcut anvil secateurs; these worked well provided they were kept sharp; if blunt they could crush stems. Pam and Sibylle stress that they should be used with the blade uppermost so that the anvil does not obscure the part of the stem being cut. Felco secateurs are now used and are comfortable and efficient, although even if sharp they do not cut string easily, an important consideration when pruning and tying. For deadheading, Pam and Sibylle find scissors with 5cm/2in long blades to be much easier to use than secateurs. Cuttings are trimmed with Stanley craft knives; their disposable blades are easily replaced. Pam, Sibylle and Sarah seldom use traditional gardener's knives, which they find difficult to manage if working up steps or a ladder and less versatile than secateurs. Other cutting tools in regular use include loppers, bill hooks (for putting a point on the end of hazel and sweet-chestnut stakes) and Sandvik bow saws and small folding saws.

Several different sorts of rakes are used including Springboks, hay rakes and rubber rakes. Iron rakes are only used on rare occasions when a fine tilth must be prepared for a seedbed. Pam and Sibylle consider rubber rakes to be underrated and have used them since their Waterperry days; they are excellent on gravel, good on grass and especially handy for getting out leaves from the bottoms of hedges, a situation where a wire Springbok

rake would hook itself on to low branches.

Reinforced plastic sheets are sometimes used for collecting and carrying rubbish such as leaves or grass clippings; the four corners can be drawn together, making it easy to cart refuse around the garden, even in places where wheelbarrows would be cumbersome. However, Pam, Sibylle and Sarah all feel that hessian squares are even more versatile: they are not so easily blown away in gusty weather, are a more natural colour, weigh less and are not damaged by thorny prunings. Because they rot if stored wet, they must always be hung up in the toolshed to dry.

Of course, there are many more tools used at Sissinghurst: some are traditional, such as oak boards (to pick up leaves), or trugs; some are commonsensical such as a spirit level to set lines for the tops of hedges; some, such as a bolster chisel to deadhead fascicularias, are fanciful. All are carefully chosen and imaginatively used.

&

The planting at Sissinghurst is transient and depends on constant reworking and rejuvenation by skilled and sensitive staff. Plants are chosen and placed with artistry and, as seen in this chapter, equipment is selected with precision to give the best results. It is rare for such a garden to outlive its creators; Sissinghurst proves conclusively that this is possible, and that the garden can retain its spirit and individuality.

Sissinghurst's Plants

Rosa *'Sissinghurst Castle'*

Viola *'Vita'*

Thalictrum aquilegiifolium
'White Cloud'

Keen-eyed gardeners will occasionally discover a chance seedling or sport that is quite different from anything they have seen before. Few such finds are truly good garden plants and most are lost to cultivation without ever becoming established. However, Sissinghurst's gardeners have never allowed good new varieties to die out. They have also always scrupulously avoided naming any plant that was less than first rate. Of numerous plants that have been called 'Sissinghurst' over the years, only a few genuinely commemorate the garden; these and a handful of other plants raised here are all of considerable merit and have been generously passed on, to guarantee their enjoyment by countless other gardeners. Their provenance is described here.

One might expect to find plants celebrating Harold and Vita's family and friends throughout the garden. However, Vita seems never to have striven to collect these; the main consideration in her choice of flowers was their beauty; associations with people of her own time seemed to have held little appeal, though commemorative names redolent of a more romantic past undoubtedly attracted her. She and Harold had no qualms about scrapping the 'Night' roses, originally called 'Lady Sackville' after Vita's mother. There is nothing to suggest that she grew *Narcissus* 'Lady Sackville', a Small-cupped yellow daffodil raised before 1921, nor does there seem to be any record of *Lythrum* 'Lady Sackville' in the garden (this variety is too tall to be useful now in the Purple Border). However, she did order *Viola* 'Lady Sackville' shortly before her death.

In some cases, the name 'Sissinghurst' has been erroneously attached to plants with perfectly good names of their own, perhaps because plants or cuttings were taken from the garden without their true epithets attached: this has happened to an artemisia and *Tanacetum parthenium* 'Rowallane'. *Penstemon* 'Sissinghurst Pink', so called because the garden's stock of 'Evelyn' seemed to be superior, is not distinct from that variety and does not merit a separate name. However, the following varieties associated with the garden are all validly named.

Iris 'Sissinghurst'

This Dwarf Bearded cultivar was raised by John Taylor, then living at Hythe in Kent, and given to the gardeners after it was named in 1969. Only 13-15cm/5-6in high, it has flowers of a rich, plummy reddish-purple. Used at the front of the Purple Border, it blooms in mid to late spring.

Phlox 'Violet Vere'

On a visit to the Chelsea Flower Show in the late 1980s, Pam and Sybille saw a pot of an outstanding purple phlox some 23cm/9in high in a florist's shop near Sloane Square. Never having seen a carpet-forming phlox of such rich colour, they bought the pot and propagated plants to carpet an area in the Top Courtyard at the foot of the tower. Here in dappled shade beneath *Rosa* 'Geranium' it throve and flowered generously. When exhibited at the Royal Horticultural Society in 1990, it was given an Award of Merit subject to the provision of a cultivar name. In spite of efforts to find an existing name, the gardeners could find no record of such a phlox having been grown in the British Isles. It may prove to be a previously named American plant. Pam chose to name it after her mother, whose ninetieth birthday fell on 1st May that year.

Pulmonaria officinalis 'Sissinghurst White'

Found originally by Hampshire plantswoman Mrs Amy Doncaster, this clone was supplied to Washfield Nursery, Hawkhurst, as *P. o.* 'Alba', not then a legitimate name according to the rules of nomenclature. Acquired from there by the gardeners, plants were submitted to the Royal Horticultural Society's pulmonaria trial from both Sissinghurst and Washfield. The Sissinghurst stock performed remarkably well and in 1976 was given an Award of Merit, subject to the provision of a cultivar name. With white flowers opening from pale pink buds, it has evenly silver-spotted leaves, those at the base being heart-shaped or cordate. (*P. saccharata*, to which this cultivar is sometimes wrongly ascribed, has elliptical basal leaves.) This excellent variety is used in the White Garden and cut back after flowering to encourage the production of healthy new foliage.

Rosa 'Sissinghurst Castle'

Found growing among nettles and brambles when Vita first came to Sissinghurst, this Gallica rose reaches about 90cm/3ft, suckering freely if grown on its own roots. Reintroduced to the nursery trade in 1947, it has been suggested that its true name is 'Rose des Maures', though eminent rosarian Graham Thomas has been unable to find that name in French literature. It lacks the quality of the finest French Gallica roses of similar colour, raised by breeders such as Vibert and Laffay during the 1830s and 1840s, and is therefore likely to predate these. Redouté's illustrations of roses grown by the Empress Josephine at La Malmaison show comparable varieties dating from about 1810. In spite of its unsophisticated form, its sumptuous colour and slightly muddled flowers have great charm, and it combines agreeably with the blush-pink Hybrid Musk rose 'Kathleen' in two beds in the Orchard.

Rosmarinus officinalis 'Sissinghurst Blue'

Vita was intrigued by the upright rosemary that seeded itself in the tower steps some time during the mid 1950s. With flowers deeper than the common rosemary yet not so rich a blue as the rather prostrate narrow-leaved Corsican or broad-leaved Tuscan varieties that grew nearby, its other parent remains a mystery. Common rosemary certainly grew in the garden, but 'Sissinghurst Blue' has ascending stems reminiscent of 'Miss Jessopp's Upright', a variety not known to have been grown at Sissinghurst. Reaching about 90cm/3ft, it is intermediate in hardiness between the tender deep-blue varieties and common rosemary. The gardeners felt that it 'survived better in beastly places' such as the brickwork of the steps, where a sparse diet and a good summer baking encouraged tougher growth. However, replacing it there after a severe winter can be difficult unless it is protected from passing feet by a huddle of pots. 'Sissinghurst Blue' received the Royal Horticultural Society's Award of Merit in 1983.

Thalictrum aquilegiifolium 'White Cloud'

In about 1977, the gardeners bought four plants of *T. a.* var. *album* from Prichard's nursery at Riverslea, Christchurch in Hampshire. Apparently raised from seed, the four showed considerable variation, one being far superior to any other stock of this variety that the gardeners had seen. The best plant was cosseted in the nursery until enough had been propagated to plant a whole group in the White Garden. Named 'White Cloud' (the other well-known cultivar of this species is Alan Bloom's 'Thundercloud'), it was given the Royal Horticultural Society's Award of Merit in 1983. As with many other thalictrums, the plant's display depends not on petals but on the filaments that carry the stamens. In 'White Cloud', these are significantly thicker and considerably longer than usual, creating a far more showy effect.

Verbena 'Sissinghurst'

This was collected abroad by the Director of the Glasshouse Crops Research Institute, Littlehampton, Sussex and given in the mid 1970s to the gardeners, who sent it to Wisley for identification. Grown in the garden there, the provenance 'Sissinghurst' on its labels was taken to be a cultivar name and soon became so widespread that it could not be changed without causing confusion and irritation to many. It was given an Award of Merit by the Royal Horticultural Society when shown in 1982 by the Royal Botanic Gardens, Kew. It has occasionally been called 'Tenerife', an erroneous name perhaps arising from confusion with *V. tenera*, of which it is perhaps a hybrid. It is not hardy and has to be overwintered under glass. Suitable for planting in containers or at the front of the border where it can scramble among other plants, it makes a particularly effective combination with silver-leaved *Artemisia stelleriana* 'Mori'.

Viola 'Vita'

Vita ordered plants of *V.* 'Lady Sackville' in about 1960. The gardeners planted them in Delos next to *V.* 'Nellie Britton' (syn. *V.* 'Haslemere'). After the death of Miss Britton, who had owned a nursery at Washfield in Devon, her colleague Hilda Davenport-Jones brought her plants to Hawkhurst, near Sissinghurst, where Washfield Nursery, now run by Elizabeth Strangman and Graham Gough, is still a source of many choice introductions to Sissinghurst.

Not long after Vita's death, a chance seedling arose between the two plants with flowers 3.5cm/1¼ in across, substantially bigger than those of 'Nellie Britton', and of a deeper and purer pink. The gardeners felt that 'Vita' would be an appropriate name for this child of 'Lady Sackville' and gave stock to viola nurseryman Richard Cawthorne who propagated it. It has been confusingly offered as 'Lady Saville'. *V.* 'Sissinghurst' is also listed by some nurseries, though it is unknown to any of Sissinghurst's gardeners.

Rosmarinus officinalis
'Sissinghurst Blue'

Verbena *'Sissinghurst'*

Bibliography

Brown, Jane *Sissinghurst: Portrait of a Garden*, Weidenfeld & Nicolson, London, 1990

Brown, Jane *Vita's Other World*, Penguin Books, London, 1985

Glendinning, Victoria *Vita*, Weidenfeld & Nicolson, London, 1983

Jenkins, Jennifer and James, Patrick *From Acorn to Oak Tree*, Macmillan, London, 1994

Lane Fox, Robin (ed.) *V. Sackville-West: The Illustrated Garden Book*, Michael Joseph, London, 1986

Lees-Milne, James *Harold Nicolson: A Biography*, Vols I and II, Chatto & Windus, London, 1980

Lord, Tony *Best Borders*, Frances Lincoln, London, 1994; Viking, New York, 1995

Nicolson, Nigel (ed.) *Harold Nicolson: Diaries and Letters (Vol. 1 1930–39, Vol. 2 1939–45, Vol. 3 1945–62)* Collins, London, 1966, 1967, 1968

Nicolson, Nigel *Portrait of a Marriage*, Weidenfeld & Nicolson, London, 1973

Nicolson, Nigel *Vita and Harold*, Weidenfeld & Nicolson, London, 1992

Nicolson, Nigel *Sissinghurst Castle Garden*, The National Trust, London, 1994 (reprinted with amendments 1995)

Nicolson, Philippa (ed.) *V. Sackville-West's Garden Book*, Michael Joseph, London, 1968

Sackville-West, Victoria *The Land*, Heinemann, London, 1926

Sackville-West, Victoria *The Garden*, Michael Joseph, London, 1946

Sackville-West, Victoria *In Your Garden*, Michael Joseph, London, 1951

Sackville-West, Victoria *In Your Garden Again*, Michael Joseph, London, 1953

Sackville-West, Victoria *More For Your Garden*, Michael Joseph, London, 1955

Sackville-West, Victoria *Even More For Your Garden*, Michael Joseph, London, 1958

Scott-James, Anne *Sissinghurst: The Making of a Garden*, Michael Joseph, London, 1975

Stevens, Michael *V. Sackville-West*, Michael Joseph, London, 1973

Index

Each chapter contains numerous references to Harold and Vita, Pam Schwerdt and Sibylle Kreutzberger; only the most important are included in the index. Page nos in **bold** refer to principal references. Page nos in *italics* refer to illustration captions and planting plans. For an explanation of hardiness zones (not given for annuals), e.g. **Z7**, see page 167.

HARDINESS ZONES (Z)

Hardiness zone ratings are a rough guide to the appropriate minimum temperature a plant will tolerate. Hardiness depends on factors such as the depth of a plant's roots, its water content at onset of frost, duration of cold weather, wind force, and length of (and temperatures encountered) the preceding summer. These ratings, based on those devised by the US Department of Agriculture, are allocated to plants according to their tolerance of winter cold in the British Isles and Western Europe. In climates with hotter and/or drier summers, as in Australia and New Zealand, some plants will survive colder temperatures; their hardiness in these countries may be one or, rarely, two zones lower than quoted.

Sissinghurst's winter climate corresponds with **Z8**, as do most areas in the British Isles except central London, the extreme south and west (**Z9**) and the Highlands of Scotland (**Z7**). However, in each **Z8** area there are sheltered microclimates, such as the foot of a sunny wall, which are effectively one zone milder and where **Z9** plants may usually be grown.

In south-east England, the English Channel is all that separates the land mass from continental Europe. This narrow body of water is less able to moderate the climate during periods when prevailing winter winds are from the north-east; thus Kent and East Anglia benefit less from the warm Gulf Stream and suffer severe winters rather more often than is usual for most of the British Isles. In roughly one winter in ten, most **Z8** and **Z9** plants can be lost. Even **Z6** and **Z7** plants such as figs, crocosmias and some roses, normally considered reasonably hardy in England, can be killed or severely damaged at Sissinghurst.

CELSIUS	ZONE	°FAHRENHEIT
below - 45	1	below -50
-45 to -40	2	50 to -40
-40 to -34	3	-40 to -30
-34 to -29	4	-30 to -20
-29 to -23	5	-20 to -10
-23 to -18-	6	-10 to 0
18 to -12	7	0 to 10
-12 to -7	8	10 to 20
-7 to -1	9	20 to 30
-1 to 4	10	30 to 40
above 4	11	above 40

Acknowledgments

To save Sissinghurst from the pressures of yet more visitors, the National Trust avoids publicity; in spite of this, I felt it was more important to provide a record of its development, planting and techniques of maintenance than to place an embargo on its beauty and the inspiring story of its survival. I am grateful for the National Trust's permission to publish and for the support and encouragement of Regional Director for Kent and East Sussex Peter Griffiths, Chief Gardens Adviser John Sales, Gardens Adviser Jim Marshall and Head Gardener Sarah Cook.

The survival of Sissinghurst reflects great merit on all involved, especially its donor Nigel Nicolson and its gardeners past and present. I am indebted to Nigel Nicolson, Sarah Cook, Pam Schwerdt and Sibylle Kreutzberger, all of whom I interviewed at considerable length; Nigel Nicolson kindly allowed me to peruse Harold and Vita's papers and loaned the photograph of his parents by Cecil Beaton. Pam and Sibylle have been particularly forbearing, responding patiently to many days of questions, some pertinent, others doubtless idiotic. Their sacrifice has stopped me from pestering Sarah Cook for even longer hours, allowing her to get on with the more important work of running the garden.

Sissinghurst's gardeners and office staff have all been most helpful, particularly Visitor Services Manager Bob Woods and Property Secretaries Shirley Temme and Samantha Snaith.

Thanks are due to Ann Richards and James Bennett who have valiantly typed some 200,000 words of interviews on which most of the text is based. I am very grateful to all at Frances Lincoln who encouraged me to write this book and produced it with characteristically high standards of professionalism. My thanks go particularly to Celia Levett, Louise Tucker, Caroline Hillier, Erica Hunningher, Alison Freegard, Jo Christian, Penelope Miller and James Bennett.   T.L.

PHOTOGRAPHY

With only a few exceptions, the photographs were taken between April 1994 and July 1995 using a Canon T90 camera. Fuji Velvia, a fine-grained and therefore rather slow (ASA50) professional 35mm film, was used, supplied by Jessops of Leicester, Cheltenham branch, and processed by Central Photographic Services, Cheltenham, to both of whom my thanks are due.

Almost thirty visits were necessary to see the garden through the seasons and in varied lights. I was fortunate to be allowed in when the garden was closed to the public, usually in the early morning. With a relatively slow film such as Velvia, it was necessary to select quite bright days (although brilliant sunlight was avoided) and to use a tripod. Dull weather offers little opportunity to take garden photographs with such film, except those which require a very shallow depth of field.

The T90 is not an autofocus camera. For garden photography, autofocusing is seldom an advantage: foliage and flowers do not offer the hard edges it requires. A standard 50mm lens was used for about half the photographs, though a 100mm short telephoto lens proved immeasurably useful for photographing plants and distant views; this and a 135mm telephoto lens allow details of borders to be photographed without the need to walk into the beds. The 135mm lens was used for perhaps 10 per cent of photographs, with a still smaller proportion being taken with 28mm, 200mm or 300mm lenses, all of them in the Canon FD range. The 28mm lens is useful in confined spaces or to take in a wide panorama, though it can give a distorted image, making a relatively intimate area such as the Cottage Garden seem like a wide-open prairie.

Visitors are not allowed to take tripods into the garden because these block paths and spoil the enjoyment of others. However, monopods are allowed; cutting out vertical and much lateral shake, they offer a good chance of achieving sharp pictures. Photographers are asked to consider others and not to block the paths; nor should they remove labels and put them back in the wrong place, nor tread on beds and borders. The garden's opening hours can be a limitation, generally coinciding with the worst possible light when the sun is high in the sky, contrasts are harsh and there is no opportunity for flattering backlighting. Those wanting to photograph the garden without the distraction of too many other visitors and when the light is best should either arrive at opening time on weekend mornings, when, at present, the garden opens early, or try late weekday afternoons when there is less crowding. My inclination would be to be first in the queue to get into the garden; then I could rush to whichever areas I wanted to portray in overall or panoramic views before they became busy; thereafter I could concentrate on details of planting, photographs in which visitors are unlikely to obtrude. Always take enough film to Sissinghurst. A dozen or so years ago, I arrived to meet plantsman the late Marvin Black in the Top Courtyard; visiting from Seattle, he was setting up his camera to photograph the Purple Border. When the time came to leave several hours later, Marvin had worked his way around almost to the end of the border; he had used eight films. There is much to photograph here, not just views of the garden but the individual plants, many of them unusual and grown to a state of perfection seldom seen elsewhere.   T.L.

PUBLISHERS' ACKNOWLEDGMENTS

The Publishers thank Curtis Brown Ltd for permission to quote from 'The Garden' by Vita Sackville-West (Michael Joseph, 1946). They are grateful to Nicky Cooney for all the watercolour plans, except the one on page 123, for which they thank Jean Sturgis. Thanks are due to Zoe Bowers, Sally Cracknell, Margherita Gianni, Penelope Miller and Patti Taylor for their assistance in producing this book.

Editors   Jo Christian, Alison Freegard, Celia Levett
Art Editor   Louise Tucker
Production   Annemarieke Kroon, Kim van Woerkom
Editorial Director   Erica Hunningher
Art Director   Caroline Hillier